International Financial Intermediation

Studies in International Economics

TITLES PUBLISHED

International
Financial
Intermediation

RALPH C. BRYANT

THE BROOKINGS INSTITUTION
Washington, D.C.

Library of Congress Cataloging-in-Publication data
Bryant, Ralph C., 1938–
  International financial intermediation.
  (Studies in international economics)
  Bibliography: p.
  Includes index.
  1. Intermediation (Finance)   2. International
finance.   I. Title.   II. Series: Studies in international
economics (Washington, D.C.)
HG3891.5.B79   1987   332'.042   87-10358
ISBN 0-8157-1138-7
ISBN 0-8157-1137-9 (pbk.)

9 8 7 6 5 4 3 2 1

THE BROOKINGS INSTITUTION is an independent organization devoted to nonpartisan research, education, and publication in economics, government, foreign policy, and the social sciences generally. Its principal purposes are to aid in the development of sound public policies and to promote public understanding of issues of national importance.

The Institution was founded on December 8, 1927, to merge the activities of the Institute for Government Research, founded in 1916, the Institute of Economics, founded in 1922, and the Robert Brookings Graduate School of Economics and Government, founded in 1924.

The Board of Trustees is responsible for the general administration of the Institution, while the immediate direction of the policies, program, and staff is vested in the President, assisted by an advisory committee of the officers and staff. The by-laws of the Institution state: "It is the function of the Trustees to make possible the conduct of scientific research, and publication, under the most favorable conditions, and to safeguard the independence of the research staff in the pursuit of their studies and in the publication of the results of such studies. It is not a part of their function to determine, control, or influence the conduct of particular investigations or the conclusions reached."

The President bears final responsibility for the decision to publish a manuscript as a Brookings book. In reaching his judgment on the competence, accuracy, and objectivity of each study, the President is advised by the director of the appropriate research program and weighs the views of a panel of expert outside readers who report to him in confidence on the quality of the work. Publication of a work signifies that it is deemed a competent treatment worthy of public consideration but does not imply endorsement of conclusions or recommendations.

The Institution maintains its position of neutrality on issues of public policy in order to safeguard the intellectual freedom of the staff. Hence interpretations or conclusions in Brookings publications should be understood to be solely those of the authors and should not be attributed to the Institution, to its trustees, officers, or other staff members, or to the organizations that support its research.

Foreword

MODERN economic growth has been closely associated with the expansion and increasing sophistication of financial activity. To a progressively greater extent, decisions to save have been made independently of decisions to invest in tangible physical assets. Financial intermediaries, such as banks and insurance companies, and financial markets, such as stock exchanges and interbank trading in overnight funds, have more and more efficiently transmitted funds from one part of the economy to another, thereby reconciling the divergent needs of ultimate savers (primarily households) and ultimate investors (mainly businesses).

The existing literature on the structure and policy regulation of financial intermediation has been preoccupied with its domestic aspects. But the international aspects—lending and borrowing across national borders, with assets and liabilities denominated in foreign and domestic currencies—have become progressively more important. Strong interdependence among nations' financial systems is one of the most salient facts about the world economy in the second half of the 1980s. Scarcely a single macroeconomic or regulatory policy issue that formerly was viewed solely as a domestic matter can now be intelligently discussed without reference to international flows of funds and the policy environments in foreign countries.

In this study, Ralph C. Bryant presents an overview of the international dimensions of financial intermediation. He documents the progressive internationalization of banking and other financial activity. He then analyzes why this process has been occurring, assesses how far it has gone, and evaluates whether, for individual nations and for the world, the trend has been helpful or harmful. He concludes with a discussion of how national governments and international organizations can best regulate, supervise, and tax financial institutions in an increasingly integrated worldwide financial system.

A paper drawn from an early draft of this manuscript was delivered at the Second International Conference sponsored by the Institute for Monetary and Economic Studies, Bank of Japan, held in Tokyo on May 29–31, 1985. That paper was published in Yoshio Suzuki and Hiroshi Yomo, eds., *Financial Innovation and Monetary Policy: Asia and the West* (University of Tokyo Press, 1986).

Ralph C. Bryant is a senior fellow in the Brookings Economic Studies program. He appreciates the help of numerous colleagues and friends during the course of his research and writing. In particular, he acknowledges the valuable comments or other assistance of Edward M. Bernstein, Barry P. Bosworth, Joseph Bisignano, Matthew Canzoneri, Gary Dymski, Allen B. Frankel, Tamar Frankel, Dale W. Henderson, Gerald Holtham, Barbara Koremenos, Rodney H. Mills, Ellen Nedde, Walter S. Salant, Robert Solomon, Hiroo Taguchi, and Linda Mix Tesar. Barbara Koremenos, Jan van Eck, and Linda Mix Tesar contributed able research assistance; the latter, in particular, provided indispensable help in the collection and analysis of empirical data, especially the statistical backup for the tables in chapter 3. Evelyn Taylor helped with excellent typing and office assistance. Nancy Davidson shepherded the manuscript through the publication process. Victor M. Alfaro verified the factual content, and Toni Warner Gillas prepared the index.

This book has received generous financial support from the National Science Foundation and the Ford Foundation.

The views expressed here are those of the author and should not be attributed to the supporting foundations or to the officers, trustees, or other staff members of the Brookings Institution.

BRUCE K. MACLAURY
President

April 1987
Washington, D.C.

Contents

Tables

Figures

CHAPTER ONE

Introduction

THE economic links between the United States and other nations have been growing much more rapidly than the American economy itself. A gradual trend toward increasing openness of the economy has probably been operative for at least the last century, interrupted only by two destructive world wars and the intervening years of turbulence and depression in the 1920s and 1930s. Without doubt, economic interdependence has increased markedly since the late 1940s.

What has been true for the American economy has also been true for the economies of other industrial nations and a majority of developing nations. Seen from the vantage point of the mid-1980s, the trend toward greater economic interdependence is one of the key facts characterizing the world economy in the second half of the twentieth century.

The most familiar manifestations of the increasing openness of national economies involve international trade in goods and services. Most nations' exports and imports have been growing more rapidly than their national outputs. Correspondingly, the aggregate flow of trade across national borders for the world as a whole has been increasing faster than total world production.

The international debtor-creditor relationships of national economies are less well documented and understood than international trade in goods and services. But increases in financial interdependence have been even more rapid than those for trade. To a degree virtually unimaginable in the 1940s and 1950s, lending and borrowing across national borders, with assets and liabilities denominated in several foreign currencies as well as domestic currency, have progressively integrated nations' financial markets. Relative to earlier decades, there is much less scope for an individual nation to maintain financial conditions within its borders different from those prevailing abroad.

1

International transactions of banks, or those indirectly arranged by banks, have been the cutting edge of this growing financial interdependence. Other types of financial intermediaries, such as security dealers, insurance companies, and pension funds, have also contributed importantly to the trend. So far, however, commercial banks and merchant banks have played a role overshadowing nonbank financial institutions.

Another broad secular trend has been occurring simultaneously with the growing integration of the world economy and financial system. The last four decades have been characterized by increasing political pluralism—a marked expansion in the number of governmental decisionmaking units in the world and a greater diffusion of power among them. Increasing political pluralism has in turn been accompanied by rising nationalism.

A great enlargement in the number of independent nation states, reflecting the dissolution of colonial empires, has been a highly visible aspect of this trend. For example, in July 1944 only 44 nations participated in the Bretton Woods conference, accepting the original Articles of Agreement of the International Monetary Fund (IMF). By the end of 1970, however, the number of members had grown to 118, and had reached 151 as of July 1986.

Less visible but equally important, the political and economic hegemony of the United States—at its height at the end of World War II—gradually declined during the ensuing four decades. The United States accounted for a third or more of the world's total production of goods and services immediately after the war; by the early 1980s, its share had fallen to about 22–24 percent. Concurrently, the political and economic influence of the colonial powers continued to wane. Most fundamentally, increasing pluralism led to a world political situation in which one or a few nations no longer effectively dominated international decisionmaking.[1]

---

1. As a suggestive illustration of the greater diffusion of economic and political power, consider again the International Monetary Fund. The United States alone had over 30 percent of the total quotas and votes in the initial years of IMF operations. By 1984 this share had fallen below 20 percent. The two countries that instituted and dominated the negotiations establishing the IMF, the United States and the United Kingdom, together had over 46 percent of the quotas and votes at the outset. The proportion in 1984 was less than 27 percent. The falling shares of the United States and the United Kingdom were offset to some extent by upward adjustments in the shares of other industrial nations, especially Germany and Japan. After the 1950s, however, the largest reallocation of shares was in favor of nonindustrial nations. In the mid-1980s, the oil-exporting nations and the developing nations that are not oil exporting jointly controlled about 36 percent of the quotas and 37¼ percent of the votes in the IMF. To be sure, the political influence wielded by a country or group of countries in the IMF is not perfectly correlated with voting power. Nonetheless, it is broadly true that the United States and a handful of other major nations no longer dominate IMF decisions to the extent characteristic of earlier decades.

Unfortunately for the peace of mind of nations' policymakers and citizens, interaction between the trends of increasing economic interdependence and increasing political pluralism tends to generate discord. The economic significance of national boundaries has been reduced by growing interdependence even as their political significance has been enhanced by increasing pluralism and the associated forces of nationalism. Each trend has thus exacerbated a mismatch between the economic and the political structures of the world: the effective domains of economic markets coincide less and less well with national governmental jurisdictions.

This mismatch makes decisions by nations' governments more difficult and the consequences of their decisions more uncertain. It also creates pressures for the strengthening of intergovernmental cooperation and international institutions. Yet increasing political pluralism simultaneously tends to undermine the chances of effective responses to such pressures. Increasing pluralism means that more nations than before typically have to be involved in any given cooperative effort. Decisionmaking in large groups is considerably more difficult than in smaller groups. The greater diffusion of political and economic power creates stronger incentives for individual nations to act as "free riders," thereby reducing the probability that all nations will act collectively to foster their common interests.

This book is an outgrowth of a broad research program analyzing these trends and their implications. The focus here is on the financial aspects of interdependence. In particular, I survey the international dimensions of financial intermediation (a concept explained in detail in chapter 2). I identify the main issues posed by these international dimensions and provide needed background to place the issues in appropriate perspective. Some of the issues are analytical—how to interpret the financial trends of recent decades and what judgments to make about the likely evolution of the world financial system. At least as important, I consider issues that are normative—what policies national governments should adopt in the light of the progressive internationalization of financial intermediation. My overview addresses both types of issues, trying to meet the needs of economic analysis and public policy.[2]

Many parts of the book will, I hope, be useful to economist colleagues, helping them interpret recent developments in international finance. Other parts, however, will be old hat to them. Alas, if here and there I should bore

---

2. In an earlier book, *Money and Monetary Policy in Interdependent Nations,* I examined the consequences of increasing economic interdependence for the conduct of national monetary policy. (Full references to the works cited throughout appear in the Bibliography.)

my fellow economists, that cannot be helped. For a major part of my purpose is pedagogical: I hope to facilitate a better understanding of this important subject among a wider audience of noneconomists, many of whom may currently regard it as too arcane or too inaccessible to merit their attention.

The plan of the book is as follows. Chapter 2 defines financial intermediation and summarizes its basic characteristics. Little is said about international aspects. The discussion in chapter 2, however, is an essential foundation for all the subsequent chapters.

Chapter 3 presents illustrative empirical evidence about the progressive internationalization of financial intermediation during the last several decades. That evidence includes some newly compiled comparative data on international banking. The purpose of chapter 3 is to provide an analytical overview of empirical trends. That goal requires a wide-ranging examination of the available evidence. Yet it precludes consideration of many interesting points that would warrant discussion in a more detailed treatment. Readers wanting further evidence and discussion can consult the references cited in the footnotes in chapter 3, especially the statistical sources identified in the footnotes to the tables.

Chapter 4 outlines alternative explanations for why internationalization has occurred and discusses their relative importance. Chapter 5 provides a preliminary assessment of the degree of interconnectedness among national financial systems as of the mid-1980s.

Chapter 6 is, speaking loosely, an effort to construct a "report card"—an identification of the most important benefits and costs—for international financial intermediation.

Chapters 7 and 8 turn to aspects of international financial intermediation of direct concern in the formation of government policies. Chapter 7 summarizes some basic rationales for the regulation and supervision of financial activity and the extensions of those rationales made necessary by cross-border and cross-currency financial transactions. Chapter 8 identifies international collective-goods problems in the regulation, taxation, and supervision of financial intermediation and discusses nascent cooperative efforts to deal with them.

In chapter 9, I conclude with some speculative judgments about broad choices for the evolution of government policies and intergovernmental cooperation.

As the preceding outline makes clear, I traverse a wide territory. I regret that I am not able to deal satisfactorily with all parts of the subject. The deficiencies in my treatment stem from the imperfect state of scholarly knowledge. Here I fault my fellow economists and other social scientists. Had they been more intrepid and insightful in their analysis, I would have had a more solid, comprehensive body of knowledge from which to steal my overview.

My position is like that of cartographers in the early sixteenth century. They and their patrons badly needed a new map of the world. Yet their information was insufficient to draw a map correct in all details. Their rationale is mine, too. Even a rough new chart, with some of the continents and islands correctly described, is a better aid to navigation than the old maps showing the earth as flat.

CHAPTER TWO

Financial Intermediation

TO PROVIDE a foundation for the analysis in the rest of the book, this chapter summarizes the basic characteristics of financial intermediation and outlines the vital role that financial institutions play in the process of economic development.

Concepts and Definitions

In modern complex economies, most decisions to save are made independently of decisions to invest in durable physical assets (tangible capital). The ultimate savers are primarily households. They set aside some fraction of current income, rather than spending it on current consumption, so as to increase future possibilities for consumption, either by themselves or their heirs. The ultimate investors are primarily business enterprises. They purchase and employ tangible capital goods to facilitate their production of goods and services. Business enterprises borrow—that is, they issue financial instruments as liabilities—to be able to purchase and employ more physical capital than would otherwise be possible. Some of the financial liabilities issued by businesses are debt instruments. The remainder are equity claims—evidences of fractional ownership of the net worths of the businesses.

Financial intermediation, broadly conceived, is the complex process through which the differing needs of ultimate savers and ultimate investors are reconciled. *Financial intermediaries*, such as banks, savings and loan associations, and insurance companies, and *financial markets*, such as stock exchanges and the interbank overnight-funds market, are institutions that facilitate this reconciliation.

The assets of a financial intermediary are debt instruments or equities issued by ultimate investors—and, in an increasingly complex financial system, by other intermediaries as well. The liabilities of a financial intermediary are assets of the ultimate savers—and, in a complex financial system, of other intermediaries. Unlike the ultimate investors, whose main assets are physical capital goods, the financial intermediaries have both their assets (for example, loans) and their liabilities (for example, deposits) predominantly in the form of financial instruments.[1]

Financial markets facilitate the trading of financial instruments that have standardized features and are readily negotiable (hence "marketable"). Many such instruments are *securities,* legal documents representing evidence of a debt or equity claim on an ultimate investor or a financial intermediary. Financial markets require a variety of supporting services, often provided by specialized institutions—for example, firms of brokers and dealers that execute market transactions and rating firms that evaluate the riskiness of particular securities.

Financial activity is a rough synonym for financial intermediation. *Financial institutions* include both financial intermediaries and financial markets. *Financial system* and *financial sector* refer loosely to the multiple activities of financial institutions engaged in the promotion of financial intermediation.

In a hypothetical economy without financial instruments of any kind, the behavior of spending units would be severely restricted. Each unit would have to invest in tangible assets whatever part of its current income was not consumed. No unit could invest more in tangible assets than its current saving because there would be no way to finance the excess expenditures. In the complete absence of financial instruments, therefore, no unit would be able to indulge its needs and preferences for an intertemporal pattern of spending that differed from the time profile of its income. Under such arrangements, resources would be allocated inefficiently. The economywide levels of saving and investment, and hence the growth rate of output, would thus be substantially less than under arrangements where ultimate investors can borrow through the issuance of *primary securities.*[2]

1. For a more detailed description of the activities of financial intermediaries, see, for example, James Tobin and William C. Brainard, "Financial Intermediaries and the Effectiveness of Monetary Controls"; or John G. Gurley and Edward S. Shaw, *Money in a Theory of Finance,* chap. 6.

2. *Primary securities* is the term used by Gurley and Shaw to denote the financial obligations issued directly by ultimate investors and borrowers (for example, bonds and equities issued by nonfinancial corporations and mortgages issued by households).

An economy in which the only financial instruments were money and primary securities would also be constricted, although to a lesser degree, in its possibilities for growth and efficient resource allocation. By issuing claims against themselves, financial intermediaries offer ultimate savers a wider menu of combinations of risk, return, maturity, and liquidity than would be available if the savers had to lend directly to the ultimate investors. Many intermediaries engage in *maturity transformation* so that most or all of their liabilities have shorter maturities than their assets. And the liabilities of intermediaries tend to have smaller default risk and greater predictability of value than their assets. Ultimate savers can therefore hold financial assets of greater liquidity than the primary securities issued by the ultimate investors.

Financial intermediaries accomplish this transformation between primary securities and the financial assets held by the ultimate savers because they can, for example, reduce the risk per dollar of lending through the pooling of independent risks. Financial intermediaries facilitate the transformation because they develop specialized expertise in the collection and evaluation of information about the creditworthiness of ultimate investors. And financial intermediaries can further reduce the costs associated with maturity transformation through their greater efficiency in negotiating, accounting, and collecting. The activities of financial intermediaries thus make it possible for ultimate investors to finance their purchases of tangible assets at lower rates and easier terms than if they were forced to borrow directly from the ultimate savers. Similarly, financial intermediaries provide ultimate savers much greater flexibility to adopt intertemporal paths for their consumption that differ from the intertemporal paths of their income.

The markets that trade securities and other financial instruments are quintessentially "auction markets." Trading tends to be centralized and conducted by numerous participants. Transaction costs are relatively low. Short sales are often permitted. Prices are quoted continuously and adjust immediately in response to changes (actual or expected) in market supplies and demands.

In contrast, real tangible assets and many types of goods and services are traded in "customer markets." Trading is typically less centralized. Products are more differentiated. Transaction costs are higher. Because products have "price tags" that are not changed continuously, market clearing in the first instance occurs through quantity changes rather than price adjustments.[3]

---

3. For general analysis of the differing behavior of auction markets and customer markets, see Arthur M. Okun, *Prices and Quantities: A Macroeconomic Analysis.*

The auction characteristics of financial markets allow individual savers a flexibility in the holding of securities analogous to the flexibility associated with their direct claims on financial intermediaries. For an individual holder, a negotiable security is liquid if he can sell it in the market, at his discretion, without substantially affecting the market price. Similarly, an ultimate investor may be able to borrow funds more cheaply and easily than would otherwise be possible if he can issue negotiable securities traded in an actively functioning financial market. The de facto liquidity provided by financial markets thus complements the maturity transformation of financial intermediaries in reconciling the differing needs of ultimate savers and ultimate investors.

Financial markets provide liquidity not merely for ultimate savers and investors but also for financial intermediaries themselves. Individual intermediaries as asset holders enjoy the same liquidity advantages as ultimate savers when they have the option—backup insurance, as it were—of buying or selling marketable securities. And some of the instruments traded in financial markets, instead of primary securities, are the debt or equity obligations of financial intermediaries. Intermediaries can thus raise additional funds via the securities markets.

It can sometimes be helpful to distinguish between *direct intermediation* and *indirect intermediation*. Direct intermediation occurs when a financial intermediary is interposed as a separate asset-holding entity in the chain of financial links between ultimate investors and ultimate savers. It is a straightforward case of direct intermediation, for example, when a commercial bank extends a multiyear loan to a nonfinancial firm and holds the loan on its own balance sheet until maturity. Indirect intermediation occurs when financial institutions play an essential role in placing primary securities in the asset portfolios of ultimate savers, yet do not acquire and hold those securities on their own balance sheets. It is a straightforward illustration of indirect intermediation when merchant banks underwrite a new issue of bonds for a nonfinancial firm, but retain none of the new securities in their own portfolios.

Indirect intermediation through financial markets not only complements, but can substitute for, lending by financial intermediaries for their own accounts. Instead of obtaining a new loan from a commercial bank, an ultimate investor can raise additional external finance by issuing marketable securities. Instead of holding relatively liquid assets in the form of deposit claims on intermediaries, an ultimate saver can purchase marketable securities.

The "securitization" of liabilities of ultimate investors leads to a different sharing of risks among savers, financial institutions, and the ultimate investors than would otherwise prevail. The explicit maturity transformation characteristic of direct intermediation entails extensive risk bearing by financial intermediaries themselves. With indirect intermediation, financial institutions shift some of the risks to the purchasers and issuers of the securities.

The distinction between direct and indirect intermediation can be blurred in practice. For example, suppose commercial banks initiate loans to nonfinancial firms, hold the loans on their balance sheets for a transitional period, and then "pool" the loans together, issuing a standardized security, representing a pro rata claim on the pool of loans, to be traded on a financial market. Still more complex are note issuance facilities or commercial-paper facilities organized for nonfinancial firms by financial intermediaries. For example, suppose a bank legally binds itself to assist a firm in periodically issuing commercial paper (short-term, negotiable debt obligations of the firm tradable in a secondary market), but with a commitment to purchase any residual amounts of the issues that cannot be sold to others (or alternatively to provide the borrower with a guaranteed standby direct loan). In normal times the underwriting bank plans not to hold any of the paper itself; that credit risk is assumed by the purchasers of the paper (who could lose if the borrower were to fail before the paper matures). Over a longer term, however, the underwriting bank does bear credit risk, since if things go badly it may have to lend to a borrower in whom other investors have lost confidence. These cases are examples where direct and indirect intermediation are subtly combined. They may also be described as an "unbundling" of several intermediation functions. The bank performs the initial risk evaluation and prepares the legal documents, for example, but shifts some of the risk of actually holding the primary securities onto other investors.

Financial Intermediation and Economic Development

Economists and historians agree that the process of modern economic growth has been closely associated with the expansion and increasing diversification of financial intermediation. The rough parallelism between economic growth and financial development involves complex causal relationships, some of which are not well understood. The causation is almost certainly not unidirectional. Growth in the production of goods and services and the accumulation of physical capital have stimulated expansion and adaptation of the activities of financial institutions. At the same time, innovations in financial intermediation have catalyzed the process of real growth.

The pioneering literature on the financial aspects of the growth process is dominated by the work of Raymond Goldsmith and that of John Gurley and Edward Shaw. Several generalizations emerge from that literature and its subsequent elaboration.[4]

First, as economic development proceeds, the financial superstructure of an economy tends to expand relative to the real infrastructure. In other words, the network of financial interrelations among decisionmaking agents in the economy acquires greater density at an even more rapid rate than the network of goods and services transactions. Goldsmith evaluates this phenomenon with his "financial interrelations ratio," the ratio of the aggregate market value of all financial instruments to the value of tangible net national wealth. Increases in the financial interrelations ratio, however, may not continue without limit. Once an advanced stage of development is attained, the financial superstructure may grow only commensurately with the real infrastructure. These Goldsmith generalizations are closely related to the Gurley-Shaw conclusion that the ratio of outstanding primary securities to income rises sharply in the early stages of the financial development of a capitalist economy, but then eventually reaches a plateau.

Second, financial institutions tend to become relatively more important as economic growth proceeds. In particular, the share of financial intermediaries in the issuance and ownership of financial assets tends to rise over time. This trend reflects the growing separation and institutionalization of the functions of saving and investing. In the advanced industrial countries, the proportion of total financial assets accounted for by financial intermediaries has continued to increase even after the rise in the financial interrelations ratio has ceased.

A third manifestation of the links between financial and economic development is an increasing diversity in the types of financial institutions and in

---

4. These generalizations are drawn in part from Goldsmith's own summary in *Financial Structure and Development*. Goldsmith's other books include *A Study of Saving in the United States*, *Financial Intermediaries in the American Economy Since 1900*, *The Determinants of Financial Structure*, *The National Balance Sheet of the United States, 1953–1980*, and *Comparative National Balance Sheets: A Study of Twenty Countries, 1688–1978*. The Gurley-Shaw analysis is summarized in their *Money in a Theory of Finance*; see also John G. Gurley and Edward S. Shaw, "Financial Intermediaries and the Saving-Investment Process," and "The Growth of Debt and Money in the United States, 1800–1950: A Suggested Interpretation." See also Simon Kuznets, *Economic Growth of Nations: Total Output and Production Structure;* Rondo Cameron with Olga Crisp, Hugh T. Patrick, and Richard Tilly, *Banking in the Early Stages of Industrialization: A Study in Comparative Economic History;* and Rondo Cameron, ed., *Banking and Economic Development: Some Lessons of History*. For a recent theoretical paper, see Robert M. Townsend, "Financial Structure and Economic Activity."

the types of instruments in which they specialize. At an early stage of development, banks with narrowly defined functions tend to dominate the financial structure. As economic and financial growth proceed, there is a decline in the banking system's share of the assets of all financial institutions and a corresponding rise in the share of newer types of institutions, such as thrift intermediaries, insurance companies, government and private retirement funds, investment companies, finance companies, and securities brokers and dealers. Commensurate with the increasing specialization of the financial system, the relative share of direct intermediation in total financial activity may decline, while financial markets and indirect intermediation become more important. At any rate, the declining relative importance of the banking system entails a smaller role for direct intermediation through commercial banks.

Evidence about the relative importance and catalytic role of securities markets in financial systems is inconclusive. More research needs to be done, for a variety of countries, before generalizations about indirect intermediation can rest on solid ground. In principle, the extent of securitization of the liabilities of ultimate investors could be strongly influenced by factors other than the stage of development of the financial system.

Consider, for example, the information available to economic agents in a society. Information is unevenly distributed in all societies, including in particular the information necessary to assess the creditworthiness of borrowers. Because information is differentially available, different agents have widely differing abilities to assess the risks of investments. The expertise of financial intermediaries in collecting and evaluating information is, as already noted, one major reason why intermediaries play a vital role in the process of economic growth.

Societies differ, however, in the social conventions and legal requirements that govern the availability of information. Those differences can importantly influence the structure of the financial system. Imagine two societies, one of which has laws requiring firms to disclose comprehensive information about their income statements and balance sheets, whereas the other does not. The society with extensive disclosure requirements, because of its less uneven distribution of information, would have less skewness in differential ability to assess and monitor the creditworthiness of individual firms. Other things being equal, financial markets and indirect intermediation might be considerably more developed in the ample-information society. The valuations of securities in that society's markets could better incorporate information about creditworthiness. In the society without disclosure requirements, on the other hand, access to information about the creditworthiness of individual firms would be highly skewed. To an even greater degree than in the ample-information society, financial intermediaries would have a comparative advantage relative to the general public in evaluating investment proposals. Other things being equal, a smaller proportion of financial intermediation in the restricted-information society would be channeled through financial markets.[5]

Geographical Transmission of Financial Technology

The financial development of economically less advanced regions has been catalyzed by the transmission of financial technology and expertise from advanced regions. The primary mechanism for that transmission has been the establishment within host regions of financial institutions owned or managed by "foreigners" (in numerous cases, actual branches or subsidiaries of institutions with head offices located in the advanced regions). Local offices of foreign commercial banks have often been the single most important catalytic influence. This process was prominently evident in the economic development of Europe itself.[6] Among today's nation states, only a handful—Great Britain, France, the United States, possibly Germany and a few other European countries—have had development experiences in which financial institutions owned and managed by indigenous residents dominated the evolution of the national financial system.[7]

No less than in advanced regions, the causal links between real growth and financial activity in newly developing regions are complex and bidirectional. Entry by foreign financial institutions into a host region, however, may be associated with especially strong stimuli to real growth originating with financial activity. In effect, financial intermediaries can lead rather than passively follow real-sector activity. In an essay on entrepreneurship in the economic development of Germany, Gerschenkron illustrates this point:

The German investment banks—a powerful invention, comparable in economic effect to that of the steam engine—were in their capital-supplying

5. Economic theorists in recent years have devoted increasing attention to the lending and borrowing decisions of economic agents in conditions where information is imperfect and unevenly distributed. This emphasis promises to yield new insights and, possibly, overturn some of the conclusions derived from older analyses in which informational considerations were ignored. See, for example, Joseph E. Stiglitz, "Information and Economic Analysis: A Perspective"; and Joseph E. Stiglitz and Andrew Weiss, "Credit Rationing in Markets with Imperfect Information."

6. Fernand Braudel, *Civilization and Capitalism: 15th–18th Century*.

7. Goldsmith, *Financial Structure and Development*, pp. 360–67.

functions a substitute for the insufficiency of the previously created wealth willingly placed at the disposal of the entrepreneurs. But they were also a substitute for entrepreneurial deficiencies. From their central vantage points of control, the banks participated actively in shaping the major—and sometimes even not so major—decisions of individual enterprises. It was they who very often mapped out a firm's paths of growth, conceived far-sighted plans, decided on major technological and locational innovations, and arranged for mergers and capital increases.[8]

Notwithstanding the catalytic roles that can be played by foreign financial institutions in host regions, many other causal factors interact with the financial ones. The vigorous growth of financial activity, while doubtless a necessary condition, is not a sufficient condition for real-sector development.[9]

8. Alexander Gerschenkron, *Continuity in History and Other Essays,* p. 137. The importance of financial institutions as catalysts in the industrial development of Europe in the nineteenth century is also an important theme in Gerschenkron, *Economic Backwardness in Historical Perspective: A Book of Essays.*

9. See, for example, Charles P. Kindleberger, "Financial Institutions and Economic Development: A Comparison of Great Britain and France in the Eighteenth and Nineteenth Centuries," and *The Formation of Financial Centers: A Study in Comparative Economic History.*

CHAPTER THREE

The Progressive Internationalization
of Financial Intermediation

THE existing literature on the structure and regulation of financial intermediation has focused on domestic aspects—that is, intermediation where the lenders, the borrowers, and the intermediating parties are all residents of a single nation and the asset-liability relationships are assumed to be denominated exclusively in the national currency unit. The international aspects have frequently been neglected. Increasingly, however, this relative lack of attention to the international dimensions has become an anomaly.[1]

In his work on the financial structure of national economies, for example, Raymond Goldsmith devotes comparatively little attention to international assets and liabilities. One reason for this relative neglect may have been Goldsmith's perception that the international dimensions of intermediation had not increased in importance in the twentieth century. Writing in the mid-1960s, Goldsmith summarized his conclusions on this point:

> Foreign financing, as either a source of funds supplementing those domestically available or as an outlet for funds not easily utilizable within the country, has played a substantial role in some phase of the development of most countries. As a result of both economic and political trends the ratio of foreign to domestic financing, and particularly that of foreign long-term financing, has, however, failed to show a definite movement since World War I for the world as a whole, after increasing rapidly through most of the nineteenth century, an increase closely connected with the railway age.[2]

---

1. Important exceptions to the neglect of international aspects in the literature include Charles P. Kindleberger, "Balance-of-Payments Deficits and the International Market for Liquidity"; Emile Despres, Charles P. Kindleberger, and Walter S. Salant, "The Dollar and World Liquidity: A Minority View"; Walter S. Salant, "Capital Markets and the Balance of Payments of a Financial Center"; Walter S. Salant, "Financial Intermediation as an Explanation of Enduring 'Deficits' in the Balance of Payments"; and Charles P. Kindleberger, *The Formation of Financial Centers: A Study in Comparative Economic History.*
2. Raymond W. Goldsmith, *Financial Structure and Development,* p. 47.

With the added perspective of two more decades, it is now clear that the postwar period as a whole was characterized by a resumption of the nineteenth century pattern of increasing financial openness. Goldsmith's views about cross-border financial activity, like the analogous conclusions of Simon Kuznets about the long-run trend of international trade in goods and services relative to output, were formed early in the period after World War II and were perhaps unduly influenced by the consequences for financial variables of the troubled years of the two world wars and the intervening depression.

The broad trends of increasing interdependence can be illustrated in a variety of ways for virtually all countries or regions. In the figures and tables in this chapter, I present some selected examples. I begin with a reminder of the growing openness of nations' goods markets and then concentrate on increasing financial interdependence through banking channels.

Foreign Trade Proportions

Figure 3-1 shows the ratio of international trade in goods and services to gross domestic output (GDP)—sometimes called the foreign trade proportion—for each of the seven largest industrial countries and for a "world" aggregation of countries. Marked differences in countries' experiences are evident. For example, the United States and Japan are less "open" than the other large industrial countries when trade proportions are used as a yardstick. Trade openness for Japan, and also for the United Kingdom, did not rise between the mid-1950s and early 1970s. Movements in countries' ratios are partly cyclical. Notice, for example, the sharp increases in the ratios in 1973–74 when the world economy was booming and commodity prices, especially for energy, were rising rapidly. The declines for most industrial countries in 1982–83 can be partly explained by the severe worldwide recession of those years—which in turn, with lagged effects, was still contributing to a decline in the estimated world ratio through 1984 and 1985.

The most striking feature of figure 3-1, however, is the generally upward trend in all countries' ratios, especially in the period since the early 1970s. For each of the countries shown, the level of the foreign trade proportion is markedly higher today than in the early postwar period.

Both the numerators and the denominators of the ratios illustrated in figure 3-1 are measured in current prices. The ratios thus can vary because of changes in relative prices as well as changes in the relative quantitative impor-

Figure 3-1. *Trade in Goods and Services as a Proportion of Gross Domestic Product, Major Industrial Countries, 1953–85*[a]

Ratio in percent

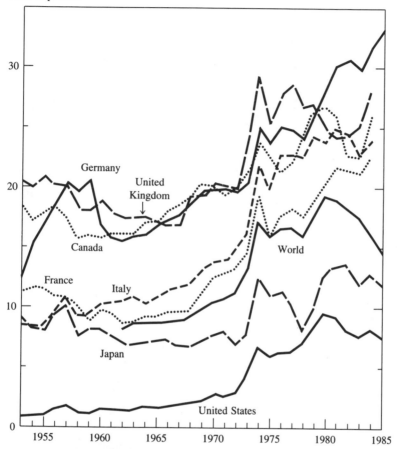

Sources: Data for trade and output for the world, International Monetary Fund, *International Financial Statistics, Supplement on Output Statistics,* no. 8 (Washington, D.C.: IMF, 1984), updated with figures for 1984 and 1985 (partially estimated by the author) from IMF, *International Financial Statistics Yearbook 1986.* Figures for United States from national income and product accounts in U.S. Department of Commerce, Bureau of Economic Analysis, *Survey of Current Business,* various issues.

a. For the seven individual countries, "trade" is measured as the average of exports and imports (of both goods and services). "World" trade is a total for all countries (other than those in the Soviet bloc) of exports of goods and services.

tance of traded goods. Broadly speaking, before the early 1970s the prices of internationally traded goods rose more slowly than the prices of nontraded goods and hence more slowly than the average of all prices. The experience after the early 1970s was the reverse: the prices of traded goods, especially

Figure 3-2. *Ratios of Exports and Imports of Goods and Services to Gross Domestic Product, Current and Constant Prices, United States, 1948–86*

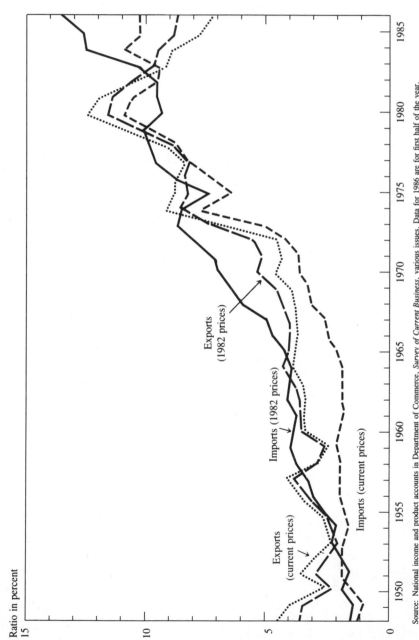

Ratio in percent

Exports
(1982 prices)

Imports (1982 prices)

Exports
(current prices)

Imports (current prices)

Source: National income and product accounts in Department of Commerce, *Survey of Current Business*, various issues. Data for 1986 are for first half of the year.

following the large increases in world oil prices in 1973–74 and 1979–80, rose more rapidly than the average of all prices.

Interpretation of the ratios is also clouded by the measurement of trade as the average of exports and imports. Changes in exchange rates and differences among countries' growth rates can powerfully influence the quantities of a country's exports and imports, especially the shorter-run evolution of its trade and current-account balances. The differential movements of exports and imports are concealed within an average for trade as a whole.

Figure 3-2 illustrates the importance of these points for the case of the United States. It shows separately the ratios to GDP of exports and imports of goods and services, measured in both current prices and constant prices. The effects of the differential trends in the prices of traded and nontraded goods can be seen in the contrasting behavior of the current-price and constant-price ratios before and after the early 1970s. The nominal and price-adjusted ratios both fluctuate in response to variations in economic activity in the United States and the rest of the world (for example, 1972–74, 1974–76, and 1980–83). The effects of swings in the exchange value of the dollar manifest themselves especially strongly in the export and import ratios calculated in constant prices. For example, during 1980–85 the sharp decline in the quantity of exports and the sharp increase in the quantity of imports—both relative to GDP—were in part attributable to an enormous appreciation in the exchange value of the dollar (see figure 6-1 for the exchange value of the dollar in 1973–86).

Despite the variety of influences on the ratios shown in figure 3-2, the single most striking feature of the chart is, again, the upward secular trend in all the ratios. The U.S. economy, like almost all other national economies, is much more extensively linked to the world economy through goods and services transactions than it was three or four decades ago.

World Aggregates for Output, Trade, and International Banking

As illustrative evidence documenting the faster pace of increases in financial interdependence, consider first the three curves charted in figure 3-3. The series for output and for goods-and-services trade are the same world aggregates used to derive the world ratio shown in figure 3-1. The data for international banking are derived from statistics published by the Morgan Guaranty Trust Company. The series is typically referred to as the "gross Eurocurrency

Figure 3-3. *International Banking, World Exports of Goods and Services, and World Output, 1964–85*

Billions of U.S. dollars (log scale)

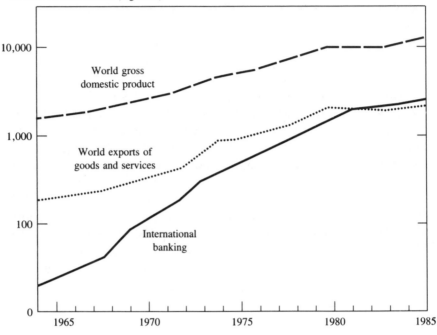

Sources: For world aggregates, see figure 3-1. For international banking data, Morgan Guaranty Trust Company of New York, *World Financial Markets*, various issues.

market''; it is the most comprehensive of the regularly published aggregates for international banking.[3]

Observations for selected years for the three series plotted in figure 3-3 are shown in table 3-1, together with rates of growth for various subperiods. Over the twenty-one-year period as a whole, international banking grew at a compound rate of some 26 percent per year. The comparable growth rates for trade and output were, respectively, only about 12½ percent and 10½ percent. Thus

3. I use this series only illustratively. It refers merely to international banking rather than all types of international financial intermediation and indeed just to a part of the banking activity that has one or another international characteristic (see below for further discussion). Each of the three ''world'' variables in figure 3-3 is a crude aggregate subject to a variety of measurement problems. For the purposes of the comparisons here, however, those measurement problems do not alter my qualitative conclusions.

over the last two decades international banking activity grew roughly twice as fast as trade and two and one-half times as fast as the value of economic activity.

Virtually all series for the aggregate dimensions of international banking for which statistics can be compiled exhibit very high rates of growth during the last two decades. For example, table 3-1 shows a second indicator of growth in the Eurocurrency markets, the Bank for International Settlements (BIS) series for net international bank credit extended by banks in the so-called BIS reporting area. The absolute value of this series is about half the Morgan Guaranty series for the gross size of the Eurocurrency market, in part because the BIS series has been adjusted to exclude large amounts of interbank claims. Note, however, that its rate of growth is roughly similar.

The data for output, trade, and international banking exhibit significant differences over various subperiods. For example, the faster growth of international banking than of trade was less dramatic in 1972–80 than in 1964–72. Banking was severely affected, but less so than trade, by the worldwide recession in the early 1980s and by the associated debt-servicing difficulties of developing nations. (The value of trade declined absolutely during 1980–83, whereas international banking continued to grow at a reduced but still substantial rate.) Notwithstanding such differences during various subperiods, the internationalization of banking was a powerful trend throughout the two decades.

The absolute values of the series shown in figure 3-3 and table 3-1 are nominal magnitudes and thus significantly influenced by inflation. The amounts are expressed in U.S. dollars, moreover, and changes between the dates shown are thus influenced by exchange-rate movements of the dollar relative to other currencies. Since inflation and exchange-rate changes affected all of the series, however, neither phenomenon can account for the large relative differences in the growth rates between the international banking aggregates on the one hand and the trade and output measures on the other.

The scatter diagram in figure 3-4 provides another perspective on the faster pace of financial interdependence by comparing actual data points with points showing what the growth of the international banking series would have been if it had expanded (or contracted) each year since 1964 in exact proportion to the growth of goods-and-services trade. If international banking had grown merely at the pace of trade, it would have been on the order of only $230 billion in the mid-1980s—less than one-tenth of its actual size (some $2,500 billion).

Table 3-1. *Economic Activity, International Trade, and International Banking, Selected Years, 1964–85*

Indicator	Amount (billions of U.S. dollars at current prices and exchange rates)					Compound annual rate of growth			
	1964	1972	1980	1983	1985	1964–72	1972–80	1980–85	1964–85
Gross domestic product									
World excluding Soviet bloc[a]	1,605	3,336	10,172	10,140	12,825	9.6	15.0	4.7	10.4
International trade in goods and services									
World excluding Soviet bloc[a]	188	463	2,150	1,986	2,190	12.0	21.2	0.4	12.4
International banking									
BIS series for net international bank credit, BIS reporting area[b]	12	122	810	1,240	1,485	33.6	26.7	12.9	25.8
Morgan Guaranty series for gross size of international banking market[c]	20	208	1,559	2,253	2,598	34.0	28.6	10.8	26.1

a. Source: International Monetary Fund, *International Financial Statistics, Supplement on Output Statistics,* no. 8 (Washington, D.C.: IMF, 1984), and data from IMF, *International Financial Statistics Yearbook 1986.* Both the output and trade series incorporate rough estimates for some countries. "Trade" is a country aggregation of statistics for exports of goods and services. The 1985 figures are partly estimated by the author.

b. Source: Bank for International Settlements, *Annual Reports* and quarterly statistical releases on international banking developments. In concept this series nets out interbank redepositing among the banks in the reporting area. The reporting area in recent years has included banks in the Group of Ten countries plus Luxembourg, Austria, Denmark, Ireland and the offshore branches of U.S. banks in the Bahamas, the Cayman Islands, Panama, Hong Kong, and Singapore. Banks in Finland, Norway, and Spain were added to the reporting area as of December 1983. Only the Group of Ten countries were included in the reporting area in the 1960s and early 1970s. The figures for 1964 and 1972 are partly estimated by the author.

c. Source: Morgan Guaranty Trust Company of New York, *World Financial Markets,* various issues. This measure differs from the BIS series for net international bank credit in two major ways: it includes redepositing among the reporting banks and it defines the reporting area to cover a larger number of countries and banks. The figures for 1964 and 1972 are partly estimated by the author.

Figure 3-4. *International Banking and World Trade in Goods and Services, 1964–85*

International banking (billions of U.S. dollars, log scale)

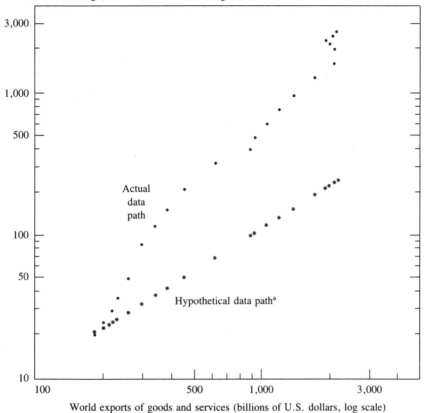

World exports of goods and services (billions of U.S. dollars, log scale)

Sources: IMF, *International Financial Statistics, Supplement on Output Statistics,* no. 8; IMF, *International Financial Statistics Yearbook 1986;* and Morgan Guaranty Trust Company, *World Financial Markets,* various issues.
a. Hypothetical growth of international banking in exact proportion to the growth of goods-and-services trade.

Eurocurrency and International Banking

International financial intermediation can be defined in numerous ways. The same is true for international banking.

Much of the existing banking and academic literature, and virtually all of the journalistic discussion, has been preoccupied with "Eurocurrency" banking or the "Eurocurrency markets." The impression is frequently given that Eurocurrency banking comprises all the international aspects of banking. The existing literature also tends to perceive Eurocurrency banking as entirely different from the regular or ordinary banking characteristic of financial activity within nations. These impressions are unfortunate. Eurocurrency banking is not a phenomenon sui generis, but merely one part of a general nexus of financial interrelations linking open national economies.

Eurocurrency banking has been defined conventionally as the denomination of the assets and liabilities of a bank office in a currency other than the currency unit of the nation where the office is located. The statistical data used to describe the Eurocurrency markets have often included only claims or liabilities denominated in foreign currencies vis-à-vis foreign residents.

From an analytical perspective, there is nothing logically compelling about the conventional definition. When a bank office has claims on or liabilities to foreign residents denominated in the domestic currency, those cross-border assets and liabilities are unambiguously international in character. Similarly, when a bank office has foreign-currency claims on or liabilities to domestic residents, the currency denomination of those assets and liabilities gives the banking relations an external aspect. Eurocurrency deposits and loans as conventionally defined, therefore, are certainly not the only type of banking activity with a significant international dimension.

To be sure, the banking regulations and banking supervision procedures in most nations differentiate between domestic-currency and external-currency assets and liabilities, or between resident customers and nonresident customers (see chapters 7 and 8). Some countries' regulations and supervision make both types of distinction. Such differences create differential incentives for the growth of the various categories of assets and liabilities. Regulations apart, the question of whether obligations are denominated in domestic currency or external currency can be of critical importance for many aspects of financial and economic behavior.

The establishment of asset and liability relations with foreigners and the denomination of obligations in external currencies, however, is a pervasive feature of life in interdependent national economies. There is no good reason for isolating one aspect of international banking and analyzing it independently of the rest of the nexus of financial relations linking nations together. Indeed, there is no compelling reason for analyzing the international aspects of banking independently of ordinary domestic banking.

To study international banking in a comprehensive way, an analyst should have available a detailed breakdown of the balance sheets of banks in each national jurisdiction cross-classified by currency denomination, by residency of customer, and by type of customer. In principle, the data should be assembled in a way that integrates the domestic as well as all international aspects of banking for a given jurisdiction. Unfortunately, such data are not published by most countries (and in some instances not even collected).[4]

In the last several years, I have worked sporadically to compile such data as are available in published national sources for the major industrial nations and the most important offshore banking centers. An illustration of the integrated figures one would like to have is shown in table 3-2 for the single date December 31, 1982. Each row shows the total assets, including interbank claims, of all banking offices located within a particular country (column 5). This total-assets figure is broken down into traditional domestic assets (column 4) and the three broad types of claims having either a currency-denomination or a residence-of-customer characteristic that makes the claim international (columns 1, 2, and 3). Table 3-2 also shows the total of claims with some international characteristic (column 6) and the relative importance of these claims in the total balance sheet (column 7).[5]

The data frequently associated with Eurocurrency banking are some variant or some subset of the data in column 1 (often the subtotal for countries whose banking data are given to the BIS for their quarterly release, *International Banking Developments*). At the end of 1982, these banking claims amounted

4. The Bank for International Settlements publishes large amounts of data for international banking in its quarterly *International Banking Developments* and its semiannual surveys of the maturity structure of international bank lending. The International Monetary Fund now also publishes large amounts of relevant data, including helpful compilations of the geographical distribution of cross-border banking (compiled not only by the country of location of the reporting banks but also by the geographical location of the banks' customers). Both the BIS and the IMF improved the coverage of their statistics in 1984–85. Although the BIS and IMF data are indispensable, both omit the domestic aspects of banking. Users of the international-institution data confront many difficulties if they attempt to use the international data in conjunction with data from national statistical sources. For two recent descriptive surveys of the available data for international banking, see Rodney H. Mills, "Foreign Lending by Banks: A Guide to International and U.S. Statistics"; and Joslin Landell-Mills, *The Fund's International Banking Statistics*.

5. Construction of table 3-2 (or its equivalent for other dates) encounters numerous difficulties. Several of these create potential inconsistencies of treatment across countries. For example, some countries use a comprehensive definition of "bank," including many types of thrift intermediaries in their banking statistics; others use a narrow definition, restricting it to the traditional commercial banks. There is thus considerable variation across countries in the financial institutions that fall into the bank reporting net. There is also variation across countries in the types of assets (and liabilities) actually included by the reporting institutions; different countries have differing reporting criteria. Many of the figures presented in table 3-2 are partially estimated since the requisite breakdowns by residency and currency denomination are often not fully available. As noted in the acknowledgments, Linda Mix Tesar provided helpful assistance with many of the tables in this chapter. I am especially grateful to her for assistance in the construction of table 3-2 and the numerous backup tables for individual countries not shown here.

Table 3-2. *Assets (including Interbank Claims) Reported by Banking Offices in Fifteen Industrial Countries and Eight Offshore Banking Centers, December 31, 1982*

Billions of U.S. dollars at end-1982 exchange rates unless otherwise indicated

Country or group of countries	Assets with one or more international characteristic			Traditional domestic assets (claims on home residents denominated in home currency) (4)	Total assets (gross size of banks' balance sheets) (1+2+3+4) (5)	Subtotal of assets with some international characteristic	
	Claims on foreign residents denominated in foreign currencies (1)	Claims on foreign residents denominated in home currency (2)	Claims on home residents denominated in foreign currencies (3)			Amount (1+2+3) (6)	Percent of total balance sheet [(6÷5)×100] (7)
A. Five major European banking centers	**716**	**160**	**242**	**1,957**	**3,075**	**1,118**	**36**
United Kingdom	437	26	183	248	893	646	72
Germany	19	64	2	1,054	1,140	86	8
France	124	24	40	466	654	188	29
Switzerland (excluding trustee accounts)	33	38	5	184	260	76	29
Luxembourg	102	8	12	6	128	122	96
B. Seven other European countries	**177**	**29**	**69**	**826**	**1,101**	**275**	**25**
Austria	20	8	8	106	141	35	25
Belgium	61	5	22	42	130	88	68
Denmark	5	*	2	25	33	7	22
Ireland	3	*	3	14	19	5	28
Italy	33	1	18	495	547	53	10
Netherlands	49	13	8	97	168	72	42
Sweden	6	1	9	48	63	16	25

C. Twelve European countries (BIS reporters) (A+B)	**893**	**188**	**311**	**2,783**	**4,176**	**1,392**	**33**
D. Japan	66	25	87	1437	1,615	178	11
E. Canada	37	2	26	171	236	65	27
F. United States	8	356	*	1745	2,109	363	17
G. Fifteen industrial reporting countries (C+D+E+F)	**1,003**	**571**	**425**	**6,136**	**8,135**	**1,999**	**25**
H. Eight offshore banking centers	**499**	**9**	**69**	**82**	**660**	**577**	**87**
Singapore	80	2	28	18	128	109	86
Hong Kong	56	2	28	47	133	86	65
Bahrain	45	5	8	4	62	58	94
Lebanon	4[a]	[a]	12[b]	[b]	16	6	60
Bahamas	132	*	*	2	134	132	98
Cayman Islands	128	...	*	...	128	128	100
Panama	44	...	3	...	47	47	100
Netherlands Antilles	11	*	*	1	12	11	89
I. Swiss trustee accounts	93[a]	[a]	...	...	93	93	100
J. Grand total (G+H+I)	**1,593**	**583**	**494**	**6,218**	**8,887**	**2,669**	**30**

* Data not reported with this breakdown but the amount is believed small (less than $½ billion).

Sources: Details do not always add to totals due to rounding of underlying figures. Many figures in the table are partially estimated by the author. National source data were used where the requisite breakdowns were available. In all cases the figures for column 5 come from national sources. For some of the countries in the BIS reporting area, figures for columns 1 and 2 are from the BIS quarterly tables on *International Banking Developments*. When not available from the national-source data, figures for column 3 were based on the series for "international banking analyzed by centre" published by the Bank of England in its annual review article (see, for example, *Bank of England Quarterly Bulletin*, vol. 25 [March 1985], p. 66]. The figures in column 4 for many countries were obtained as a residual (column 5 less the sum of columns 1, 2, and 3).

a. Figure in column 1 is sum of columns 1 and 2.
b. Figure in column 3 is sum of columns 3 and 4.

to roughly $1 trillion. If the comparable assets of banks in the main offshore centers and the trustee accounts of Swiss banks are included, the total figure is some $1.6 trillion.[6]

As can be seen by contrasting the first three columns of table 3-2, the data conventionally associated with Eurocurrency banking are larger than the magnitudes of other international types of lending. Yet for many countries, and certainly for the world as a whole, the figures for the other types of lending are sizable. Even if one treats the United States with its large dollar lending to foreigners as a case apart, bank offices in other countries have more than $200 billion of foreign claims denominated in local currencies (column 2). Foreign-currency claims on domestic residents add up to another $500 billion, with the amount especially large in the United Kingdom ($183 billion), but the remainder widely distributed across all the industrial countries other than the United States (column 3).

If one takes into account all the aspects of banking that have a cross-border or cross-currency characteristic, the grand total in December 1982 came to nearly $2.7 trillion. By the spring of 1986 the comparable figure was larger by at least another $800 billion and conceivably by as much as an additional $850 billion to $875 billion.

The relative importance of banking assets with international characteristics varies greatly from one geographical location to another. Such assets dominate the balance sheets of banks in London, Luxembourg, Singapore, Hong Kong, and Bahrain. For the Bahamas, the Cayman Islands, Panama, and the Netherlands Antilles, they are virtually the whole of the balance sheet. At the end of 1982 they are estimated to have accounted for one-fourth or more of banks' balance sheets in Belgium (68 percent), the Netherlands (42), Switzerland (29 percent even without the trustee accounts), France (29), Ireland (28), Canada (27), Austria (25), and Sweden (25) (column 7). The industrial countries for which this balance-sheet proportion was lowest at the end of 1982 are Germany (8 percent), Italy (10), and Japan (11). The estimated proportion for the United States was 17 percent.[7]

6. The role of Swiss banks in operating trustee accounts is formally that of an agent. In many instances, however, the banks are thought to have a decisive influence in advising the clients where and how to place the funds; some analysts therefore include these accounts with other banking data. These accounts represent claims on residents of countries other than Switzerland, but the reported data do not indicate a breakdown by currency denomination. In line K of table 3-2, I have assumed that almost all these assets are denominated in U.S. dollars and other foreign currencies, rather than in Swiss francs.

7. No data are collected in the United States for banks' claims on and liabilities to domestic residents denominated in foreign currencies. The amounts are assumed to be still very small.

In the rest of this book the term "international banking" will denote any bank asset—or a liability with corresponding attributes—that would fall into the categories shown in columns 1, 2, or 3 of table 3-2, or a similarly constructed table covering a larger number of countries. Analogously, "international financial intermediation" may be defined—loosely, but sufficiently for the purposes of this book—as any asset or liability of a financial intermediary or a participant in securities markets that has a cross-border or cross-currency dimension (or both).

Table 3-2 does not show a breakdown between claims of banking offices on other banks and claims on nonbanks. It therefore cannot reveal the important fact that Eurocurrency banking, and international banking in general, are first and foremost *interbank* phenomena. To speak roughly, less than one-third of the claims in most entries shown in columns 1, 2, and 3 represent claims on nonbank economic units. To give a concrete example, the amount of external lending (claims on nonresidents) of banking offices in the United States, Japan, Canada, and twelve European countries reporting to the Bank for International Settlements was some $1.6 trillion at the end of December 1982 (the sum of columns 1 and 2 on row G). Of that amount, only 30 percent (some $460 billion to $480 billion) represented lending to nonbanks. The remaining 70 percent was lending to other banking offices or to official monetary institutions.

Analysts who speak of the "net" rather than "gross" size of the Eurocurrency market wish to abstract from some or all of the interbank claims, thereby focusing on assets and liabilities vis-à-vis nonbanks. Over a period of many years, the BIS has calculated and published such a measure in its annual reports and quarterly statistical releases (see the series "net international bank credit" in table 3-1). The relative importance of interbank claims in international banking has changed only marginally since the initial collection of the data in the mid-1960s.[8]

On the liability side of Eurobanks' balance sheets, the bulk of deposits are akin to time certificates of deposit. Unlike a bank's demand or sight liabilities denominated in the currency of the nation where the bank is located, Eurocurrency deposits are not transactions balances that can be widely used as a means of payment.[9] Even after estimates of interbank redepositing are subtracted from estimates of the gross size of Eurocurrency magnitudes, only a

---

8. A detailed discussion of the distinction between the gross and net sizes of the Eurocurrency market may be found in Helmut W. Mayer, "The BIS Concept of the Eurocurrency Market."

9. This statement applies even to the bulk of call Eurocurrency deposits (those without a fixed maturity and redeemable immediately at the request of the depositor).

modest fraction (in the mid-1970s, about one-third) of net Eurocurrency deposits is owned by nonbanks. This point also applies more broadly to other deposits that are "international" but not "Eurocurrency."

As presently conducted, therefore, international banking plays a much more prominent role in channeling funds among financial institutions themselves than in providing direct intermediation and maturity transformation between ultimate nonbank savers and ultimate nonbank investors. Nor is international banking as yet an important mechanism for facilitating nonbanks' holdings of assets usable for transactions purposes. Such a development seems likely in the future but is not a reality in the mid-1980s. These basic facts are frequently overlooked in superficial discussions that ignore the importance of interbank redepositing and describe Eurocurrency deposits as "stateless money."[10]

International Banking by Nationality of Ownership

The data shown in table 3-2 are organized by the countries in which banking offices are located. When reading that table, one should recall that the country distribution of the ultimate ownership of banking offices does not closely correspond to the geographical location of the offices. A significant fraction of the assets shown are on the balance sheets of branches or subsidiaries of foreign-owned banks rather than of locally owned banks.

For most countries and dates, figures that distinguish between foreign-owned and locally owned banks are not publicly available. In recent years, however, the Bank for International Settlements obtained additional data for this breakdown from countries that are regular reporters in the BIS quarterly analysis of international banking developments. In 1985 and 1986, the BIS in turn included some of these data in published documents. Tables 3-3 through 3-5 summarize some highlights of that new information.

Table 3-3 provides an overview of the number of institutions or banking offices owned by foreign banking organizations operating in selected host

10. In *Money and Monetary Policy in Interdependent Nations,* chaps. 3 and 7–9, I discuss the issues involved in defining the stock of money for particular nations or regions. Cross-border and cross-currency deposits create especially severe conceptual difficulties for those who seek a definition of money to use as an intermediate target in the conduct of national monetary policy. For further discussion of the analytical issues, see my essay "Eurocurrency Banking: Alarmist Concerns and Genuine Issues."

Table 3-3. *Institutions or Offices Owned by Foreign Banks Operating in Selected Host Countries, December 1960–June 1985*

Host country	December 1960	December 1970	December 1980	June 1985
	Number of institutions[a]			
Belgium	14[b]	26	51	57
Canada	0	0	0	57
Italy[c]	1	4	26	36
Netherlands	n.a.	23	39	40
Switzerland	8	97	99	119
United Kingdom	51[d]	95	214	293[e]
	Number of banking offices[f]			
France	33	58	122	147
Germany	24	77	213	287[g]
Japan[h]	34	38	85	112
Luxembourg	3	23	96	106
United States	n.a.	n.a.[i]	579	783[j]

Source: Bank for International Settlements, *Recent Innovations in International Banking*, report prepared by a study group established by the central banks of the Group of Ten countries (Basel: BIS, 1986), p. 151.

n.a. Not available.

a. Figures are for the number of foreign-owned banking institutions ("families") operating in the host country through branches or majority-owned subsidiaries unless otherwise specified. An institution maintaining offices at several locations is counted only once. Figures are for end of month.

b. December 1958.

c. Figures are for branches only. At end of June 1985, five foreign-owned subsidiaries were operating in Italy.

d. December 1962.

e. The figure for June 1985 is 357 if joint ventures and consortium banks are included.

f. Foreign-owned banking institutions represented by more than one entity in a host country are counted more than once. Figures are for end of month.

g. At end of June 1985 these offices represented 95 different foreign-owned banking institutions.

h. Figures are for branches only. At end of June 1985, 76 different foreign-owned banking institutions were operating in Japan.

i. In the early 1970s about 50 offices of foreign-owned banking institutions were operating in the United States.

j. At end of June 1985 these offices represented approximately 350 different foreign-owned banking institutions.

countries.[11] The growth in foreign banking presence is perhaps especially striking for the United Kingdom and the United States. An easing of government restraints on the activities of foreign-owned banks in the late 1970s or 1980s explains much of the recent growth for Canada and Japan. Nonetheless, the expansion in numbers of foreign-owned entities in the domestic banking system has been impressive in each of the eleven countries shown in the table.

11. The two parts of table 3-3 are not conceptually comparable. The six host countries in the first rows of the table reported information to the BIS about the number of foreign-owned banking *institutions*—in effect, "families"—operating within their borders; if a foreign-owned institution maintained offices at several locations in those countries, it was nevertheless counted only once in the classification. The host countries in the second part of the table reported the number of foreign-owned *offices*; an institution represented by several offices in those countries was thus counted several times. The footnotes to table 3-3 provide further information about comparability.

Another measure of the growing importance of foreign-owned banks is provided in table 3-4. The figures are estimates of the proportion of total assets of resident banking institutions accounted for by foreign-owned institutions. For example, foreign-owned institutions had only 7 percent of the assets of banking offices located in the United Kingdom at the end of 1960; the proportion rose to 38 percent by 1970, 56 percent by 1980, and 63 percent by June 1985. Among the eleven host nations shown in the table, only Canada, Germany, Italy, and Japan had proportions of less than 10 percent by 1985, and even those four countries experienced substantial increases over the last two and one-half decades.[12]

For December 1983, the earliest date for which such special-survey comparative data are available, table 3-5 provides a classification of aggregate international banking activity by nationality of ownership. In concept, the coverage of the data is similar to the coverage in the first three columns of table 3-2; that is, the figures include all assets of reporting bank offices that are international (cross-border or cross-currency) in character. The difference between the tables is that table 3-5 allocates the data by country of ownership of the parent banking entity, whereas table 3-2 allocates the data by location of the banking offices.[13] For example, the figures for France shown in table 3-5 represent the international business of French parent banks and of their branches and subsidiaries located in France or in the other thirteen reporting countries. Consortium banks that cannot be classified according to parent country are shown separately. The figures in the table also include international business on the balance sheets of affiliates located within the reporting area of banks with head offices outside the reporting area; the data for those banking organizations do not include the business of their outside-area parent institutions.[14]

The figures in table 3-5 show banking organizations with U.S. ownership having the largest share of aggregate international business in December 1983

12. For Germany and Japan, moreover, the available data include only branches (instead of branches plus subsidiaries) of foreign-owned banks.

13. The country coverage of reporting bank offices for the data in table 3-2 is somewhat broader than that for table 3-5.

14. I have used data for December 1983 in table 3-5 to make it somewhat less difficult to compare the December 1982 data in table 3-2 with figures classified by bank ownership. More recent data comparable to those in table 3-5 are now available. See Bank for International Settlements, *International Banking Developments, Third Quarter 1985* (January 1986), pt. 2, pp. 9–17, for the updated figures through September 1985. In this publication, the reporting area was extended to include Austria and Spain, with separate data shown for the international activities of banks with head offices in those two countries. Figures for U.S. banks were also improved.

Table 3-4. *Relative Importance of Assets of Foreign-Owned Banking Institutions Operating in Selected Host Countries, December 1960–June 1985*[a]

Percent

Host country	December 1960	December 1970	December 1980	June 1985
Belgium	8.2[b]	22.5	41.5	51.0
Canada	. . .	. . .	. . .	6.3
France	7.2	12.3	15.0	18.2[c]
Germany[d]	0.5	1.4	1.9	2.4
Italy	n.a.	n.a.	0.9	2.4
Japan[d]	n.a.	1.3	3.4	3.6
Luxembourg[e]	8.0	57.8	85.4	85.4
Netherlands[f]	n.a.	n.a.	17.4[g]	23.6
Switzerland	n.a.	10.3	11.1	12.2
United Kingdom	6.7	37.5	55.6	62.6
United States[h]	n.a.	5.8[i]	8.7	12.0

Source: Bank for International Settlements, *Recent Innovations in International Banking*, p. 152.
n.a. Not available.
a. Percent of total assets of all banking institutions (domestic- and foreign-owned) at end of month.
b. December 1958.
c. December 1984.
d. Only branches of foreign-owned banking institutions.
e. Banks owned by Belgian residents are not considered foreign-owned banking institutions.
f. Only universal branches of foreign-owned banking institutions.
g. December 1983.
h. Only agencies and branches of foreign-owned banking institutions.
i. December 1976.

(29½ percent), with Japanese banks accounting for another large share (21 percent). Banks with U.S. and Japanese ownership, along with those with French, British, and German ownership, represented 74 percent of the total international banking business caught in this reporting net.

The rankings of the countries shown in table 3-5 are affected by numerous factors, some of them potentially misleading. For example, U.S. and Japanese banking organizations tend to have much larger claims on and liabilities to related offices than do banking organizations owned by other nations. This characteristic inflated the numbers for the United States and Japan relative to other countries. Moreover, a flaw in the data collection artificially inflated the U.S. figures and reduced the figures for other countries for December 1983.[15]

15. Data for the subsidiaries of foreign-owned banks in the United States were not distinguished from data for other U.S. banks, and were thus included with the positions of U.S.-owned banks. The subsequent update of these data in the BIS publication cited (ibid.) correctly classified the figures for U.S. subsidiaries of foreign-owned banks according to the nationality of their parent banks.

Table 3-5. *International Assets Reported by Banking Offices in Main BIS Reporting Countries, by Nationality of Ownership, December 1983*[a]

Billions of U.S. dollars at end-1983 exchange rates

Parent country	Type of international asset					Total international assets of offices in all reporting countries
	Claims on related offices[b]	Claims on other nonaffiliated banks	Claims on nonbanks[c]	Claims on official monetary institutions	CDs[d]	
United States[e]	234	213	180	1	2	631
Japan	120	194	133	2	3	451
France	24	104	56	5	*	190
United Kingdom	19	82	65	3	2	171
Germany	11	70	62	1	*	144
Canada	22	29	37	*	1	89
Italy	2	57	20	*	1	80
Switzerland	13	36	20	2	5	77
Netherlands	5	36	21	*	n.a.	62
Belgium	2	18	18	. . .	n.a.	38
Luxembourg	*	3	2	. . .	n.a.	5
Sweden	1	6	11	*	n.a.	18
Denmark	2	5	2	. . .	n.a.	9
Other BIS reporting countries[f]	2	4	5	*	*	12
Consortium banks	2	21	19	1	*	43
Other developed countries	3	9	11	*	*	23
Middle East	2	11	5	*	*	18
Latin America	9	3	9	. . .	*	21
Eastern Europe	. . .	3	2	3	n.a.	8
Others	7	19	12	*	1	40
Unallocated	. . .	3	4	. . .	. . .	6
Total	480	925	695	21	16	2,136

Source: Bank for International Settlements, Monetary and Economic Department, *The Nationality Structure of the International Banking Market and the Role of Interbank Operations* (Basel: BIS, 1985), p.4.

n.a. Not available.

* Less than $0.5 billion.

a. Details do not always add to totals due to rounding of underlying figures. International assets are defined as cross-border assets in all currencies plus foreign-currency assets vis-à-vis local residents. The assets classified in the table are the international assets reported by banking offices located in fourteen of the BIS reporting countries (Belgium, Luxembourg, Canada, Denmark, France, Germany, Ireland, Italy, Japan, the Netherlands, Sweden, Switzerland, the United Kingdom, and the United States) and the cross-border assets reported by the branches of U.S. banks operating in the Bahamas, the Cayman Islands, Panama, Hong Kong, and Singapore. The classification is according to the nationality of ownership, not the geographical location, of the banking offices.

b. Cross-border claims only; positions on related offices were not reported by banking offices located in Germany and Italy.

c. Includes claims of banking offices in the United States on official monetary institutions.

d. Holdings of bank offices in the United Kingdom only.

e. Includes U.S.-chartered subsidiaries of foreign banks and U.S. banks' branches in certain offshore centers.

f. Includes banks owned in Austria and Ireland as well as reporting-area banks whose data could not be allocated to individual countries.

By September 1985, Japanese banks' share of total international banking business (measured as in table 3-5), had risen to some 26 percent, while the U.S. share had dropped to 23 percent.[16] French, British, and German banks continued to have the third, fourth, and fifth largest shares, with the top five countries together accounting for 72 percent of total international banking business.

The nationality-of-ownership data shown in table 3-5 confirm the broad generalization made earlier about the modest importance of transactions with nonbanks. For the aggregate of banks' international assets classified in the table, slightly less than one-third ($695 billion out of $2,136 billion) represented claims on nonbank entities. In their cross-border and cross-currency transactions, banks are much more extensively engaged in channeling funds among themselves than in providing direct intermediation between ultimate nonbank savers and ultimate nonbank investors.

In earlier history, foreign-owned financial institutions, especially banks, played a key role in transmitting financial technology across borders and in opening up domestic financial systems to international influences. The figures shown in tables 3-3 through 3-5 provide further evidence of the pervasive international character of banking in the 1980s, continuing this historical trend. Today, as in the past, foreign-owned financial intermediaries are especially likely to initiate cross-border and cross-currency transactions. Now, as then, foreign-owned intermediaries tend to have a larger part of their business with foreign residents or in foreign currencies than do domestically owned intermediaries. Now, as then, foreign-owned intermediaries are more likely to transfer financial innovations from abroad into domestic financial systems.

International Financial Intermediation in the United States

Examination of the experiences of individual countries underscores the points about increasing financial interdependence made above. Table 3-6 summarizes the most comprehensive data available on the assets and liabilities of U.S. residents vis-à-vis foreign residents, known as the international investment position of the United States. In the early postwar period, well over half of the external assets of the U.S. economy were owned by the U.S. govern-

16. Reflecting that change in relative position, Japanese-owned banks had also become the major bank group in several of the world's principal financial centers, including London. Japanese-owned banks were likewise the largest foreign owners of International Banking Facilities in the United States.

Table 3-6. *External Assets and Liabilities of the U.S. Economy, Selected Years, 1952–85*
Billions of dollars outstanding at year end, unless otherwise indicated

Item	1952	1962	1972	1975	1978	1981	1983	1985
U.S. assets abroad	**59.1**	**96.7**	**198.7**	**295.1**	**447.8**	**719.7**	**874.1**	**952.4**
U.S. official reserve assets[a]	24.7	17.2	13.2	16.2	18.7	30.1	33.7	43.2
Other assets of U.S. government	11.7	19.2	36.1	41.8	54.2	68.5	79.3	87.4
Assets of private U.S. residents	22.7	60.3	149.4	237.1	375.0	621.2	761.1	821.8
Direct investments	14.7	37.3	89.9	124.1	162.7	228.3	207.2	232.7
Foreign securities	4.7	11.9	27.4	34.9	53.4	63.5	84.3	114.1
Claims reported by nonbanks on unaffiliated foreigners	1.8	3.9	11.4	18.3	28.1	35.9	35.1	28.2
Claims reported by banks[b]	1.5	7.3	20.7	59.8	130.8	293.5	434.5	446.7
Foreign assets in the United States	**20.8**	**46.3**	**161.7**	**220.9**	**371.7**	**579.0**	**785.6**	**1,059.8**
Foreign official assets[c]	5[E]	14[E]	63.0	86.9	173.1	180.4	194.6	202.3
Other foreign assets in the U.S.	26[E]	32[E]	98.7	134.0	198.7	398.6	591.0	857.5
Direct investments	3.9	7.6	14.9	27.7	42.5	108.7	137.1	183.0
Securities other than U.S. Treasury securities	n.a.	n.a.	50.7	45.7	53.6	75.4	114.7	207.8
Liabilities reported by U.S. nonbanks to unaffiliated foreigners	n.a.	n.a.	10.7	13.9	16.0	30.6	26.9	29.1
Liabilities reported by U.S. banks to nonofficial foreigners[d]	4.6[E]	9.2[E]	22.4	46.7	86.6	183.9	312.3	437.7
Net external-asset position	**38.3**	**50.4**	**37.0**	**74.2**	**76.1**	**140.7**	**88.5**	**-107.4**

U.S. gross domestic product[e]	349.5	570.2	1,201.6	1,580.9	2,219.1	3,000.5	3,355.9	3,957.0
Memoranda								
Ratio of external assets other than those held by the U.S. government to GDP (percent)	6.5	10.6	12.5	15.0	16.9	20.7	22.7	20.8
Ratio of external liabilities to GDP (percent)	6.0	8.1	13.5	14.0	16.8	19.3	23.4	26.8

Source: U.S. Department of Commerce, Bureau of Economic Analysis, *Survey of Current Business*, various issues.

E. Estimated by author.

n.a. Not available.

a. The U.S. gold stock is valued at $35 per ounce before May 1972, at $38 per ounce between May 1972 and October 1973, and thereafter at $42.22 per ounce. Foreign currency reserves are valued at exchange rates at time of purchase through 1973 and at current exchange rates thereafter.

b. Includes claims on foreign residents of banking offices in the United States owned by foreigners and (since December 1981) of International Banking Facilities and claims on foreign residents held in custody by U.S. banking offices for customers resident in the United States.

c. Includes U.S. government securities owned by foreign institutions and claims of foreign official institutions on banking offices in the United States.

d. Includes U.S. Treasury securities held by nonofficial foreigners. Also includes liabilities to foreign residents of banking offices in the United States owned by foreigners and (since December 1981) of International Banking Facilities and liabilities of U.S. nonbanks to nonofficial foreigners held in custody and reported by U.S. banking offices.

e. Billions of dollars in current prices, annual flow.

ment. Over the ensuing years, however, the external assets of private Americans grew much faster than those of the government. Direct investments grew rapidly, especially in the 1960s. The most vigorous growth took place in the external claims reported by banking offices in the United States, but other types of financial claims grew strongly as well.

On the liability side of the external balance sheet, an important factor was the role of the U.S. dollar as a reserve currency. Dollar-denominated securities and deposits in the United States held by foreign governments in their international reserves expanded, with intermittent fits and starts, throughout the four decades from 1945 to 1985. The assets in the United States of foreigners other than foreign official institutions are partly in the form of direct investments. These grew especially rapidly after the late 1970s. On the liability side too, however, transactions going through banks were dominant for most of the postwar period.

By definition, the term "U.S. residents" includes the offices in the United States of foreign-owned financial institutions and nonfinancial corporations, just as the term "foreign residents" includes the offices abroad of U.S.-owned financial institutions and nonfinancial corporations. In the 1970s, in particular, foreign banks came into the United States on a large scale. Earlier, in the 1950s and the 1960s, American banks had established numerous offices abroad. Beginning in December 1981, banks in the United States (including the agencies and branches of foreign banks) were permitted to establish International Banking Facilities (IBFs).[17] All of these developments importantly influenced the external assets and liabilities reported by banking offices located in the United States.

The last two rows in table 3-6 show private external assets and total external liabilities of the United States as a proportion of gross domestic product. In the early 1950s, these asset and liability magnitudes were, respectively, 6½ and 6 percent of GDP. Two decades later, these ratios had doubled. Measured in this way, financial openness increased substantially further in the 1970s and 1980s. By the early 1980s, private external assets and external liabilities were both above 20 percent of the value of GDP. By 1985, the ratio of external liabilities to GDP was nearly 27 percent and still rising rapidly.

Throughout the period from 1945 to 1982, the United States had a sizable and generally increasing net creditor position vis-à-vis the rest of the world. The surplus of external assets over external liabilities was more than $135 billion in 1981 and 1982. By 1983, however, the United States was beginning

17. See Sydney J. Key, "International Banking Facilities."

Figure 3-5. *Net External-Asset Position of the United States, 1946–86*[a]

Billions of dollars

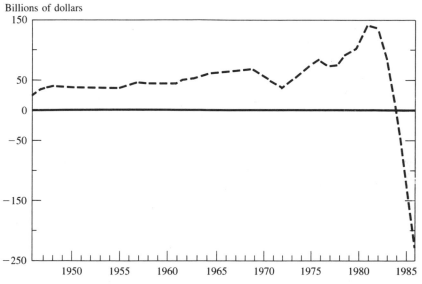

Source: Department of Commerce, Bureau of Economic Analysis, *Survey of Current Business,* October 1977, August 1980, and June 1986. Figure for 1986 is a rough estimate made in September 1986.
a. Claims of U.S. residents on foreigners less foreigners' claims on U.S. residents.

to run large deficits in the current account of its balance of payments, which in turn caused a sharp reversal in the net external-asset position. Figure 3-5, a chart of the net external-asset position over the entire postwar period, shows clearly the extent to which the 1983–86 figures were "off the map" of recent historical experience.[18]

Table 3-7 focuses more narrowly on international banking conducted in the United States. As a point of reference for the international banking series, the final rows in the table provide figures for real-sector economic activity and for

18. One of the dominant causes of the 1980s deterioration in the U.S. current-account balance was the very large appreciation of the exchange value of the dollar from the summer of 1980 through February-March 1985 (see figure 6-1). That appreciation in turn was importantly attributable to slack fiscal policy and tight monetary policy in the United States, combined with strong moves toward fiscal contraction in Europe and Japan. Even though some one-half to two-thirds of the 1980–85 appreciation in the dollar's exchange value had been reversed between the first quarter of 1985 and the third quarter of 1986 and even though some progress had been made during 1985–86 in adjusting the U.S., European, and Japanese macroeconomic policies that had led to the large payments imbalances, it nonetheless seemed probable as of this writing (September 1986) that the U.S. current account would remain in sizable deficit at least through 1988, and possibly through 1989 and 1990. It was not implausible to foresee the United States falling into a net external debtor position as large as $500 billion to $800 billion before the end of the 1980s.

Table 3-7. *Indicators of International Banking, United States, Selected Years, 1952–85*

Billions of dollars at end of year unless otherwise indicated

Indicator	1952	1962	1972	1975	1978	1981	1983	1985	Compound annual rate of growth, 1952–85
A. Claims of U.S. banking offices on foreign residents[a]									
1. Total reported[b]	1.5	7.3	20.7	59.8	130.9	293.5	434.5	449.0	18.9
2. Banks' own claims	1.0[E]	6.2[E]	15.5[E]	51.5[E]	119.3	256.6	398.5	419.3	20.0
B. Liabilities of U.S. banking offices to foreign residents[a]									
1. Total reported[c]	9.3	22.0	61.7	96.2	169.2	247.4	374.8	449.8	12.5
2. Banks' own liabilities denominated in dollars	6.1[E]	11.7[E]	25.0[E]	51.0[E]	78.7	163.8	279.1	340.4	13.0
C. Total assets of foreign branches of U.S.-chartered banks[d]	1.3[E]	4.3[E]	78.2	176.5	306.8	462.8	477.1	458.1	19.4
D. Consolidated claims on unaffiliated foreigners at domestic offices and foreign branches of U.S.-chartered banks[e]	1.7[E]	7.5[E]	71.5[E]	167.0	266.2	415.2	437.3	403.5	18.0

Memoranda

E. Total assets at domestic offices[f]								
1. U.S.-chartered commercial banks	189.6[E]	298.1[E]	740.8	957.2	1,278.2	1,692.3	2,032.3	2,383[E]	8.0
2. All U.S. commercial banking institutions	191.0[E]	302.7[E]	763.6	1,004.8	1,380.1	1,881.8	2,281.1	2,680[E]	8.3
F. Gross domestic product (annual rate during calendar year)[g]	349.5	570.2	1,201.6	1,580.9	2,219.1	3,000.5	3,355.9	3,957.0	7.6
G. International trade in goods and services (annual rate during calendar year)[g]	17.6	29.6	79.8	145.8	225.4	365.9	355.6	409.2	10.0

E. Partially estimated by author.

a. Banking institutions reporting these data include U.S.-chartered commercial banks; U.S. agencies and branches of foreign banks; domestic offices of Edge and Agreement corporations; New York investment company subsidiaries of foreign banks; and (after December 1981) International Banking Facilities. The United States includes Puerto Rico, the Virgin Islands, and other overseas U.S. territories and possessions. Source: Board of Governors of the Federal Reserve System, *Banking and Monetary Statistics, 1941–70*; *Annual Statistical Digests*, various issues; and *Federal Reserve Bulletin*, various issues.

b. Includes claims held in custody for domestic customers.

c. Includes custody liabilities such as U.S. government securities owned by foreigners.

d. Series contains minor discontinuities due to changes in reporting requirements. Source: Board of Governors of the Federal Reserve System, *Federal Reserve Bulletin*, various issues, and *Annual Statistical Digests*, various issues. Estimates for 1952 and 1962 are based on end-year condition reports published in Federal Reserve Board *Annual Reports*.

e. These data are adjusted to exclude "intrafamily" assets and liabilities (the claims on their foreign branches held by U.S. offices of a banking organization and the claims of one foreign branch of a banking organization on other foreign branches of the same organization). Reporting institutions include only U.S.-chartered banks. Source: Board of Governors of the Federal Reserve System, *Annual Statistical Digests*, various issues, and *Federal Reserve Bulletin*, various issues.

f. Data for 1952–1983 are based on end-year condition reports. The figures for 1985 were estimated by the author on the basis of the last-Wednesday-of-month series. Sources: Federal Deposit Insurance Corporation, *Statistics on Banking*, various issues (data formerly published in annual report); and Board of Governors of the Federal Reserve System, *Federal Reserve Bulletin*, various issues.

g. Source: National income and product accounts in U.S. Department of Commerce, Bureau of Economic Analysis, *Survey of Current Business*, various issues. International trade (in both goods and services) is defined as the arithmetic average of exports and imports.

Table 3-8. *International Banking in Relation to Banks' Total Assets and International Trade, United States, Selected Years, 1952–85*

Ratios in percent

Indicator	1952	1962	1972	1975	1978	1981	1983	1985
International banking as a proportion of total assets at banks' domestic offices								
1. Own claims of U.S. banking offices on foreign residents (to total assets at domestic offices of all commercial banking institutions)	0.5^E	2.0^E	2.0^E	5.1^E	8.6	13.6	17.5	15.6
2. Own dollar liabilities of U.S. banking offices to foreign residents (to total assets at domestic offices of all commercial banking institutions)	3.2^E	3.9^E	3.3^E	5.1^E	5.7	8.7	12.2	12.7
3. Consolidated claims on unaffiliated foreigners at domestic offices and foreign branches of U.S.-chartered banks (to total assets at domestic offices of U.S.-chartered banks)	0.9^E	2.5^E	9.7^E	17.4	20.8	24.5	21.5	16.9
International banking in relation to international trade in goods and services								
4. Own claims of U.S. banking offices on foreign residents (all commercial banking institutions)	5.7^E	20.9^E	19.4^E	35.3^E	52.9	70.1	112.1	102.5
5. Own dollar liabilities of U.S. banking offices to foreign residents (all commercial banking institutions)	34.7^E	39.5^E	31.3^E	35.0^E	34.9	44.8	78.5	83.2
6. Consolidated claims on unaffiliated foreigners at domestic offices and foreign branches of U.S. chartered banks	9.7^E	25.3^E	89.6^E	114.5	118.1	113.5	123.0	98.6
Memorandum								
7. U.S. international trade in goods and services as a percent of U.S. GDP	5.0	5.2	6.6	9.2	10.2	12.2	10.6	10.3

Source: Derived from table 3-7. The correspondence between rows in this table and rows in table 3-7 is as follows (row numbers in table 3-7 in parentheses): row 1 (A2/E2); row 2 (B2/E2); row 3 (D/E1); row 4 (A2/G); row 5 (B2/G); row 6 (D/G); row 7 (G/F).
E. Underlying series partially estimated by author.

the total assets at domestic offices of U.S.-chartered banks and of all commercial banking institutions with offices in the United States.

Over the whole period from the early 1950s through 1985, the U.S. banking sector expanded at an annual rate of about 8 percent. Growth in the 1950s was slower; by the 1970s, when higher inflation was causing all nominal magnitudes to grow at more rapid rates, the banking sector was expanding by some 10 percent per year. Throughout the postwar period until about 1982 or 1983, however, the international banking aggregates grew at rates well above the domestic: typical annual rates of growth were 15–20 percent, or even more.[19]

As international banking expanded rapidly, the U.S. banking sector gradually became more open to the rest of the world. Several indicators of this trend are presented in table 3-8. The banks' own dollar liabilities to foreigners rose from only 3 percent in the early 1950s to more than 12 percent of the total assets of the U.S. banking sector by 1983 (row 2). The banks' own claims on foreigners as a proportion of the sector balance sheet rose still more dramatically, from less than 1 percent in the early 1950s to some 8 to 9 percent in the late 1970s and to over 17 percent by 1983 (row 1). Still another suggestive measure is the growth in claims on unaffiliated foreigners at both the domestic offices and the foreign branches of U.S.-chartered banks from less than 1 percent of total assets at the domestic offices in the early 1950s to well over 20 percent by the late 1970s (row 3).

Rows 4 through 6 in table 3-8 relate the international banking series (end-year stocks) to the international trade in goods and services of the U.S. economy (annual flows). The external assets of U.S. banking offices in the early 1950s represented only some 5 to 6 percent of the value of U.S. international trade. Consolidated banking claims on unaffiliated foreigners at the domestic offices and foreign branches of U.S.-chartered banks were only one-tenth the value of trade. By the late 1970s, these two banking series had risen to, respectively, well over 50 percent and well over 100 percent of the annual

19. The main exceptions to this generalization, the growth of the cross-border assets and liabilities of U.S. banks during the second half of the 1960s and early 1970s, are readily explained by the controls on capital outflows in force at that time (in particular the Federal Reserve program of voluntary foreign credit restraint for banks). Because of those controls, banks expanded the balance sheets of their foreign offices (see, for example, row C) at the expense of their domestic offices; but the consolidated claims on foreigners of the domestic and foreign offices combined (for example, row D) continued to grow very rapidly—in fact, even faster than in the 1950s. It is sometimes asserted that the rapid growth of international banking for American banks did not begin until the late 1960s or the 1970s. The data in table 3-7 (and more detailed data underlying those figures) show that such a view is incorrect.

Table 3-9. *Financial Assets of All Banking Offices in the United Kingdom, Selected Years, 1963–83*
Billions of pounds sterling at end of year unless otherwise indicated

Asset	1963	1968	1972	1975	1978	1981	1983	Compound annual rate of growth, 1963–83
Claims on foreign residents	**1.8**	**7.9**	**25.4**	**62.1**	**106.0**	**224.9**	**342.3**	**30.0**
Denominated in foreign currencies	1.2	7.0	23.6	59.0	100.9	216.2	323.6	32.3
Denominated in sterling	0.7	0.9	1.7	3.2	5.1	8.7	18.8	17.9
Claims on U.K. residents	**14.1**	**21.6**	**49.6**	**82.3**	**113.2**	**212.2**	**288.5**	**16.3**
Denominated in foreign currencies	0.4	2.7	12.9	29.6	40.8	82.6	119.5	33.0
Claims on other U.K. banking offices	0.4	2.1	10.4	21.3	29.6	68.7	92.7	31.3
Claims on U.K. residents outside banking sector	. . .	0.6	2.6	8.3	11.3	13.9	26.7	31.3
Denominated in sterling	13.6	18.9	36.6	52.7	72.4	129.6	169.0	13.4
Claims on other U.K. banking offices	2.4	4.2	11.6	16.0	22.9	37.5	54.5	17.0
Claims on U.K. residents outside banking sector	11.3	14.7	25.0	36.7	49.5	92.1	114.5	12.3
Total financial assets	**15.9**	**29.5**	**74.9**	**144.4**	**219.2**	**437.1**	**630.9**	**20.9**
Memoranda								
U.K. gross domestic product, current prices, annual flow during calendar year	30.6	44.0	64.1	106.3	167.8	253.5	300.0	12.1
Exchange rate, U.S. dollar per pound sterling, end of year	2.797	2.384	2.349	2.024	2.035	1.908	1.451	. . .

Sources: Bank of England, end-quarter sector-finance accounts; International Monetary Fund, *International Financial Statistics*, various issues. The data from the sector-finance accounts exclude small amounts of tangible assets.

flow of trade; by 1983, the ratios were 112 percent and 123 percent. The liabilities of U.S. banking offices had already become a large fraction of U.S. trade early in the postwar period. They increased moderately faster than trade during the 1970s and then much faster in the 1980s.[20]

After 1982, the external assets of banking offices in the United States grew much more slowly than in earlier years, and in numerous instances even declined. U.S.-owned banks also reduced their lending to foreigners from branches and other offices located abroad. This sharp change is evident from a comparison of the figures for 1983 and 1985 in tables 3-7 and 3-8. Several new trends in international banking during the 1980s, to be discussed below, contributed to this turnaround. Another part of the explanation can be traced to the world recession in the early 1980s and the resulting crises that developing countries experienced in servicing their external debts. To an even greater extent than Japanese and European banks, U.S. banks seem to have responded to the financial uncertainties associated with those events by pulling in their horns.

Banking in the United Kingdom and Germany: Two Contrasting Cases

The internationalization of banking has proceeded further in the United Kingdom than in any other country. Cross-border and cross-currency transactions booked on the balance sheets of banking offices located in Germany have been relatively modest. Thus the cases of the United Kingdom and Germany provide an interesting contrast.

Table 3-9 presents an analytic breakdown of the financial assets of banking offices located in the United Kingdom.[21] After the decline of Amsterdam in

---

20. The establishment of IBFs explains some of the unusual movements between 1981 and 1983 of the ratios shown in table 3-8. Whereas in the 1960s and early 1970s banks had had incentives to book lending to foreigners on the balance sheets of their overseas branches, the creation of IBFs led them to shift some of this lending back to U.S. locations. IBF claims on and liabilities to non-U.S. residents are included in the figures for rows A and B of table 3-7. At the end of December 1985, 166 IBFs had total assets of $260 billion; of this amount, some three-fifths was held by IBFs established by the U.S. agencies and branches of foreign-owned banks.

21. Data in the format of table 3-9 are not available for years before 1963. The figures exclude tangible assets and are therefore not quite a complete balance sheet. The excluded items are not large enough, however, to affect the major trends in the banks' balance sheets. The figures were compiled from a computer printout of the sector-finance data for the British banking sector. I am grateful to the staff of the Bank of England for making these data available to me.

the eighteenth century, London became the leading financial center for the "world economy" of European and American capitalism. London's supremacy was not seriously challenged until well into this century.[22] Given this history, even in the 1950s and early 1960s the banking system in the United Kingdom was much more internationally oriented than in other countries. But it was nonetheless dominated by traditional domestic banking: in December 1963 claims on British residents denominated in pounds sterling represented 86 percent of the total assets of banking offices.

By 1963 Eurocurrency activity was already growing rapidly, with London emerging as the hub. Many innovations in international banking originated in London; those originating elsewhere were quickly adopted in London. Sterling-denominated banking with overseas residents moved up and down in conjunction with fluctuations in the exchange value of sterling. Although not keeping pace with the dizzying growth in foreign-currency banking, overseas sterling business remained quantitatively significant.

By the mid-1980s, the relative importance in the United Kingdom of traditional domestic and international banking had been completely reversed. At the end of 1983, sterling claims on British residents, including interbank claims among the banking offices that are associated with this traditional domestic-currency banking, had fallen to one-fourth of the total assets on balance sheets. The opposite side of the coin was the dominance of banking assets with an international dimension, in particular assets denominated in the U.S. dollar and other foreign currencies. Figure 3-6 charts these balance-sheet proportions year by year.

Banking in Germany is much less international in orientation than banking in the United Kingdom. Table 3-10 presents year-end asset data for all banking offices in Germany for 1952–85. Traditional domestic banking—deutsche mark claims on German residents—has been, and continues to be, the preponderant part of the balance sheet. In December 1985, for example, the sum of all assets with a cross-border or cross-currency dimension (lines A4, A5, and B5) represented only some 8½ percent of total assets.

To be sure, a careful study of banking in Germany would partially mitigate the sharp contrast between the data shown in tables 3-9 and 3-10 and would reveal that the German banking system has extensive links with the outside world. For one thing, the data in table 3-10 are unusually comprehensive. To a greater extent than in most other nations, numerous small financial interme-

---

22. Fernand Braudel, *The Perspective of the World;* and Charles P. Kindleberger, *The Formation of Financial Centers: A Study in Comparative Economic History.*

Figure 3-6. *Asset Balance Sheet of All Banking Offices Located in the United Kingdom, 1963–83*

Percent of total financial assets

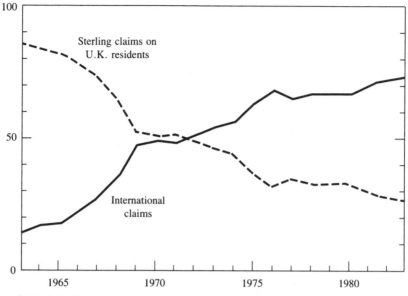

Source: Bank of England, end-quarter sector-finance accounts.

diaries are regarded as banks in the German statistics. Thus when German data are compared with other nations' data, as in table 3-2, the international parts of the balance sheets of the larger German banks tend to be masked.

Even more important, the larger German banks conduct much of their international business from branches or subsidiaries located outside Germany. When the balance sheets of banking organizations are consolidated and classified by the country of location of the head office (table 3-5), the large German banks appear among the group of dominant international banks (together with the largest American, Japanese, British, and French banks). Luxembourg is particularly important as a location in which German-owned banks book large amounts of assets and liabilities with cross-border and cross-currency characteristics—including assets and liabilities vis-à-vis customers resident in Germany.

A closer look at table 3-10, moreover, shows that the international parts of the balance sheets of banking offices in Germany have grown more rapidly than traditional domestic banking. Over the twenty-three years from 1962 to 1985, claims on foreigners grew at a compound annual rate of over 16 percent,

Table 3-10. *Assets of All Banking Offices in the Federal Republic of Germany, Selected Years, 1952–85*

Billions of deutsche marks at end of year unless otherwise indicated

Asset	1952	1962	1972	1975	1978	1981	1983	1985	Compound annual rate of growth, 1952–85
A. Claims on foreign residents	**0.2**	**8.7**	**50.2**	**102.3**	**136.2**	**194.2**	**208.9**	**283.2**	**24.6**
By type of customer									
1. Foreign banks	0.2	3.0	22.7	65.8	72.1	101.5	106.4	165.7	22.6
2. Foreign nonbanks	...	5.6	26.7	34.4	61.4	88.7	96.7	111.5	...
3. Other foreign claims[a]	...	0.1	0.8	2.1	2.7	4.0	5.8	6.0	...
By currency denomination									
4. Deutsche mark	n.a.	n.a.	36.8E	76.2E	101.9	146.4	160.3	220.4	...
5. Foreign currencies	n.a.	n.a.	13.3E	26.1E	34.4	47.8	48.7	62.9	...
B. Claims on domestic residents	**63.6**	**317.3**	**1,010.2**	**1,352.0**	**1,851.9**	**2,344.3**	**2,672.4**	**3,045.1**	**12.4**
By type of customer									
1. Domestic banks	12.3	73.2	250.5	362.7	505.4	605.0	697.7	808.0	13.5
2. Domestic nonbanks	44.7	215.3	672.2	883.6	1,199.0	1,592.0	1,808.5	2,041.0	12.3
3. Other domestic claims[b]	6.8	28.8	87.5	105.7	147.5	147.3	166.2	196.2	10.7
By currency denomination									
4. Deutsche mark[c]	n.a.	n.a.	n.a.	1,349.4E	1,848.4E	2,339.8E	2,667.0E	n.a.	...
5. Foreign currencies[d]	n.a.	n.a.	n.a.	2.6E	3.5E	4.5E	5.4E	n.a.	...
C. Total assets and liabilities (A+B)	**63.8**	**326.1**	**1,060.3**	**1,454.3**	**1,988.2**	**2,538.4**	**2,881.3**	**3,328.3**	**12.7**
Memorandum									
D. Claims on foreign residents as a proportion of total balance sheet (percent)	0.3	2.7	4.7	7.0	6.9	7.6	7.3	8.5	...

Sources: *Monthly Report of the Deutsche Bundesbank* (table III.2); Statistical Supplements to the *Monthly Report of the Deutsche Bundesbank*, Series 3: Balance of Payments Statistics (tables 7a and 7b).
E. Partially estimated by author.
n.a. Not available.
a. Includes cash balances and participations. Obtained as the residual of row A less rows A1 and A2.
b. Obtained as the residual of row B less rows B1 and B2.
c. Estimated as row B less row B5.
d. Estimated from figures on foreign-currency lending to domestic residents published by the *Bank of England Quarterly Bulletin* in its annual March articles "Developments in International Banking and Capital Markets."

significantly faster than the 10½ percent growth rate for total assets; the contrast was still greater, 25 percent versus 13 percent, for the entire period from 1952 to 1985. Assets with international characteristics were less than 3 percent of the balance sheet in the early 1960s, versus the 8½ percent ratio at the end of 1985.

Notwithstanding the important qualifications, the conclusion still stands that Germany as a jurisdiction for international banking is a pale shadow of the United Kingdom.

International Financial Intermediation in Japan

The Japanese financial system differs in many respects from national financial systems in Europe and North America. Outsiders' understanding of it is limited. Moreover, it is difficult to assemble consistent statistical time series for the whole postwar period and thereby gain an adequate historical perspective. Given the large and growing importance to the world economy of Japanese banks and securities firms, however, this chapter would be seriously incomplete without presentation of a few illustrative statistics for Japan.

Table 3-11 presents summary data for the international investment position of Japan for 1972–85.[23] These figures provide suggestive evidence that the openness of the Japanese financial system did not change much in the early and mid-1970s, but increased significantly thereafter. Note, for example, that by 1985 the ratios of external assets and liabilities to GDP were each more than two and one-half times greater than their values seven years earlier at the end of 1978. This impression of accelerating financial interdependence of Japan and the rest of the world is consistent with the views of many analysts inside and outside Japan.[24]

Table 3-12 provides aggregate figures for the asset side of the balance sheets of banking offices located in Japan. Banks are defined broadly for the purposes of the table, including not only the large so-called city banks oriented to international business but also the regional, trust, and long-term credit banks and some of the banklike financial institutions serving small business

23. Data for external assets and liabilities for years before 1972 have not been published.
24. See, for example, Eisuke Sakakibara and Akira Kondoh, *Study on the Internationalization of Tokyo's Money Markets;* Jeffrey A. Frankel, *The Yen/Dollar Agreement: Liberalizing Japanese Capital Markets;* J. David Germany and John E. Morton, "Financial Innovation and Deregulation in Foreign Industrial Countries"; and Keimei Kaizuka and Tadao Hata, "Internationalization in Financial Activities in Japan."

Table 3-11. *External Assets and Liabilities of the Japanese Economy, Selected Years, 1972–85*

Billions of U.S. dollars at end of year unless otherwise indicated

Asset	1972	1975	1978	1981	1983	1985
Total Japanese assets abroad	**43.6**	**58.3**	**118.7**	**209.3**	**272.0**	**437.7**
Government sector (including reserve assets)	23.2	20.7	50.3	57.1	58.4	64.5
Private sector	20.4	37.7	68.4	152.2	213.5	276.7
Direct investments	2.6	8.3	14.3	24.5	32.2	44.0
Other claims abroad	17.9	29.4	49.0	127.7	181.3	329.2
Total foreign assets in Japan	**29.7**	**51.3**	**82.5**	**198.3**	**234.7**	**307.9**
Foreign claims on government sector	2.5	3.3	11.5	27.6	33.1	39.1
Foreign claims on private sector	27.3	48.0	71.0	170.7	201.6	268.8
Direct investments	1.7	2.1	2.8	3.9	4.4	4.7
Other foreign claims	25.6	45.9	68.1	166.8	197.3	264.0
Memoranda						
Japanese gross domestic product[a]	**304.8**	**499.8**	**971.3**	**1,167.0**	**1,180.0**	**1,329.3**[E]
Ratio of external assets to GDP (percent)	14.3	11.7	12.2	17.9	23.1	32.9[E]
Ratio of external liabilities to GDP (percent)	9.7	10.3	8.5	17.0	19.9	23.2[E]

Sources: Eisuke Sakakibara and Akira Kondoh, *Study on the Internationalization of Tokyo's Money Markets* (Tokyo: Japanese Center for International Finance, 1984), p. 86-2; Bank of Japan, Research and Statistics Department, *Economic Statistics Annual, 1985* (March 1986), p. 260. Data for 1985 from *Economic Statistics Annual, 1986* (March 1987).

E. Partially estimated by author.
a. Annual flow during calendar year at current exchange rates.

and agriculture, forestry, and fisheries. Data for the Japanese offices of foreign-owned banks are included in the table for 1979 and subsequent years. Table 3-12 provides the same disaggregation of total assets shown in table 3-2. For its estimates of the cross-border and cross-currency components, it relies on figures supplied by the Japanese government to the Bank for International Settlements.[25]

25. The institutional coverage of Japanese banking offices underlying the figures supplied to the BIS may differ in minor ways from the coverage of the Japanese-source data I have used in constructing the total-assets figures for row C of the table. (See the footnotes to the table for further discussion.) Alternative data for international lending by Japanese banks published in the annual reports of the International Finance Bureau of the Japanese Ministry of Finance (quoted in, for example, the paper by Kaizuka and Hata, "Internationalization in Financial Activities in Japan") differ from the data in table 3-12 by including assets booked by overseas branches of Japanese banks (as well as assets booked at banking offices located in Japan) and by excluding all assets other than loans (whereas the data in the BIS statistics include deposits, bondholdings, and other credits as well as loans).

The interpretation of changes in the openness of the Japanese banking system suggested by table 3-12 corresponds broadly to the inferences for the whole financial system drawn from table 3-11. Internationalization progressed slowly until the 1970s but increased rapidly thereafter. The timing of the accelerated expansion of international banking from offices in Japan is known to have coincided with the Japanese government's relaxation of various regulatory and supervisory constraints. By the end of 1985, cross-border and cross-currency assets accounted for some 13 percent of the total assets of Japanese banking offices, a proportion more than double the 5 to 6 percent characteristic of the mid-1970s.[26]

New Trends in the 1980s

Until now, this chapter has focused mainly on the cross-border and cross-currency assets on the balance sheets of banks. A balanced overview of international financial intermediation, however, must also identify some new trends that became evident in the mid-1980s.

The new trends had three related aspects. First, some international lending that would formerly have taken the form of assets on banks' balance sheets became "securitized" (chapter 2). Bank-intermediated financial flows thus became less dominant while flows through capital markets began to grow faster than other forms of international financial activity. Second, former lines of distinction between banking activities and securities markets became increasingly blurred. Third, a variety of new financial instruments facilitated this evolution of international lending and borrowing.

Note issuance facilities (NIFs) are a prominent example of the new finan-

---

26. As with earlier tables in this chapter, interpretation of the data in table 3-12 is complicated by fluctuations in exchange rates. Large changes in the exchange value of the yen can cause substantial changes in the yen value of assets denominated in foreign currencies independently of changes in the amounts of the foreign-currency assets themselves. To illustrate with an especially striking example: when expressed in yen, the value of the external assets denominated in foreign currencies (row A1 in table 3-12) *fell* by 13 percent between December 1975 and December 1978 (from 5,767 to 5,014 billion yen), whereas the value of the assets expressed in U.S. dollars *increased* by 36 percent (from $18.9 to $25.7 billion). The apparent decline in the proportion of international business on Japanese banks' balance sheets between 1975 and 1978 is due entirely to the large appreciation of the yen during that period (see row E). When one adjusts for the valuation effects of the yen appreciation in 1975–78, it becomes clear that the volume of international business in those years increased substantially *faster* than the balance sheet as a whole. Careful studies of changes in the volume of international financial activity from one period to another require systematic adjustments for exchange-rate valuation effects.

Table 3-12. *Assets of All Banking Offices in Japan, Selected Years, 1973–85*

Billions of yen at end of year unless otherwise indicated

Asset	1973	1975	1978	1981	1983	1985	Compound annual rate of growth, 1973–85
A. Claims on foreign residents	**4,788**	**6,225**	**6,575**	**18,633**	**25,311**	**39,057**	**19.1**
1. Denominated in foreign currencies[a]	4,564	5,767	5,014	14,008	18,166	24,253	14.9
2. Denominated in yen[a]	224	458	1,561	4,625	7,146	14,804	41.8
B. Claims on domestic residents	**149,037**	**192,037**	**265,197**	**344,509**	**407,730**	**486,585**	**10.4**
1. Denominated in foreign currencies[a]	2,800	5,188	4,878	16,519	24,870	28,866	21.5
2. Denominated in yen[b]	146,237	186,850	260,320	327,990	382,860	457,719	10.0
C. Total assets (A+B)[c]	**153,825**	**198,262**	**271,772**	**363,142**	**433,041**	**525,642**	**10.8**
Memoranda							
D. Japanese gross domestic product, current prices, annual flow during calendar year	112,498	148,328	204,403	257,363	280,257	317,084[E]	9.0
E. Exchange rate, yen per U.S. dollar, end of year	280.00	305.15	195.10	220.25	232.00	200.60	. . .
F. Claims with some international characteristic (A1+A2+B1) as a proportion of total balance sheet (percent)	4.9	5.8	4.2	9.7	11.6	12.9	. . .

Sources: Bank of Japan, Research and Statistics Department, *Economic Statistics Annual, 1985* (Tokyo, 1986), pp. 77–80; and *Annuals* for earlier years (rows C and E); Bank for International Settlements, *International Banking Developments*, July 1986 and earlier issues (rows A1, A2, and B1); International Monetary Fund, *International Financial Statistics Yearbook 1986*, p. 421 (row D).

E. Partially estimated by author.

a. Data obtained from the BIS compilation of statistics in *International Banking Developments*, various issues (with U.S.-dollar amounts converted to yen using the exchange rates on row E).

b. Obtained as the residual of row C less rows A1, A2, and B1.

c. The financial institutions treated as banks for the purposes of this table are city banks, regional banks, trust banks, long-term credit banks, the offices in Japan of foreign-owned banks, Sogo banks, Shinkin banks, the Zenshinren Bank, the Shoko Chukin Bank, and the Norinchukin Bank. Data for the Japanese offices of foreign-owned banks have not been published for years before 1979 (and were assumed equal to zero for those years).

cial instruments. A NIF is a medium-term arrangement enabling a borrower to issue a series of short-term debt obligations (typically referred to as Euronotes). NIFs are often backed or underwritten by a commitment from a group of banks to ensure that the borrowers will have access to funds when they are required. The underwriting banks are exposed to a liquidity risk (they might be called upon to provide funds at short notice) and a credit risk (the borrower might need to call upon them if his creditworthiness had deteriorated). Several different manifestations of the basic arrangement exist in practice.[27] Eurocommercial paper facilities, another type of new instrument, are like NIFs in that they provide for a borrower to issue short-term Euronotes. Eurocommercial paper facilities, however, are not backed by commitments or guarantees from banks.

Innovative financial instruments of other types have greatly facilitated the hedging of exchange-rate and interest-rate risks. Such instruments include currency swaps, interest-rate swaps, currency and interest-rate options, and forward rate agreements (FRAs).

Swap instruments require two counterparties to agree to exchange streams of interest payments over time according to predetermined procedures. A currency swap involves two streams, both at fixed interest rates, but denominated in different currencies.[28] An interest-rate swap involves streams denominated in the same currency but on different interest-rate bases—for example, a stream of fixed-rate payments in U.S. dollars and a stream of variable-rate payments at the London interbank offer rate (LIBOR) for Eurodollars. When the interest-payment streams are in different currencies and on different interest-rate bases, the arrangement is known as a cross-currency interest-rate swap (for example, a stream of fixed-rate payments in deutsche marks and a stream of variable-rate payments in U.S. dollars at LIBOR).

27. For example, variants of NIFs include revolving underwriting facilities (RUFs) and "multiple-component" facilities. RUFs separate the functions of underwriting and distribution. The bank that is lead manager for a RUF acts as sole placing agent for any Euronotes issued; the underwriting banks take up notes that cannot be placed elsewhere (or extend loans of an equivalent amount). A multiple-component facility permits a borrower to draw funds in several different forms—for example, short-term advances and bankers' acceptances—all of which have been included with a NIF; borrowers with these facilities gain flexibility in choosing the maturity, currency, and interest-rate base for their drawings.

28. For many years currency swaps involving simultaneous spot and forward transactions have been common in exchange markets. The innovations termed "currency swaps" or "cross-currency swaps" that have become newly important in the 1980s are different from those traditional transactions; the new-style currency swaps involve streams of interest payments over the life of a contract, and may or may not involve exchange of principal either initially or at maturity.

Options are contracts conveying a right, but not an obligation, to buy or sell a specified financial instrument at a fixed price (the "exercise" or "strike" price) before or on a certain future date. Options traded on organized exchanges are standardized contracts, with predetermined exercise prices set according to predefined formulas and with standard maturities. Options are traded with an actual currency or financial asset as the underlying financial instrument. Some options also exist with a futures contract on a currency or financial asset as the underlying instrument.

FRAs are agreements between two counterparties, one wishing to protect itself against a future rise in interest rates and the other against a future fall. Without a commitment to lend or borrow the principal amount, the parties agree to an interest rate for, say, a three-month period beginning six months hence; at maturity, they settle by paying (or receiving) only the difference between the interest rate agreed earlier and the then current interest rate.[29]

One significant consequence of the proliferation of international financial instruments was an "unbundling" of the different risks that were combined in traditional cross-border and cross-currency bank lending. The distinction between direct intermediation and indirect intermediation through securities markets (chapter 2), already blurred within national financial systems, was thereby blurred still further in international finance. Banks could more easily shift certain of the risks of international lending to the purchasers of the securitized assets. Ultimate borrowers could more finely adjust their exposures to interest-rate and exchange-rate risks according to their particular objectives and expectations. Ultimate providers of the funds could likewise hedge or adjust their asset positions in accordance with their needs and expectations. In effect, risks were redistributed to those best placed to bear them. Liquidity was enhanced for both asset holders and liability issuers.[30]

The financial innovations of the 1980s, by facilitating the separation and shifting of risks, encouraged securitization—a conversion into marketable securities of what was already, or what otherwise would have been, direct intermediation by a bank or other intermediary. In international finance after the early 1980s, securitization diminished the importance of traditional forms of bank lending but greatly enhanced the role of banks in preparing, under-

29. All these new instruments are discussed in detail in Bank for International Settlements, *Recent Innovations in International Banking,* chaps. 1–4.

30. For additional references on the recent innovations in international finance and their consequences, see Bank of England, "Developments in International Banking and Capital Markets in 1985"; Maxwell Watson and others, *International Capital Markets: Development and Prospects;* and Morgan Guaranty Trust Company of New York, "International Bank Lending Trends."

writing, and placing marketable securities. As noted earlier, banks still assumed significant risks when committing themselves to backstop NIFs. Swaps and options on currencies and interest rates likewise entailed risks. But the securitized lending and innovative transactions for the most part did not appear on banks' balance sheets. The risks were contingent and off-balance-sheet.

Why did the trend toward securitization gather momentum? Several factors seem to have played a role. The deregulation of financial activity in many countries permitted various security transactions—by both banks and their nonbank customers—that formerly had not been possible or profitable. Supervisory authorities encouraged banks to strengthen their capital ratios, which gave banks incentives to meet customers' demands for credit in ways that did not place the resulting claims directly on the banks' balance sheets. Competition seems to have intensified, both among banks and between banks and other types of financial institutions. Many of the improvements in communications technology may have weakened banks' comparative advantage in acquiring information about other nations' financial systems. The perceived creditworthiness of some large banks declined relative to that of prime nonbank borrowers, in part because of concerns about banks' exposures to heavily indebted developing countries. Finally, geographical shifts in the pattern of payments imbalances may also have played a role. In the 1970s, OPEC countries accumulated much of their balance-of-payments surpluses in the form of bank deposits; developing country borrowers with large deficits went directly to the banks for loans. More recently, payments surpluses accrued to countries like Japan and Germany, and the United States became a large net borrower; residents of these countries preferred to lend and borrow via securities transactions.

Table 3-13 provides some evidence on the extent of substitution of securities-market transactions for direct lending by banks. The figures in the table pertain to new lending facilities (not including rollovers of existing lending) arranged during 1981–85. The total amounts arranged are broken down into three components: international bond issues, note issuance facilities of all types, and syndicated bank lending. As shown in the last line of the table, securities-market facilities were only about one-fourth of new lending in 1981. The proportion rose steadily in subsequent years and by 1985 was over nine-tenths of the total. The growth during 1984 and 1985 of NIFs and floating rate notes was especially impressive.

Although securitization led to a sharp reduction in direct intermediation through banks, the banks themselves began holding larger amounts of marketable securities in their portfolios. Data on banks' holdings of international

Table 3-13. *New Lending Facilities Arranged in International Financial Markets, 1981–85*

Billions of dollars at end of year unless otherwise indicated

Facility	1981	1982	1983	1984	1985
A. International bond issues	44.0	71.7	72.1	108.1	163.6
Fixed rate straight issues	32.1	56.4	50.0	65.5	100.4
Floating rate notes	7.8	12.6	15.3	34.1	55.9
Convertible bonds[a]	4.1	2.7	6.8	8.5	7.3
B. Note issuance facilities[b]	1.0	2.3	3.3	18.9	49.5
C. Syndicated bank lending[c]	131.5[d]	100.5	51.8	36.6	21.2
Voluntary loans	131.5	89.3	38.1	30.1	18.9
"Nonspontaneous" loans[e]	. . .	11.2	13.7	6.5	2.3
D. Total of new facilities (A+B+C)	176.5	174.5	127.2	163.6	234.3
Memorandum					
Securities-market facilities as a percent of total new facilities	25.5	42.4	59.3	77.6	91.0

Source: Bank for International Settlements, *Fifty-Sixth Annual Report* (Basel, 1986), pp. 101–07.
a. Excludes bonds with equity warrants.
b. Covers all Euronote facilities including underwritten facilities (NIFs, RUFs, and multiple-component facilities with a note issuance option) and nonunderwritten or uncommitted facilities and Eurocommercial paper programs.
c. Does not include existing loans newly negotiated where only spreads are changed.
d. Includes $35 billion of U.S. takeover-related standbys.
e. The new-money element of rescue packages arranged for heavily indebted countries by the International Monetary Fund and other governmental entities in cooperation with commercial banks.

bonds and other marketable securities have only recently been collected; the country coverage of reporting banks is still seriously incomplete. But the partial figures now available suggest that banks' outstanding holdings of such securities were at least $157 billion at the end of 1985.[31]

As it did within domestic financial systems, securitization of lending also tended to erode traditional regulatory distinctions between banks and other financial institutions. Some observers have termed this trend "universalization" (after "universal" banking systems that do not have regulations separating banking and securities-market transactions). All types of financial institutions found it easier to circumvent national regulations in their international transactions than in their domestic transactions. Especially in their cross-border and cross-currency business, therefore, banks moved into a wider range of financial activities, poaching more extensively on the traditional preserves of security brokers and dealers. Similarly, nonbank financial institutions increasingly encroached on traditional banking business.

The 1980s trends in international finance identified here were undoubtedly

31. Bank of England, "Recent Innovations in International Banking," p. 209.

beneficial in several ways. But they also raised new issues—or, more precisely, old issues in new guises. For example, suppose that for many future years a large share of lending to prime-quality borrowers continued to be channeled through securities markets rather than directly through banks. The average quality of banks' remaining assets might then decline significantly. The information relationships between debtors and creditors in securities markets, it can be argued, are less close and less focused on long-run fundamentals than the relationships between banks and ultimate debtors. A less broadly based banking system might thus be less able to respond promptly to emergency liquidity needs.

As a second illustration, the unbundling of risks associated with securitization may raise new difficulties for the monitoring of the sizes and interactions of risks. Participants in financial markets might therefore underestimate the risks. Such underestimates could in turn lead to market underpricing of new financial instruments. For these reasons, too, the new trends may have increased the vulnerability of national financial systems and the world financial system. As observed by the Bank of England, "The presumed superior liquidity of securitized assets has not yet been tested," and "there is a danger that it may disappear when it is most needed."[32]

The securitization of lending, with its unbundling of different types of risks and its growth of off-balance-sheet business, has also impaired the usefulness of the existing statistics on international financial intermediation. By taking a growing proportion of credit transactions off banks' balance sheets, the new trends have reduced the content of available information on the international exposures of individual institutions. Many nonbank financial institutions, although playing an increasingly important role in the volume of financial activity, have remained outside the existing reporting system for statistics. The enhanced negotiability of assets has made it more difficult to keep track of their ownership. And the assets reported by banks have less accurately reflected the country and industry distribution of the liabilities of borrowers.

---

32. Ibid., p. 210.

CHAPTER FOUR

Why Has Internationalization Occurred?

WHY has international financial intermediation grown so rapidly? This chapter identifies alternative explanations and offers judgments about their relative importance.

Saving, Investment, and Financial Intermediation in a Single Integrated Capital Market

To provide a benchmark for analysis, consider first a hypothetical self-contained economy whose financial system is fully integrated. In such an economy, all financial intermediation is domestic (by assumption the economy is completely closed to the rest of the world). The financial system may be likened to a reservoir. When the current-period consumption of households and other economic agents falls short of their income, the resulting savings flow into the reservoir. Businesses and other economic agents whose current-period spending exceeds their income draw funds out of the reservoir as they borrow to finance their excess spending. The existence of the reservoir permits the saving and investment decisions of individual agents to be taken independently—even though, when measured ex post (after the decisions have been made and inconsistencies among them eliminated), aggregate savings and aggregate investment are necessarily equal for the economy as a whole.

Risk pooling, risk evaluation, and maturity transformation by financial intermediaries play a central role in maintaining the reservoir. The same is true of financial markets and the specialized financial firms supporting them. In effect, financial institutions attract and funnel the savings into the reservoir and make it easier for ultimate investors to withdraw funds from it. Without the institutions, the economy's saving and investment transactions would be fragmented into numerous local puddles that are partially or wholly disconnected from each other, rather than one single reservoir.

Many economic and noneconomic forces affect saving and investment decisions, and thus influence the level of savings in the reservoir and associated interest rates for lending and borrowing. In particular, the reservoir's level rises and falls with the pace of activity in the real sectors of the economy.

In a superefficient financial system having no market imperfections and very low communications and transactions costs, the fluid in the reservoir would behave like water. Following a change in underlying circumstances somewhere in the economy, the fluid in all parts of the reservoir would adjust almost instantaneously to reestablish a single uniform level. Savers would move funds so adeptly from low-return to higher-return locations and borrowers would shift so promptly from high-cost to lower-cost sources of financing that market interest rates and yields on investments (adjusted for risk premiums) would speedily become equalized throughout the reservoir.

However, in a system where there are asymmetries in the distribution of information and in access to financial institutions, and where there are significant communications and transactions costs, the fluid in the reservoir should be imagined as viscous—more like thick molasses than water. Given sufficient time for adjustment to changes in underlying circumstances, a uniform level of the viscous fluid will prevail. Nonetheless, if in one region the "taking out" activity during any particular short run substantially exceeds or falls short of the "putting in" activity, the level in that region can be temporarily lower or higher than elsewhere in the reservoir.

Suppose investment opportunities become more favorable in a particular region of the economy. This situation might occur because (for example) a technological innovation differentially benefits the region or because new, commercially exploitable supplies of natural resources are discovered in the region. Ex ante (that is, before the new information has become widely available and all plans have become correspondingly adjusted), the region will have an excess demand for savings: desired withdrawals from the reservoir by the residents of the favored region will be temporarily larger than planned inflows. The region will pull savings from other parts of the reservoir as investors in the projects with higher than average expected returns successfully bid funds away from investors whose projects in other regions are less promising. Investment within the favored region will not be limited by the current flow of regional savings. Indeed, during the transitional adjustment period there need be little relation between the investment and saving of the region's residents. If one could calculate balance-of-payments accounts for the favored region, one would observe a net savings inflow (a current-account deficit). Eventually, rates of return on investment (adjusted for risk premiums) will converge throughout all regions of the economy. But as long as perceived rates of return are unusually high in the favored region, the reservoir will not have a uniform level and funds will flow from the rest of the reservoir to the favored region.

Postwar National Financial Markets

The depression of the 1930s and World War II caused severe disruptions in world economic activity. In the early postwar period, cross-border transactions in goods and services were thus hampered by frictions and obstacles. Financial transactions between nations were impeded even more; in numerous cases exchange and capital controls prohibited them altogether. Individual national economies were partially isolated from each other.

The financial system of each nation was in effect a different reservoir. Within each reservoir, savings flows were viscous and in some instances impeded by market imperfections. But internal conditions were sufficiently flexible to encourage an eventual convergence of returns on investment projects throughout most parts of each nation's economy. In any case, the mobility of funds within each reservoir was much greater than the mobility of funds from one reservoir to another.[1]

The reasons for the separation of national reservoirs can be classified into two broad groups. Nonpolicy factors—geography, technology, information and education, and even cultural and social traditions—interposed large "economic distances" between the national reservoirs. Second, government policies inhibited the cross-border transfer of funds. In effect, nations' governments erected and maintained "separation fences" around their reservoirs.

Communications and transportation costs were the most important nonpolicy factors interposing economic distance between nations. Financial transactions across borders require the transmission of messages. The physical transport of pieces of paper, and often people themselves, is also required. Money and time are expended to accomplish this transmission and transport.

---

1. The analogy of a single reservoir for each nation in which rates of return (adjusted for risk) were relatively uniform within each national economy does violence to the facts, even for the immediate postwar period. No nation's financial system corresponded closely to the textbook description of a fully integrated capital market. For the discussion here, however, I simplify by omitting any further mention of the market imperfections and lack of complete integration within each nation. My analogy of reservoirs and viscous savings flows is similar to the "hydraulic" imagery in Arnold C. Harberger, "Vignettes on the World Capital Market."

The greater the economic distance, the larger the fraction of the total costs of a transaction due merely to communications and transportation.

The various nonpolicy factors inhibited movements of funds across borders, but not by design. In contrast, the government policies embodied in separation fences were explicitly intended to disconnect the reservoirs. Some countries maintained separation fences that were high and nearly insurmountable. Others had fences that were lower and partially permeable. Very few nations, however, had no separation fence at all.

Postwar attitudes about international capital flows were supportive of government policies to maintain separation fences. The most widely accepted economic analyses of the 1920s and 1930s identified "disequilibrating" capital flows as a prime cause of the unfavorable economic performance of those years.[2] Virtually all countries came out of the war with extensive exchange and capital controls.

The architects of postwar international monetary arrangements did not believe that unfettered capital movements would be desirable. They welcomed capital flows representing direct payments or receipts for current-account transactions and those closely associated with direct investments. They wished to encourage long-term capital exports from countries with strong external economic positions. But they feared—and recommended restraints on—other types of capital movements, particularly those motivated by short-run differentials in interest rates or prospects of capital gain due to exchange-rate changes. Writing in 1941 about prospective postwar arrangements, for example, Keynes insisted that "nothing is more certain than that the movement of capital funds must be regulated."[3] In May 1944, in a speech supporting a joint statement about plans for an International Monetary Fund negotiated with experts from the United States and other countries, Keynes argued:

> We intend to retain control of our domestic rate of interest, so that we can keep it as low as suits our own purposes, without interference from the ebb and flow of international capital movements or flights of hot money. . . . Not merely as a feature of the transition, but as a permanent arrangement, the plan accords to every member government the explicit right to control all capital movements. What used to be a heresy is now endorsed as orthodox. . . . Our right to control the domestic capital market is secured on

2. See, for example, Ragnar Nurkse, *International Currency Experience: Lessons of the Inter-War Period.*

3. John Maynard Keynes, *Collected Writings,* vol. 25, p. 31.

firmer foundations than ever before, and is formally accepted as a proper part of agreed international arrangements.[4]

Even the government of the United States, which itself had the fewest restrictions on capital movements at the border, shared the attitude that many types of capital movements were disruptive and should be discouraged or prevented. The Articles of Agreement of the IMF negotiated at Bretton Woods embodied these attitudes and policies.

Attitudes about international trade in goods and services were markedly different. All countries shared the aspiration to liberalize trade transactions after the war. To be sure, rhetoric went well beyond actual practices. Many trade barriers did not come down promptly. The existence of barriers to trade transactions reinforced the separation of national financial reservoirs due to policy barriers against capital flows.

For individual countries, the relative separation of reservoirs in the early postwar period forced a close correspondence between national saving and national investment. Stated differently, only limited scope existed for net capital flows and corresponding imbalances in current-account transactions. The main exception to this generalization was intergovernmental assistance from the United States to other countries under the Marshall Plan and other assistance programs. Those government capital flows permitted the reconstructing economies to run sizable current-account deficits in the transitional years following the war. But there was little scope for private economic agents to effect a net transfer of savings across borders. Thus even the cross-border shipments of goods and services—and especially the ladling of savings from one national reservoir to another—were modest relative to the sizes of national outputs.

Explanations for the Growth of International Financial Intermediation

The analogy of relatively isolated national reservoirs is helpful when analyzing financial activity in the world economy of the early postwar period. But it has diminishing validity as analysis moves toward the present. Indeed, one can classify explanations for the rapid growth in cross-border financial intermediation in terms of the different ways in which the separateness of the national reservoirs has progressively eroded. Alternative explanations fall

4. Ibid., vol. 26, pp. 16–17.

under three broad headings according to whether cross-border financial activity (1) followed real-sector transactions, (2) led real-sector transactions, or (3) responded to regulatory, tax, and supervisory incentives.

Financial Activity Following Real-Sector Transactions

The generally faster postwar expansion of cross-border trade than of incomes and outputs (figure 3-1 and table 3-1) occurred because governments reduced barriers to trade. Even more important, it occurred because the effective economic distances between nations were shrinking for nonpolicy reasons such as a sharp fall in the relative price of transportation.

By itself, the faster growth of trade than of output would have given rise to a faster growth of cross-border financial activity than of domestic financial activity. To pay for cross-border shipments of goods and services, for example, a nation's residents needed to hold, borrow, or otherwise acquire cash balances denominated in foreign currencies (or foreign residents needed to acquire home-currency balances). Thus the transactions-balance requirements of trade alone would probably have induced a significant increase in international assets and liabilities. In many instances, traders sought credit to finance trade transactions. Nonfinancial traders could have extended credit directly to each other, and to some degree did so. At least as much as in domestic transactions, however, they resorted to financial institutions. Hence financial transactions such as bankers' acceptances and short-term bank loans against trade collateral expanded with the growth in international trade.[5]

When cross-border financial activity is merely the financing counterpart of trade transactions, the goods trade may be said to drive the financial activity that is supporting it. An imbalance in the current account of a country's balance of payments associated with such transactions may be described as the causal result of the export and import transactions; the capital flows can be considered a passive accompaniment. The resulting net transfers of savings between countries are the by-product of the real-sector transactions and the incentives that drive those transactions.

5. An especially important example of the links running from trade transactions to their financing occurred in the 1970s when the OPEC countries engineered sharp increases in world oil prices. These real-sector shocks led proximately to large current-account surpluses for OPEC countries, since in the shorter run those countries could not raise their imports fast enough to keep pace with their burgeoning export receipts. The surpluses had to be financed by the accumulation of financial assets in foreign countries. Many of the OPEC countries chose to hold these assets in the form of deposits with large, internationally oriented banks—thereby expanding the world aggregates for international banking.

The simplest international economic relationships involved arm's-length transactions between a home resident and a foreign resident, each of whose business was primarily domestic in orientation. But as the postwar period progressed, some nonfinancial firms developed a much deeper involvement in foreign business. Rather than merely engaging in limited export or import transactions with foreign residents, some firms oriented their business primarily to foreign residents. And to facilitate this more ambitious involvement, they established production facilities or sales and trading offices abroad.

Because some of their most important nonfinancial customers were establishing offices abroad, banks and other financial institutions themselves had incentives to set up physical facilities abroad—branches or separately incorporated subsidiaries—to supplement the support they could give to customers from the home economy. Some of the lending and borrowing transactions with their customers were then booked on the balance sheets of the foreign offices.

As with the simple financing of international trade identified above, here too financial transactions were driven by real-sector economic decisions. The financial institutions setting up foreign offices followed their existing customers to retain, or to participate in the growth of, the customers' financial business. When financial institutions established offices within foreign economies, the real-sector activity being financed need not have been cross-border trade in goods and services. The real-sector activity and its counterpart financing may have been, wholly or in part, domestic within the host-country economies.

Financial Activity Leading Real-Sector Transactions

Although the nonpolicy factors shrinking the effective economic distances between nation states encouraged international trade in the postwar period, those forces had, arguably, an even more dramatic impact on international financial transactions.

New developments in communications technology were especially important. Innovations in electronic equipment—computers, switching devices, telecommunications satellites—permitted the processing and transmission of information, the confirmation of transactions, and the making of payments for transactions in a progressively less costly manner. Sophisticated methods of using the new equipment—such as computer software for electronics funds transfer and accounting—revolutionized the delivery of financial services. Entirely new possibilities for financial transactions became available. Early in the postwar period, for example, a large sale or purchase of foreign exchange could be executed only during the conventional business hours in the initiating party's time zone. By the mid-1980s, large foreign-exchange transactions in the major currencies could be readily consummated twenty-four hours a day. Large banks passed the detailed management of their worldwide foreign-exchange positions from one branch to another around the globe, staying continuously ahead of the setting sun.

Partly in response to such technological innovations, information and education about financial opportunities in foreign countries became much more readily and cheaply available. Those changes in turn helped to alter consumers' and producers' tastes. Foreign goods, foreign financial investments—virtually anything foreign—became much less a rarity than had been true early in the postwar period.

The implications for financial activity were far-reaching. Economic agents became more sensitive to, and had improved capacities to take advantage of, incentives for arbitrage among the national financial reservoirs. Financial instruments denominated in different currencies and issued by borrowers in different nations became less imperfect substitutes in the portfolios of increasingly sophisticated investors. Accordingly, larger amounts of cross-border ladling of funds began to occur. Moreover, much of this ladling was not directly related to cross-border trade in goods and services or other real-sector transactions. Saving units could decide to take advantage of higher expected yields on financial assets in foreign reservoirs by purchasing foreign assets or making loans to foreigners rather than investing the funds somewhere in the home reservoir. Investing units could borrow from foreign reservoirs if they could thereby obtain more favorable loan terms than at home. Increasingly, decisions about the country location of the investment and borrowing of funds were divorced from decisions about the country location of real-sector activity.

The economic distances between reservoirs were effectively shrinking for all types of economic agents. But financial institutions, and most of all large commercial banks, were best equipped to exploit the enhanced arbitrage opportunities. They had more and higher-quality information about foreign financial systems. They were better placed to introduce new communications technology. The relative costs of cross-border financial transactions thus fell most rapidly for banks and other financial institutions.

Ladlings of funds between reservoirs that were directly induced by newly profitable or newly perceived arbitrage opportunities may be described as leading rather than following real-sector transactions. The gross financial flows and the resulting net transfers of savings were (ex ante) independently initiated. The ensuing imbalance in current-account and real-sector transactions was a passive by-product of the capital flows.

In addition to arbitraging among national reservoirs by initiating financial transactions from their home bases, some financial institutions—again on their own initiative—moved abroad to establish actual physical offices within foreign reservoirs. Such offices enabled them to conduct arbitraging and inter-mediation activities directly from foreign locations.

For example, by the establishment of foreign branches, banks with head offices in a home (''parent'') country were able to facilitate their collection of funds from and their lending of funds to the residents of foreign (''host'') countries. Many of those foreign residents may not have had any real-sector transactions with economic agents resident in the parent country. Such inter-nationally oriented banks wanted not merely to service home customers with international transactions or foreign facilities; they also wanted new foreign customers and wanted to become active borrowers and lenders in host-country financial markets.

The last four decades of international expansion by financial institutions controlled from head offices in the economically most powerful countries was merely another chapter in a centuries-old story. As in earlier history, foreign-owned establishments imported financial innovations and practices, thereby catalyzing an increased differentiation and sophistication of host-country financial systems. Important examples of the cross-border transmission of new financial instruments included negotiable certificates of deposit, variable-rate and syndicated loans, commercial paper and note issuance facilities, financial futures contracts and options contracts, and the securitization of packaged loans. Foreign financial institutions were often the first to offer new services in host-country jurisdictions (for example, the global management of firms' cash flows through integrated computer networks). The foreign institutions were also, of course, more internationally oriented than indigenous institutions. At least in their initial years of operation in host countries, the foreign institutions had a higher proportion of their business denominated in foreign currencies and conducted with nonresidents. Similarly, they could not initially rely on a natural deposit base in host countries and therefore tended to be unusually active participants in wholesale money markets.

Regulatory, Tax, and Supervisory Explanations

From the perspective of private-sector agents, the existence of a govern-ment-erected separation fence around their home reservoir imposed extra costs on cross-border financial transactions. For reservoirs around which the fence was very high and effectively maintained, the cost of transferring funds in or out was prohibitive.

For given economic distances between reservoirs attributable to nonpolicy factors, government actions to lower separation fences caused a decline in the differential costs required to get across the fence, thereby enhancing incentives for the ladling of funds between reservoirs. The partial dismantling of policy-erected barriers to international capital flows is thus another conceptually distinct category of explanation for the rapid growth of international financial intermediation in the last four decades.

Still other incentives caused by governmental policies were important. They resulted from the interaction of nonpolicy technological innovations with regulatory, tax, and supervisory restraints on the financial systems *within* some of the economies. Such incentives would have been operative even if separation fences themselves had not been altered.

These latter stimuli were important in nations having a domestic regulatory, tax, and supervisory environment that was more constraining than the environments in some foreign countries. High reserve requirements against deposit liabilities, binding interest-rate ceilings on deposits, high ratios of required capital to assets, high effective tax rates on domestic profits, and unusually strict examination procedures are examples of such constraints. Financial institutions in nations with these constraints had incentives to locate affiliated offices outside their home country and to book transactions through those offices to take advantage of the less constrained operating environments abroad.

By locating offices abroad, a financial institution gained access to possibilities for financial intermediation in the wider world economy without the encumbrances of the home environment. To be sure, financial institutions with offices in foreign host locations still had to cope with the domestic operating environments in the host nations. Those environments often hampered their business with host-country customers. And the institutions still had to cope with getting across the separation fences of third nations to conduct business with residents of those nations.

The incentives for getting outside the home regulatory environment were related to, but not the same as, the incentives for getting over the home nation's separation fence. The distinction is between continuously shuttling over the home separation fence (engaging in profitable cross-border transactions in and out of the home reservoir on an ongoing basis) versus jumping over the separation fence once and then staying outside it.

Important variants of behavior for getting outside the fence occurred as national regulatory authorities permitted banks to establish special "offshore" facilities—typically, segregated accounting units—for conducting transactions with foreign customers or transactions in foreign currencies. In effect, banks were permitted to carry out "offshore" transactions as though the facility were just outside the home separation fence—even though the facility was physically located in the home nation. Regulations, supervision, and taxation were altered to discriminate in favor of the offshore transactions. For example, in contrast with the treatment of domestic deposits, banks were not required to hold fractional reserve balances at the central bank against offshore deposits. In exchange for the ability to operate offshore facilities, the banks agreed to limit transactions between the facilities and domestic residents (including their own "onshore" offices), thereby protecting the integrity of the separation fence.

Prominent examples of this phenomenon have included the creation of Asian Currency Units in Singapore, Offshore Banking Units in Bahrain, and International Banking Facilities in the United States. But a similar phenomenon has occurred implicitly whenever national regulations or taxation have been changed to discriminate in favor of transactions with foreigners or transactions denominated in foreign currencies.

The Relative Importance of Different Explanations

To recapitulate, three categories of explanations for the progressive erosion of the separateness of national financial systems can be distinguished.

1. Financial activity following real-sector transactions:
   a. Cross-border financial transactions, many of them conducted from home-country offices of financial institutions, that were closely associated with and driven by cross-border trade in goods and services.
   b. Establishment by financial institutions of affiliated offices abroad to improve services for existing nonfinancial customers who themselves had established operations abroad.

2. Financial activity leading real-sector transactions:
   a. Cross-border financial transactions, conducted from home offices of financial institutions, that proceeded in advance and independently of cross-border trade in goods and services;
   b. Establishment by financial institutions of affiliated offices abroad in advance and independent of the current requirements of existing nonfinancial customers in the home country.

3. Regulatory, tax, and supervisory explanations:
   a. Lowering of national separation fences;
   b. Establishment by financial institutions of affiliated offices abroad to escape from more stringent regulation, taxation, and supervision in the home environment.

It is convenient to refer to categories 1 and 2 as the basic nonpolicy hypotheses about international financial intermediation and to category 3 as the government-policy hypotheses.

The first variant of each explanation can partially account for the more extensive movement of funds from one national reservoir to another. But the second variants were probably at least as important: they presuppose a still deeper involvement in foreign activities through the establishment of actual bricks-and-mortar presences outside the home-nation reservoir. Such ownership and locational penetrations of foreign economies represented more than a mere ladling of funds among the reservoirs. In effect, financial institutions installed pipes, siphons, and pumping stations to facilitate their interreservoir transfers of funds.

Which category of explanation best describes the actual facts in the last four decades? I believe that each of the three was important. If forced to rank them, I would tentatively put the second category of explanation in first place. But no one of the three can be ignored.

In particular, neither the nonpolicy hypotheses nor the government-policy hypotheses alone can carry the whole burden of explanation. The technological nonpolicy factors were so powerful, I believe, that they would have caused a progressive internationalization of financial activity even without changes in government separation fences and the inducement of differing regulatory, tax, and supervisory environments. But I also conjecture that government-policy changes were important enough to have promoted a significant integration of national financial systems even if there had been no shrinkage in the economic distances between reservoirs due to nonpolicy innovations such as the fall in relative costs of the international communication of information. Indeed, it is likely that the interaction between nonpolicy innovations and changes in government policies was itself an important part of the history. Each set of evolutionary changes reinforced the effects of the other.[6]

---

6. When each of two interacting variables changes by a large factor, the combined change requires analysis to take into account not only the partial effects of each change considered separately but also the interaction of the two changes. More formally, the third term in the identity $d(AB) = A(dB) + B(dA) + (dA)(dB)$ is far from negligible when dA and dB are themselves large in relation to A and B.

Many governments lowered their separation fences over the last four decades. For example, in 1958, following the reconstruction period of the late 1940s and 1950s, many European countries restored convertibility for current-account transactions. Those policy actions inevitably undermined the early postwar distinction between current-account payments that were welcome and capital-account transactions that were not, which in turn loosened governmental restraints on capital flows generally. Some new controls on international capital movements were imposed in the 1960s, most notably in the United States. Germany imposed some new controls on capital inflows in the early 1970s. Viewed in retrospect, however, the predominant trend was to reduce or eliminate such restrictions. The United States had eliminated all of its 1960s restrictions on capital outflows by 1974. Major oil-importing countries relaxed their controls on capital inflows after the first big oil shock in 1973–74.

Prevailing attitudes about international capital flows also changed gradually. In contrast with the early postwar period, by the 1970s more emphasis was placed on the possible benefits associated with cross-border financial transactions. In the initial years after the onset of floating among the major currencies, the potential costs seemed less worrisome. Many governments also came to doubt the administrative feasibility of controlling capital flows (whatever the potential benefits and costs).

By the mid-1980s the salience of government restrictions on capital flows—especially among the industrial countries—was altogether different from what it had been four decades earlier. The United States was strongly against any form of capital controls; it was even leaning on other major nations to reduce their remaining controls on domestic as well as international transactions. The United Kingdom eliminated its remaining exchange controls in 1979. In 1981 Germany removed restrictions on nonresidents' purchases of domestic bonds and money market instruments. By the mid-1980s the British and German governments had become advocates of unfettered capital movements. During 1984 the United States, the United Kingdom, Germany, and France abolished withholding taxes on interest income paid to nonresidents.

It is true that some industrial countries—for example, France, Italy, and Japan—were less than ardent advocates of freedom for international capital movements. But even those countries were experiencing increasing difficulty in implementing their own remaining controls. Much less could they persuade countries like the United States, the United Kingdom, and Germany to reverse the general trend away from such controls.[7]

7. Details of many of the changes in countries' controls on capital flows are summarized in

The case of Japan is especially interesting. Japan relaxed its capital controls at a pace markedly slower than the average for all industrial countries. Even in Japan, however, formal exchange controls ended in the early 1980s. By 1984–85, moreover, the Japanese government had agreed—under pressure from the United States—to a significant liberalization of its other restrictions on international capital flows.[8]

Most developing countries retained some form of separation fence for cross-border financial transactions. Yet some had eased earlier restrictions. In Latin America, for example, although Brazil and Colombia kept their exchange and capital controls more or less intact, Argentina, Chile, and Mexico experimented with the relaxation or abandonment of such restrictions.[9]

These generalizations about capital controls do not carry the analysis very far. Economists have not adequately marshaled the evidence about government separation fences and generated analytical estimates of their effects. If one could accurately assess the importance of changes in government policies in the past four decades, economists would be on much stronger ground in forming judgments about future trends and in framing recommendations for appropriate public policies.[10]

---

the International Monetary Fund's annual reports on exchange restrictions. Various documents of the Organization for Economic Cooperation and Development and the Bank for International Settlements have from time to time summarized the status of existing restrictions—for example, a periodic BIS report on "Regulations and Policies Relating to Euro-currency Markets." Other descriptive accounts include Rodney H. Mills, "The Regulation of Short-term Capital Movements: Western European Techniques in the 1960's"; Victor Argy, *Exchange-Rate Management in Theory and Practice;* Emil-Maria Claassen and Charles Wyplosz, "Capital Controls: Some Principles and the French Experience"; J. David Germany and John E. Morton, "Financial Innovation and Deregulation in Foreign Industrial Countries"; and Bank of England, "Developments in International Banking and Capital Markets in 1985."

8. References on the Japanese capital controls include Eisuke Sakakibara and Akira Kondoh, *Study on the Internationalization of Tokyo's Money Markets;* Jeffrey A. Frankel, *The Yen/Dollar Agreement: Liberalizing Japanese Capital Markets*; Keimei Kaizuka and Tadao Hata, "Internationalization in Financial Activities in Japan"; and Colin R. McKenzie, "Issues in Foreign Exchange Policy in Japan: Sterilized Intervention, Currency Substitution and Financial Liberalization."

9. See, for example, Carlos F. Diaz-Alejandro, "Latin American Debt: I Don't Think We Are in Kansas Anymore"; and Morgan Guaranty Trust Company of New York, "LDC Capital Flight" and "Growth and Financial Market Reform in Latin America."

10. One reason for the lack of analysis of the effects of changes in government separation fences and government regulatory and tax environments is the great difficulty of empirically isolating the relevant effects. A limited early effort along these lines is described in Ralph C. Bryant and Patric H. Hendershott, *Financial Capital Flows in the Balance of Payments of the United States: An Exploratory Empirical Study,* and "Empirical Analysis of Capital Flows: Some Consequences of Alternative Specifications." For an analysis of the German case in the early

What weights should be assigned to the nonpolicy explanations in categories 1 and 2 above? Did finance follow or independently lead real-sector transactions in the internationalization of financial intermediation?

The distinction between following and leading is conceptually helpful. With sufficient information about the decisions of particular financial institutions in specific contexts, one could give it empirical content. When evaluating financial history in the large, however, it is difficult to disentangle the two.

Whether international finance has been following or leading real-sector activity is an issue related to the Goldsmith-Gurley-Shaw proposition that financial intermediation tends to grow faster than output in the earlier stages of economic development. That proposition does not rest on behavior that is peculiarly domestic in nature. And, as noted above, financial activity with an international dimension has been growing much faster than either output or trade. If cross-border real-sector transactions had been growing faster than purely domestic real-sector transactions, international financial activity would have grown faster than domestic financial activity merely because of the increasing openness of the real sectors of national economies. But since international financial activity has been growing markedly faster than international trade, one is tempted to infer that the Goldsmith-Gurley-Shaw proposition can be validly extended to the world economy as a whole.

The facts on relative growth rates are consistent with the presumption that international finance has tended to lead more than to follow real-sector activity. Observers of foreign-exchange and interbank-funds markets can cite numerous instances of financial transactions that are independently initiated in response to cross-border and cross-currency arbitrage opportunities. The numerous innovations of the 1980s promoting the securitization of international lending—for example, note issuance facilities and new hedging instruments such as currency and interest-rate swaps—are likewise presumptive evidence of the initiatives taken by financial institutions.

Bankers talking about the location decisions for foreign branches and subsidiaries often portray their organizations behaving in an anticipatory way, seeking new customers and profit opportunities in advance of the current service requirements of existing customers. When studying the rapid growth of international banking in Singapore and Hong Kong, for example, I was impressed by the numerous instances in which bankers perceived themselves

---

1970s, see Michael P. Dooley and Peter Isard, "Capital Controls, Political Risk, and Deviations from Interest-Rate Parity."

as taking initiatives and exerting leadership with their customers. Several foreign-owned banks described themselves as helping their existing customers identify and evaluate business opportunities in Asia that the customers themselves might not otherwise have considered seriously. Even more important, many foreign banks were wooing new Asian-based customers and trying aggressively to capture "a piece of the action" of the burgeoning opportunities for financial intermediation within Asia.[11]

The combination of the available evidence persuades me that financial institutions themselves have often been the cutting edge of internationalization and that finance has been much more than a passive veil draped over or molded by real-sector activity.[12]

11. Ralph C. Bryant, "The Evolution of Singapore as a Financial Center."

12. In the absence of a better understanding of the effects of changes in government policies, this conclusion remains uncertain, albeit plausible. In principle, the faster growth of finance than trade could be partly due to the greater relaxation of separation-fence controls on capital flows than of restraints on goods trade.

CHAPTER FIVE

How Far Has Internationalization Progressed?

HAVE national financial reservoirs become so well connected that nations must now be pictured as participants in a single world reservoir with a more or less uniform level throughout? Is there little scope left for autonomous financial conditions within individual national economies? Existing knowledge does not yet permit satisfactory answers to these questions. I nonetheless venture a tentative judgment and briefly review the available evidence.

A Summary Judgment and Two Qualifications

The financial structure of the world economy underwent a sea change in the last four decades. Nonpolicy technological innovations dramatically reduced the effective economic distances between national financial systems. Separation fences around them were partially or wholly dismantled.

Indisputably, therefore, the conceptual analogy of nearly autonomous national savings reservoirs is no longer appropriate. To a much greater extent than in the early postwar years, the levels in national reservoirs tend to be pulled together toward a common level. A disturbing event originating in one nation's economy or financial system causes substantially larger ripples—sometimes even waves—in other nations' reservoirs.

These stronger interconnections between national financial systems are evident even to informed laymen. They are a fact of life to financial-market participants and government policymakers. Even so, financial activity in many parts of the world is still significantly segmented. The conceit of a unified world capital market, implying a nearly uniform level throughout a single world reservoir, is also an inappropriate conceptual analogy for analyzing most aspects of international financial intermediation.

The actual situation, I believe, is an intermediate position not conforming to either of the polar cases. On the spectrum running from completely separated national reservoirs at one extreme to a fully unified world reservoir at the other, the major nations and currencies are probably some two-thirds or three-fourths of the way—but no further than that—toward the single world reservoir.

This untidy state of affairs is a conceptual vexation for analysts and policy-makers. Each group must mentally simplify a complex reality when trying to understand events and reach conclusions. The easiest simplifications to apply are the assumptions of the "nearly closed" paradigm, which presumes almost autonomous national reservoirs, or the assumptions of the "small and open" or "supranational" paradigms, which presume the polar case of a unified world reservoir. Yet the assumptions of each of those approaches conflict too greatly with the actual, intermediate facts. If theorists and empirical researchers hope to illuminate actual experience, they must struggle more directly with the analytical difficulties of intermediate interdependence. Similarly, if policymakers hope to avoid seriously overestimating or underestimating the autonomy of national economic policy, they too must abandon the polar assumptions as a basis for analysis.[1]

The preceding generalizations are subject to numerous qualifications. Two warrant special emphasis in this summary overview. First, the financial links among a few major nations and currencies have strengthened to a greater extent than those among the remaining countries and currencies. The nations most affected are the United States, Germany, the United Kingdom, Japan, and a handful of other European nations. The degree of segmentation in the second half of the 1980s presumably varies significantly even from one pair of major nations to another. Generalizations at the world level are hazardous at best.

Second, the continuing process of internationalization has increasingly divorced the currency denomination of assets and liabilities from the country residency of the economic agents who hold the assets and issue the liabilities. In the early postwar years, the country-residency and currency-denomination characteristics of financial transactions were much more highly correlated. The quantitative importance of this point is suggested by the banking data summarized in columns 1 and 3 of table 3-2. In the untidy intermediate state of the world that now prevails, analysis must jointly consider the country-

---

1. For discussion of alternative paradigms for studying international economic events, including the "intermediate interdependence" paradigm, see Ralph C. Bryant, *Money and Monetary Policy in Interdependent Nations*, chap. 10.

residency and the currency-denomination dimensions. For some purposes, for example, understanding the determination of exchange rates, currency denomination is the more important of the two. But national differences in the regulation, taxation, and supervision of financial activity require analysts to pay close attention to country residency as well.

Terminology

Analysts frequently use imprecise language when discussing the interconnectedness of national financial systems. Consider the concepts of "financial market integration," "asset substitutability," and "capital mobility." These are often used loosely as synonyms. Yet they should be differentiated and used more carefully.

The concepts have their origins in the microeconomic theory developed for analyzing markets for goods and factors of production. In those contexts, the terms are not synonyms. When applied to financial systems in a world of multiple nations and currency units, moreover, the concepts have some slippery nuances.[2]

A perfectly integrated market for good X is usually defined as a geographical area within which X sells at the same price, with prices at different locations within the integrated area adjusted for costs of transportation and transacting. Price differences within a geographical area over and above those due to transportation and transactions costs can arise because of barriers to free exchange—for example, government regulations that treat parts of the area differently—or because of asymmetrically available information or differential costs of obtaining information. In such cases the market is not fully integrated. The antonym of market integration is market segmentation.[3]

If strictly applied to financial activity, a definition of market integration along these lines would refer to the degree of price (yield) dispersion within some area for the same financial instrument. U.S. government treasury bills denominated in dollars and British government treasury bills denominated in sterling are obviously not the same financial instrument. If government capital controls led to prices for U.S. government treasury bills in London that dif-

2. I first became sensitive to the distinctions in the next few paragraphs as a result of conversations in the mid-1970s with Lance Girton and Dale Henderson.

3. Alfred Marshall wrote that "the more nearly perfect a market is, the stronger is the tendency for the same price to be paid for the same thing at the same time in all parts of the market: but of course if the market is large, allowance must be made for the expense of delivering the goods to different purchasers; each of whom must be supposed to pay in addition to the market price a special charge on account of delivery." *Principles of Economics,* vol. 1, p. 325.

fered from prices for the same bills in New York, analysis could profitably use the language of market integration. If the issue for study were differential costs of transacting in U.S. treasury bills in London and New York, the same would be true. On the other hand, if the focus for study were the relationship between the prices of U.S. treasury bills and the prices of British treasury bills (in either New York or London), the concept of substitutability would be more appropriate.

Substitutability in goods markets refers to the responsiveness of the demand or supply of good X to a change in the price of good Y. Applied to financial activity, the definition of substitutability correspondingly should focus on the cross-partial derivatives of asset demands or liability supplies in the investing and wealth-allocating behavior of individual economic agents (or groups of agents). For example, for assets A_1 and A_2 with expected yields r_1 and r_2 for some individual j, A_1 and A_2 become better and better substitutes as the cross-partial derivatives $\partial[A_1/(A_1 + A_2)]/\partial r_2$ and $\partial[A_2/(A_1 + A_2)]/\partial r_1$ go toward minus infinity. When the cross-partial derivatives are infinitely large, A_1 and A_2 are said to be "perfect substitutes"—for practical purposes, the same asset.

Individual financial instruments can be analyzed as combinations of attributes such as expected yield, default risk, term to maturity, and covariance of expected return with respect to other assets. When an economic agent perceives two instruments as having an essentially identical combination of attributes, he will treat the two as perfect substitutes. If a sufficiently large number of economic agents (on the demand side, the supply side, or both) regard two assets as having virtually the same attributes, the observed prices of the two, adjusted for the costs of transportation and transacting, will be driven to equality—provided there are no barriers to their free exchange and the prices are measured on the same basis (for example, in the same currency unit).

Capital mobility is the most used, and the least clear, of the three concepts. In microeconomic production theory, economists speak of a particular factor of production being mobile if it is able to move, and does in fact tend to move, to locations where it can earn the highest possible rent. When factor mobility is high, across industries and among subregions, the rewards earned by a factor are pushed toward equality throughout the area. Carefully used, "mobility" applies to the movement within an area of particular homogeneous factors of production (for example, labor cohorts with identical skills and experience). Loosely used, "mobility" often refers to geographical movements by aggregations of factors with differing attributes (for example, large groups of laborers with heterogeneous skills and experiences).

Applied to financial activity, "capital mobility" has meant a variety of things to different analysts. Used restrictively, the term refers to the degree of movement, and hence the price dispersion, of identical financial instruments within a specified area or between two different areas. Construed in this restrictive way, perfect capital mobility is a synonym for perfect market integration.[4] But neither term refers to the overall interconnectedness of national financial systems. Used in a more comprehensive sense, capital mobility is an idea subsuming the concepts of market integration *and* high substitutability among different financial instruments. A still broader and less precise usage invokes "capital mobility" to refer to large flows of funds among different geographical areas (a loose, overall notion of interconnectedness).

Market integration is the more appropriate concept for analysis of deliberate barriers to exchanges of assets across borders—for example, estimates of the consequences of raising or lowering separation fences. Asset substitutability seems the appropriate concept for general analysis of the linkages between national financial systems (since most of the various assets held and liabilities issued are demonstrably different financial instruments).

The summary judgment expressed earlier can be stated more carefully in the language of market segmentation and asset substitutability. Because separation fences at the borders of the main industrial countries were gradually lowered in recent decades, the degree of segmentation among the financial systems in those countries is today much less than in the 1950s, or even in the 1960s. Nonetheless, enough barriers remain at national borders to render unwarranted the assumption of complete integration. Still more important, for many types of economic agents—preeminently, large financial intermediaries—assets with otherwise similar attributes such as default risk and term to maturity, denominated in such major currencies as the U.S. dollar, deutsche mark, and pound sterling, are today much less imperfect substitutes than they were early in the postwar period. (As observed already, statements about the degree of substitutability presuppose the measurement of returns in a common currency unit, and hence the formation of expectations about changes in the relevant exchange rates.) Even for the most sophisticated decisionmakers, however, assets denominated in different currencies (adjusted for expected changes in exchange rates) are not sufficiently close to being "perfect" substitutes to warrant the use of that assumption in most analytical and policy contexts.

4. This restrictive use is the one adopted by Paul Boothe and others, "International Asset Substitutability: Theory and Evidence for Canada," who define "perfect capital mobility" as "the absence of capital controls (existing or expected), default risk, and significant transactions costs" (p. 15).

The high but less than infinite substitutability among assets denominated in different currencies does not, of course, apply to all types of economic agents. Within countries, many households and some firms may still be quite insensitive to cross-border and cross-currency opportunities for lending and borrowing. The degree of substitutability will have risen to much higher levels for some firms and financial institutions than for others.

How large must the class of agents with "high substitutability parameters" be before the incipient tendency for convergence of returns on similar assets in different currencies becomes an actual convergence? Plainly, not every investor and borrower must share the perception that two assets are very good substitutes. At the margin, a group of agents for whom two assets are nearly perfect substitutes may (through arbitrage) effectively maintain the returns on those assets close to each other even when the group constitutes only a minority of those investing in or issuing the assets.

An individual investor has to see all the attributes of two assets as nearly identical before he comes to regard the two as nearly perfect substitutes. If two assets differ in default risk or country risk or incur different transactions costs, the two may be significantly imperfect substitutes even though they offer the same expected yield. This requirement in turn means that a sufficiently large class of agents—though how large, as just noted, is a tricky question—must come to perceive all the attributes of two assets as identical before the actual yields will be observed to converge toward equality.

What does the literature in international economics offer by way of empirical evidence about the interconnectedness of financial reservoirs? The existing research has taken three approaches.

Research on Exchange-Market Intervention and Portfolio-Balance Models

One strand of work has been sparked by the policy analysis of exchange-market intervention, usually in conjunction with portfolio-balance models of asset demands. Portfolio-balance theories demonstrate that changes in the relative supplies of imperfectly substitutable assets denominated in different currencies can alter exchange rates and interest rates. If interest-bearing assets denominated in different currencies are perfect substitutes in the portfolios of a sufficiently important class of investors, however, changes in the stocks of those assets unaccompanied by changes in the stocks of central bank reserve-money liabilities—"sterilized" intervention—cannot have significant, nontransitory effects on exchange rates and interest rates. The degree of substitutability among assets denominated in different currencies is thus a central issue for the efficacy of exchange-market intervention.[5]

Academic and government economists have studied this question in recent years. The resulting evidence does not permit definitive conclusions. Some studies have found evidence consistent with the hypothesis that otherwise similar assets denominated in different currencies are very good substitutes. Other studies have found limited evidence that sterilized intervention can significantly influence exchange rates and interest rates, especially in the shorter run; these studies are consistent with the hypothesis that assets are somewhat imperfect substitutes. (None of the studies is supportive of the hypothesis that assets in the major currencies are highly imperfect substitutes.) Most of the research effort has focused on just a few currencies—primarily the U.S. dollar and the deutsche mark, with some work on the pound sterling, the yen, and the Canadian dollar.[6]

The tentative conclusions reached in this research typically depend on statistical tests of significance for individual regression coefficients. Given the equation specifications and data sets used in the studies, my conjecture is that the power of these tests is low; that is, researchers have an uncomfortably high probability of erroneously accepting the null hypothesis (so-called type-II error). If this conjecture is correct, the conclusions of the empirical research may depend critically on how researchers have formulated their null hypotheses. Typically, the null hypothesis has postulated that assets denominated in different currencies are perfect substitutes (for example, a statistical test postulating that a particular regression coefficient is not significantly different from zero). Researchers often have been unable to reject that null hypothesis. Suppose, however, that the research were conducted differently and the null hypothesis were to postulate that the assets are imperfect substitutes. Researchers might well be unable to reject that hypothesis either.

5. For a recent survey of the theory applicable to exchange-market intervention, see Dale W. Henderson, "Exchange Market Intervention Operations: Their Role in Financial Policy and Their Effects."

6. For the agreed summary of the governmental research on the efficacy of exchange-market intervention, see the March 1983 "Report of the Working Group on Exchange Market Intervention." For a summary of research carried out by the Federal Reserve staff, see Dale W. Henderson and Stephanie Sampson, "Intervention in Foreign Exchange Markets: A Summary of Ten Staff Studies." For the Canadian evidence, see Boothe and others, "International Asset Substitutability: Theory and Evidence for Canada." For two academic studies that survey these issues, see Kenneth Rogoff, "On the Effects of Sterilized Intervention: An Analysis of Weekly Data"; and Maurice Obstfeld, "Can We Sterilize? Theory and Evidence."

Given the inadequacy of the empirical understanding of capital flows and exchange-rate determination, the appropriate interim judgment has to be agnostic. There can be no doubt that the degree of substitutability across currencies and across national financial markets has increased greatly and that it is no longer low. But is the degree of substitutability moderately high, very high, or nearly infinite? One cannot yet confidently say which of these latter gradations best describes reality as of the mid-1980s.

Research on Direct Comparison of Returns

A second strand of research has investigated the relationships among assets denominated in different currencies and among assets issued in different financial markets by directly comparing measures of returns or borrowing costs. Some researchers have examined nominal interest rates; others have looked at real (inflation-adjusted) rates. Some have tried to study expected returns (and hence have had to make decisions about alternative ways of inferring measurements of expectations); others have simply examined observed returns. Virtually all the work, directly or indirectly, has involved tests of some "parity condition" (a hypothesized tendency toward equality of an interest differential with some measure of expected change in an exchange rate). The various parity conditions will hold identically only for the cases of complete market integration and perfect asset substitutability.[7]

This evidence is, at least in some ways, less ambiguous. The research confirms that *covered* interest parity holds closely where the assets being compared have similar attributes except for currency denomination (for example, Eurodollar and EuroDM deposits of the same maturity in prime banks in the same financial center). There is also ample evidence that *uncovered* interest parity does not hold closely. The appropriate interpretation of this latter result, however, is unclear. Many of the studies entail a joint test of two

7. For examples of such studies, see Robert E. Cumby and Maurice Obstfeld, "International Interest Rate and Price Level Linkages under Flexible Exchange Rates: A Review of Recent Evidence"; Michael P. Dooley and Peter Isard, "Capital Controls, Political Risk, and Deviations from Interest-Rate Parity"; Frederic S. Mishkin, "Are Real Interest Rates Equal Across Countries? An Empirical Investigation of International Parity Conditions"; Robert E. Cumby and Frederic S. Mishkin, "The International Linkage of Real Interest Rates: The European-U.S. Connection"; and David G. Hartman, "The International Financial Market and U.S. Interest Rates." Maurice Obstfeld surveys and interprets this empirical work in "Capital Mobility in the World Economy: Theory and Measurement." See also Richard M. Levich, "Empirical Studies of Exchange Rates: Price Behavior, Rate Determination and Market Efficiency."

underlying hypotheses: that securities denominated in different currencies are perfect substitutes *and* that financial markets are efficient in the sense that market participants use all relevant information in forecasting asset prices and exchange rates. The rejection of this joint hypothesis does not itself resolve which of the underlying hypotheses is false (or whether both may be).

Another part of this literature has tested for the equality of expected real rates of interest across countries. Most of these tests reject the hypothesis of equality but do reveal a significant positive correlation between movements in real interest rates.

This research also does not lead to definitive conclusions about asset substitutability or market integration. It is theoretically possible for the observed cross-country and cross-currency correlations among returns—for example, among expected real rates of interest—to be significantly less than unity even when assets are good substitutes and when separation fences at national borders are unimportant.[8]

Studies of the Correlation between Domestic Investment and National Saving

The third, and most controversial, strand in the empirical literature focuses on an observed high correlation across countries between national saving and domestic capital formation. In recent years an important impetus to this research has come from a paper by Martin Feldstein and Charles Horioka.[9] In a cross section of countries, Feldstein and Horioka carried out a variety of regressions of the general form: $(I/Y) = a + b(S/Y) + u$, where I is domestic capital formation, Y is gross domestic product, S is saving by national residents, u is a disturbance term, and a and b are estimated coefficients. (Variants of the regression included, for example, additional variables, a constant term varying across countries, and measurement of the variables averaged over different time periods.) Feldstein and Horioka found values for the coefficient b in the range of 0.8 to 1.0. In statistical terms, these estimates were signif-

8. See Obstfeld, "Capital Mobility in the World Economy."
9. "Domestic Savings and International Capital Flows." The argument was subsequently expanded and modified in Martin Feldstein, "Domestic Saving and International Capital Movements in the Long Run and the Short Run." For an early commentary on the Feldstein-Horioka paper, see Arnold C. Harberger, "Vignettes on the World Capital Market."

icantly different from zero but not statistically different from unity. Subsequent researchers replicated these results, albeit with numerous modifications and variations.[10]

Feldstein and Horioka interpreted their empirical results as strong evidence that the degree of "capital mobility" was not high. In particular, Feldstein subsequently asserted that their evidence "overwhelmingly rejected the implication of perfect capital mobility. . . . It is reasonable to interpret the Feldstein-Horioka findings as evidence that there are substantial imperfections in the international capital market and that a very large share of domestic savings tends to remain in the home country."[11]

When interpreting their research, Penati and Dooley believed that they had broadly confirmed the Feldstein-Horioka conclusion. They wrote that "changes in the propensity to save or to invest on the part of residents of an industrial country result in changes in that country's investment share or saving share, while current account balances act as temporary shock absorbers." Penati and Dooley described themselves as "unable to explain why the industrial countries were still behaving like 'insular' economies in the late 1970s, even though a substantial part of the barriers to the international mobility of goods and factors of production, which existed in the 1950s, had been phased out."[12]

Caprio and Howard reexamined the cross-sectional evidence and reached conclusions at variance with those of Feldstein-Horioka and Penati-Dooley. They argued:

The Feldstein-Horioka proposition is not correct: there appears to be a significant degree of net international capital mobility in the medium run. However, the evidence presented in this paper also indicates that net international capital is not perfectly mobile. The point estimate reported here is that, on average, about half of a change in a country's domestic saving rate from one OECD business cycle to the next has been associated with movements in its current account.[13]

10. The relevant papers include Jeffrey Sachs, "The Current Account and Macroeconomic Adjustment in the 1970s"; Jeffrey R. Sachs, "Aspects of the Current Account Behavior of OECD Economies"; Alessandro Penati and Michael P. Dooley, "Current Account Imbalances and Capital Formation in Industrial Countries, 1949–81"; and Gerard Caprio, Jr., and David H. Howard, "Domestic Saving, Current Accounts, and International Capital Mobility."
11. Feldstein, "Domestic Saving and International Capital Movements in the Long Run and the Short Run," pp. 130–31.
12. "Current Account Imbalances and Capital Formation," pp. 21–22.
13. "Domestic Saving, Current Accounts, and International Capital Mobility," p. 2.

Robert Murphy also disputed the interpretation of the Feldstein-Horioka results, showing that some part of the high estimate of the b coefficient in the cross-country regressions was attributable to country size or to the disproportionate importance of observations for three large countries (the United States, Japan, and the United Kingdom), rather than to low capital mobility.[14]

As so far conducted, this entire line of research is problematic. The simplified regressions it has generated cannot reliably be given a behavioral interpretation. Many of them merely replicate the quantitatively most important part of the identity that links saving, investment, and the current-account balance:

$$I^d \equiv S^p + Z^G - BCUR,$$

where I^d is gross domestic capital formation, S^p is gross private saving, Z^G is the government budget surplus, and $BCUR$ is the net transfer of savings abroad; or, alternatively, with each variable a ratio to GDP:

$$(I^d/Y) \equiv (S^p/Y) + (Z^G/Y) - (BCUR/Y).$$

These identities always hold ex post, by definition; and with all variables properly included, each coefficient is exactly unity.

Even more problematic is the fact that the researchers doing this work assumed that inferences about the degree of capital mobility can be made merely by examining the observed correlation between national saving and domestic investment. But that assumption is wrong. It is theoretically possible for an open economy to exhibit a high observed correlation between national saving and domestic investment even though it has no government separation fence impeding international capital flows and even though assets denominated in its currency are very good substitutes for assets denominated in foreign currencies and issued in foreign nations.

In principle, a wide variety of policy and nonpolicy disturbances originating within a nation's economy—and some types of disturbances originating abroad—can influence national saving and domestic investment in the same direction independently of the flow of capital and goods across the nation's borders. Consider a country that experiences a drought and harvest failure. In the short to medium run, incomes, saving, and domestic investment would all fall. One could observe a marked correlation between national saving and domestic investment even in the presence of high capital mobility. Or consider

14. "Capital Mobility and the Relationship between Saving and Investment Rates in OECD Countries."

a comparison of countries A and B, with A experiencing much faster rates of growth in population and productivity than B. Life-cycle consumption patterns and the interaction of production-function technology with growth in the labor force could lead to faster growth of both saving and domestic investment in A relative to B, again whatever the degree of capital-market integration and asset substitutability.[15] The observed correlation of saving rates and domestic investment rates in a cross-sectional sample of countries thus could be largely attributable to cross-country variations in demographic and production-technology variables.

Additional forces could generate a high correlation between domestic investment and national saving. Suppose governments dislike sustained imbalances in the current account of the balance of payments and respond to actual or incipient imbalances by taking policy actions to adjust the imbalances. Such reactive policies could prevent net savings flows across borders from becoming as large or as protracted as they would otherwise be, thereby raising the correlation between domestic investment and national saving.[16]

Still another consideration might be relevant for appraising the saving-investment correlation that has preoccupied researchers. Although the past four decades have been characterized by a general trend toward liberalization of trade in goods and services, some significant barriers to current-account transactions remain nonetheless. These remaining impediments to flows of goods across borders could conceivably be binding enough to prevent current-account imbalances from growing as large as would otherwise be observed. This hypothesis, in other words, presumes that the observed high correlation between domestic investment and national savings is attributable to goods-market phenomena rather than a lack of integration among financial markets or a low degree of substitutability among assets denominated in different currencies.[17]

As is evident from the preceding discussion, interpretation of the historical data for nations' saving, investment, and capital flows requires great care. Imagine that a government dismantles its separation fence. Suppose in addi-

---

15. For development of one variant of this latter line of argument, see Obstfeld, "Capital Mobility in the World Economy."

16. This possibility is emphasized in Lawrence H. Summers, "Tax Policy and International Competitiveness." See also the comments by James Tobin and Uwe Westphal on the 1983 Feldstein paper.

17. For discussion of this hypothesis, see Jeffrey A. Frankel, "International Capital Mobility and Crowding Out in the U.S. Economy: Imperfect Integration of Financial Markets or of Goods Markets?"

tion that technological innovations occur that lower the relative costs of communicating and transacting with economic agents in other nations. If an analyst compared the observed correlation of national saving and domestic investment in the years before and after those changes, he should expect to find—other things being equal—a looser correlation in the second period. But even in the second period, he would be likely to observe a substantial positive correlation. Moreover, if the second period happened to be characterized by much larger disturbing events than the first and if many of those disturbances were of the sort that influence saving and domestic investment in the same direction, the analyst could even observe a higher correlation for the second period.

Further theoretical and empirical research will permit more robust interpretations of the historical data. For the time being, one cannot safely draw inferences about the degree of cross-border and cross-currency asset substitutability or about the degree of integration of national financial systems merely by examining the correlations between national saving and domestic investment.

CHAPTER SIX

Has Internationalization Been Helpful or Harmful?

IN PREVIOUS CHAPTERS I described the progressive internationalization of financial intermediation, gave reasons why it has occurred, and summarized the limited evidence about the extent of its spread. I now ask, for individual nations and for the world, whether it has been helpful or harmful.

The perceptive reader already will have realized that an answer to this normative question requires a complex balancing of heterogeneous costs and benefits. Indeed, preparing a "report card" for financial intermediaries and financial markets is a difficult task even when the focus of discussion is domestic and multicountry complications are kept in the background.[1]

Businessmen, policymakers, and laymen are increasingly expected to have a normative judgment about international financial flows, notwithstanding the complexity of the issues. Accordingly, I identify the most important benefits and costs that have to be considered when reaching a summary judgment and offer some observations about weighing the benefits and costs to strike an overall balance.

Economic Benefits

Practical observation and economic theory alike demonstrate that a nation's residents can enjoy substantial gains from transactions with foreigners. The fundamental ideas elaborating this proposition go back at least to Adam Smith and David Ricardo.[2] Nothing that has happened in the last forty years—economic and political events or scholarly research—has diminished the rel-

---

1. See, for example, James Tobin, "On the Efficiency of the Financial System."
2. Adam Smith, *An Inquiry into the Nature and Causes of the Wealth of Nations*, first published in 1776; and David Ricardo, *On the Principles of Political Economy and Taxation*, first published in 1817.

evance of the original insights. Because the basic argument is familiar and widely accepted when applied to cross-border trade in goods, here I merely restate the essential points and draw out some less familiar implications for financial transactions.[3]

If a nation's residents could not trade with foreigners, the pattern of national spending would have to match slavishly with the goods and services produced at home. But so long as relative prices differ at home and abroad, the nation's residents can unambiguously improve their consumption possibilities by exchanging goods with foreigners. Furthermore, such "exchange gains" can be augmented by "production gains." Production gains result when the structure of production in a nation becomes specialized along the lines of comparative advantage. Resource and factor endowments are used more efficiently when production is specialized, permitting the nation to sell domestic production at favorable relative prices abroad, which in turn raises national consumption possibilities still further.

Traditional expositions of the gains from trade focus on goods transactions. But the argument applies with equal force to other cross-border transactions. Some nations tend to have a comparative advantage in the provision of financial services—for example, because of intercountry differences in liquidity preferences or because of the increasing returns to scale and the external economies associated with the historical development of financial centers.[4] As with goods, trade among nations in financial services can yield exchange gains and production gains.

As a result of cross-border transactions, therefore, a nation's residents can enjoy a higher standard of living—a time path of consumption that is higher, better adapted to their particular preferences, and not rigidly tied to the peculiarities of their geographical circumstances—than would otherwise be possible. What is true for the individual nation is equally true for the world as a whole. Cross-border transactions among countries permit a more efficient allocation of world resources than could otherwise occur and thereby increase world consumption possibilities.

The potential gains from international transactions can be very substantial. The gains are likely to be proportionately larger for small countries and countries with relatively poor endowments of natural resources. But there is a

3. For a textbook exposition of the basic argument, see, for example, Richard E. Caves and Ronald W. Jones, *World Trade and Payments: An Introduction,* chaps. 2, 5–7.

4. Walter S. Salant, "Financial Intermediation as an Explanation of Enduring 'Deficits' in the Balance of Payments"; and Charles P. Kindleberger, *The Formation of Financial Centers: A Study in Comparative Economic History.*

strong presumption that most if not all nations can, and in practice do, enjoy sizable benefits.

Not that each resident in each nation invariably benefits. Practical observation and economic theory agree that particular individuals or particular factors of production can be harmed. Nor can it be justifiably claimed that each nation, on balance, invariably benefits from all the international transactions conducted by or with its residents. Because of existing market imperfections, not every movement toward freer trade will be invariably beneficial. Nor will every imposition of new restrictions unambiguously reduce welfare. Interpersonal comparisons of well-being are problematic, and aggregative comparisons between nations even more so. Assertions about the welfare of entire nations or the world as a whole are thus inescapably controversial. These important caveats notwithstanding, there is widespread acceptance of the view that the gains from trade are substantial. There is virtually no scholarly support for the argument that a typical nation can improve its standard of living by a wholesale movement toward autarky.

A nation cannot engage in cross-border transactions in goods and services without permitting a commensurate degree of openness for financial transactions. Goods and services can be exchanged with foreigners only if the corresponding financial payments and receipts can be readily consummated. For efficiency, lending and borrowing associated with the goods transactions and their settlement will also be required.

Properly construed, therefore, the fundamental points supporting the case for cross-border transactions constitute an argument for transactions on both the current and the capital accounts of the balance of payments. The "gains from trade" can be equally well labeled the "gains from cross-border finance." (Possible qualifications to this broad conclusion are considered below.)

Cross-border financial intermediation is the essential counterpart of another dimension of the gains from trade. Suppose a nation's residents were not able to engage in goods and financial transactions with the rest of the world. The time profile of the nation's aggregate consumption plus investment would then have to conform precisely to the time profile of aggregate national production. Similarly, aggregate national savings would have to be exactly equal to aggregate investment. An autarkic nation with bright investment prospects in which ex ante demand for investment spending exceeded national saving would have to accept a higher rate of inflation that restored a balance between saving and investment, or alternatively would have to ratchet its investment, production, and income downward or find some way to raise the aggregate saving rate. An autarkic nation with an ex ante excess supply of saving would be afflicted with an analogous lack of flexibility.

With cross-border financial intermediation, however, the otherwise rigid link between national savings and domestic investment can be severed. The resulting gains for the nation as a whole are analogous to the benefits that financial intermediation within a nation brings to individual households and firms. The intertemporal pattern of households' aggregate spending can be matched to national needs and preferences instead of having to conform with the intertemporal pattern of earnings. Just as individual firms can hedge against events that could alter the profitability of their operations, an entire nation can collectively hedge against the future by accumulating income-earning assets abroad. Just as adventurous individual producers willing to assume the basic risks of business enterprise can borrow funds in excess of their current cash flow, a nation with better than average investment prospects can assume greater than average risks by importing capital funds and real resources from the rest of the world, thereby raising future consumption possibilities for the nation as a whole. With individual nations able to alter the intertemporal profiles of their consumption, the world as a whole can attain an improved allocation of savings and investment, with nations with ex ante excess savings employing them in nations where the ex ante return to investment is higher.

Economic history contains numerous examples of nations for which foreign capital played a crucial role in supporting economic growth. The United States in the nineteenth century made extensive use of savings from Europe.[5] Argentina, Canada, Australia, and New Zealand had analogous experiences in the late nineteenth and early twentieth centuries. In the last several decades, examples of countries with large current-account deficits and capital imports include Brazil, Korea, and Singapore. The prospects for future growth in many of today's less developed economies depend in part on their capacities to import and constructively absorb savings from capital-rich nations.

The major benefits associated with international financial intermediation stem from the root factors identified in the preceding paragraphs. A corollary consideration, however, also deserves mention. Financial markets within nations, and the cross-border and cross-currency transactions that increasingly link the national markets together, tend to respond promptly and fully to new information. Organized markets of any sort have this capacity to provide infor-

---

5. See Robert Solomon, "The United States as a Debtor in the Nineteenth Century," and the additional references cited there.

mation signals that help to achieve a more efficient allocation of resources. But a presumption exists that financial markets, because of their "auction" characteristics (chapter 2), respond especially quickly and efficiently.[6]

The prompt transmittal of information through financial markets helps to generate the exchange and production gains from cross-border transactions. Such benefits would not be realized to the same extent in a world in which information was disseminated less fully and less promptly. There is a presumption that the transmission of information among geographically separated nations has accelerated especially rapidly in the last four decades. The information benefits from international financial intermediation have probably increased correspondingly.

Consequences for National Economic Policies

Consider now the opposite side of the ledger, the various economic costs associated with the rapid growth of cross-border and cross-currency financial transactions. Chief among such costs are the adverse consequences for the autonomy of national economic policies and the controllability of national economies.[7]

National governments are politically accountable to their own citizens, not to a cosmopolitan world community. They therefore pursue economic goals that are unabashedly national—for example, the maintenance of high employment and the reduction of inflation within the geographical boundaries of the home nation.

When the home economy is significantly open, policymakers have an especially difficult task. They enjoy de jure sovereignty in the sense that they are free to take independent actions using the policy instruments at the nation's disposal. But they do not have de facto control over the nation's ultimate economic goals.

6. For references on the concept of market efficiency and its applications to domestic financial markets, see, for example, Eugene F. Fama, "Efficient Capital Markets: A Review of Theory and Empirical Work," and *Foundations of Finance: Portfolio Decisions and Securities Prices.* For international applications of efficient-market hypotheses to exchange rates, see the surveys (and the literature cited) in Richard M. Levich, "Empirical Studies of Exchange Rates: Price Behavior, Rate Determination and Market Efficiency"; David Longworth, Paul Boothe, and Kevin Clinton, "A Study of the Efficiency of Foreign Exchange Markets"; and Paul Boothe and David Longworth, "Foreign Exchange Market Efficiency Tests: Implications of Recent Empirical Findings."

7. The analysis summarized here is developed in greater detail in Ralph C. Bryant, *Money and Monetary Policy in Interdependent Nations,* chaps. 10–13.

For example, consider the policy actions of a home central bank. When the central bank purchases or sells securities, changes its reserve requirements, or alters its discount rate, some of the consequences of the policy actions spill across the nation's boundaries into the rest of the world rather than influencing the ultimate target variables of the home government. If structural changes occur in the home economy that further increase its interdependence with the rest of the world, these spillover effects become even more important. Typically, increases in interdependence reduce the effects of the nation's policy instruments on national variables relative to their effects on variables in other countries. The *relative* potency of the home nation's policy multipliers for its own variables is diminished.[8]

In practice, a nation's ability to achieve its economic goals by changing its monetary and fiscal policies depends as much on the uncertainty associated with own-variable multipliers as on their expected values (means). Increases in interdependence typically augment uncertainty about economic structure. More specifically, following an increase in interdependence there will be an increase in the (estimated or assumed) variances of many of the coefficients in whatever analytical model is being used for policy decisions. The remaining coefficients in the policy model will typically have unchanged variances. Only infrequently will any of the coefficients have a reduced variance. Because increasing interdependence typically generates more uncertainty about the structure and coefficients of a policymaking model, it thereby creates greater uncertainty about policy multipliers. In particular, increases in interdependence will typically increase the variances and covariances of national own-variable multipliers.[9]

The autonomy of a nation's economic policy is best defined as the effec-

---

8. Define a typical home nation's own-variable policy multiplier as (dy_j^h/dx_i^h) and the corresponding cross-border multiplier as (dy_j^f/dx_i^h), where the superscripts h and f denote the home and foreign countries, y_j is some ultimate target variable (for example, the aggregate price level), and x_i is some instrument of monetary policy (for example, the amount of central-bank money supplied to the financial system). Consider the absolute values of the means of the own-variable and cross-border multipliers after the increase in interdependence (denoted by a solid overbar) relative to their absolute values before the increase in interdependence. The hypothesis stated more formally is that

$$\frac{|\overline{dy_j^h/dx_i^h}|}{|\overline{dy_j^f/dx_i^h}|} < \frac{|dy_j^h/dx_i^h|}{|dy_j^f/dx_i^h|}$$

for all home policy instruments $i = 1, \ldots . k$. See ibid., pp. 177–82.

9. Ibid., pp. 183–87.

tiveness of the nation's policy instruments in influencing national target variables. The larger in absolute value and the less uncertain the national own-variable multipliers, the greater the degree of autonomy. Increases in interdependence thus typically diminish the autonomy of home economic policy.

In an analogous fashion, the openness of a nation's economy means that policy actions taken by foreign governments and nonpolicy economic shocks originating abroad spill over into the home nation. To an uncertain degree and, frequently, in an undesired direction, these externally generated forces buffet the home government's target variables. Increases in openness, just as they reduce home autonomy, increase these spillovers from foreign economies into the home economy. The growing size and greater unpredictability of such spillovers are likewise significant constraints on the ability of a nation's government to achieve its economic goals.

These propositions lead to a general conclusion: increases in interdependence typically diminish the degree of control that a nation's policymakers can exert over national target variables. As national economies become more closely intertwined, policy decisions in any single nation thus become more difficult to make, and more uncertain in their consequences.

The financial dimensions of interdependence have especially important consequences for national monetary policies. As cross-border and cross-currency financial transactions become more extensive, a nation's central bank encounters increasing difficulties in inducing and maintaining conditions in domestic financial markets that diverge greatly from financial conditions in the rest of the world.

For the individual nation, loss of policy control over the economy can be judged a serious cost, potential if not actual. The point is especially weighty for nations whose residents place a high value on being able to go their own way—to experience a divergent macroeconomic outcome from what is happening in the rest of the world.

The reduction in the effectiveness of individual countries' economic policies can also be a major problem for the world community as a whole. Increasing economic integration generates a growing variety and intensity of collective-action problems with international dimensions. Population growth, continued urbanization, and the more intensive exploitation of natural resources generate external diseconomies not only within but across national boundaries (for example, activities in one nation that pollute the atmosphere or ocean waters of other nations). External economies generated when benefits spill across national jurisdictions probably also increase in importance (for example, the gains from basic research and from control of communicable diseases). Economies of scale realizable from international cooperation may seem more compelling (for example, in a joint U.S.-Soviet effort in scientific space research). Issues about the use of the international "commons" arise more frequently and become more urgent. Illustrations abound: how to prevent excessive exploitation of ocean fisheries, how to manage mining of the seabed and to share the resulting benefits, how to allocate the limited band for geostationary orbits for telecommunications satellites, and how to respond to the global environmental threat associated with the carbon-dioxide "greenhouse" effect and the depletion of the stratospheric ozone shield caused by releases of chlorofluorocarbons into the atmosphere.[10]

The undermining of the autonomy of macroeconomic policies and the controllability of nations' economies that results from increasing economic interdependence are among the most important manifestations of the growing salience of collective-action problems with international dimensions. As each nation's policy instruments come to have stronger effects abroad relative to those at home, the potential costs of ignoring the external effects become correspondingly greater.

By their very nature, collective-goods issues cannot be tackled by individual governments acting sequentially and noncooperatively. Yet international governmental institutions either do not exist or have been given only very weak authority. The political processes to promote cooperative consultations and coordinated actions among national governments are poorly developed. In chapter 8 I discuss some examples of international collective-goods problems that are particularly relevant for cross-border financial intermediation.

10. The increasing importance of externalities and collective goods in modern industrial societies is a major theme in Fred Hirsch, *Social Limits to Growth*. For an introduction to the analytical issues, see Mancur Olson, *The Logic of Collective Action: Public Goods and the Theory of Groups*. For illustrative references on the international dimensions of these issues, see, for example, John F. Forbes, "International Cooperation in Public Health and the World Health Organization"; Richard N. Cooper, "International Cooperation in Public Health as a Prologue to Macroeconomic Cooperation"; Oran R. Young, *Compliance and Public Authority: A Theory with International Applications;* Edward L. Morse, "Managing International Commons"; Seyom Brown and others, *Regimes for the Ocean, Outer Space, and Weather*; Edward Miles, ed., *Restructuring Ocean Regimes: Implications of the Third United Nations Conference on the Law of the Sea*; Marvin S. Soroos, "The Commons in the Sky: The Radio Spectrum and Geosynchronous Orbit as Issues in Global Policy"; Lester B. Lave, "Mitigating Strategies for Carbon Dioxide Problems"; Mancur Olson, "Environmental Indivisibilities and Information Costs: Fanaticism, Agnosticism, and Intellectual Progress"; and Thomas E. Downing and Robert W. Kates, "The International Response to the Threat of Chlorofluorocarbons to Atmospheric Ozone."

"Inappropriate" Valuations and "Excessive" Variability in Asset Prices

The maturity transformation provided by financial intermediaries permits individuals to hold their savings in the form of short-term, liquid assets while ultimate investors simultaneously issue long-term, illiquid liabilities. The negotiability of securities traded in financial markets provides liquidity to the individual saver. Financial institutions promptly transmit price signals and other information from one geographical location to another. These maturity-transformation, liquidity-enhancing, and information-efficiency attributes are essential ingredients in generating the benefits associated with financial activity.

Yet maturity transformation, negotiability, and information efficiency come symbiotically linked with risks and problems. Viewed from a negative perspective, financial activity can be said to provide excessive opportunities for liquidity and to be too efficient in arbitraging information.

One basis for a negative perspective rests on the assertion that financial transactions, when motivated predominantly by short-run considerations, can unhitch asset prices from the long-term profit and risk calculations that are the fundamental determinants of whether investments are socially advantageous. This criticism was probably first voiced centuries ago, coincident with the development of financial markets and financial intermediaries. John Maynard Keynes stated the criticism especially clearly in his *General Theory*.

Financial markets are highly useful, wrote Keynes, in providing liquidity: "Investments which are 'fixed' for the community are thus made 'liquid' for the individual." But he also perceived that financial markets thereby introduce a "precariousness" into investment decisions. "There is no clear evidence from experience," he believed, "that the investment policy which is socially advantageous coincides with that which is most profitable."[11]

The Stock Exchange revalues many investments every day and the revaluations give a frequent opportunity to the individual (though not to the community as a whole) to revise his commitments. It is as though a farmer, having tapped his barometer after breakfast, could decide to remove his capital from the farming business between 10 and 11 in the morning and reconsider whether he should return to it later in the week. But the daily revaluations of the Stock Exchange, though they are primarily made to

11. John Maynard Keynes, *The General Theory of Employment, Interest and Money*, pp. 153, 157.

facilitate transfers of old investments between one individual and another, inevitably exert a decisive influence on the rate of current investment. . . . Certain classes of investment are governed by the average expectation of those who deal on the Stock Exchange as revealed in the price of shares, rather than by the genuine expectations of the professional entrepreneur.[12]

One might think, said Keynes, that expert professionals—possessing knowledge and judgment beyond that of the average private investor—could correct any vagaries introduced into financial-market prices by ignorance or mass psychology.

It happens, however, that the energies and skill of the professional investor and speculator are mainly occupied otherwise. For most of these persons are, in fact, largely concerned, not with making superior long-term forecasts of the probable yield of an investment over its whole life, but with foreseeing changes in the conventional basis of valuation a short time ahead of the general public. They are concerned, not with what an investment is really worth to a man who buys it "for keeps," but with what the market will value it at, under the influence of mass psychology, three months or a year hence. . . . This battle of wits to anticipate the basis of conventional valuation a few months hence, rather than the prospective yield of an investment over a long term of years, does not even require gulls amongst the public to feed the maws of the professional;—it can be played by the professionals amongst themselves. . . .

Professional investment may be likened to those newspaper competitions in which the competitors have to pick out the six prettiest faces from a hundred photographs, the prize being awarded to the competitor whose choice most nearly corresponds to the average preferences of the competitors as a whole; so that each competitor has to pick, not those faces which he himself finds prettiest, but those which he thinks likeliest to catch the fancy of the other competitors, all of whom are looking at the problem from the same point of view. It is not a case of choosing those which, to the best of one's judgment, are really the prettiest, nor even those which average opinion genuinely thinks the prettiest. We have reached the third degree where we devote our intelligences to anticipating what average opinion expects the average opinion to be. And there are some, I believe, who practise the fourth, fifth and higher degrees.[13]

12. Ibid., p. 151.
13. Ibid., pp. 154–56.

The assertion that financial markets generate asset prices that get out of line with fundamental valuations and the related assertion that asset prices fluctuate excessively have been subjected to intensive study during the last decade. Empirical research has focused in particular on the fact that the prices of shares on stock exchanges appear to vary by a multiple of the underlying variability in dividends and earnings.[14] The prices of long-term bonds appear to fluctuate more than can be readily explained by the variability of short-term interest rates.[15] The valuation of firms in financial markets has sometimes drifted far away, for extended periods, from estimated valuations based on the replacement costs of the firms' actual assets and the present values of the future returns those assets could be expected to earn.[16]

A related line of empirical research has investigated the possibility that financial markets can be disrupted by "bubbles" sparked by transient speculation. Loosely defined, a bubble occurs when the actual price of an asset deviates from its fundamental valuation because of self-fulfilling expectations of changes in price. The concept of bubbles has been combined with the assumption of rational (model-consistent) expectations. The resulting hypothesis of "rational bubbles" asserts that market participants at any point in time form a probability judgment about whether an ongoing bubble will deviate still further from the equilibrium price determined by the fundamentals; such rational agents may continue to participate in the bubble so long as they expect to be able to exit from the market before the bubble bursts. Analyses not constrained by the assumption of model-consistent expectations have postulated "irrational" speculative bubbles.[17]

Most of the research on excess volatility, speculative bubbles, and financial valuations out of line with fundamentals has focused on domestic aspects. Yet the phenomena may be equally important in the case of cross-border and

14. See, for example, Stephen F. LeRoy and Richard D. Porter, "The Present Value Relation: Tests Based on Variance Bounds"; Robert J. Shiller, "Do Stock Prices Move Too Much to be Justified by Subsequent Changes in Dividends?"; and Robert J. Shiller, "Stock Prices and Social Dynamics."

15. Robert J. Shiller, "The Volatility of Long-Term Interest Rates and Expectations Models of the Term Structure"; and Kenneth J. Singleton, "Expectations Models of the Term Structure and Implied Variance Bounds."

16. Franco Modigliani and Richard A. Cohn, "Inflation, Rational Valuation, and the Market"; and William C. Brainard, John B. Shoven, and Laurence Weiss, "The Financial Valuation of the Return to Capital."

17. For discussion of the concepts, see, for example, Robert P. Flood and Peter M. Garber, "Bubbles, Runs, and Gold Monetization"; and Olivier J. Blanchard and Mark W. Watson, "Bubbles, Rational Expectations, and Financial Markets." Related issues are analyzed in Stephen W. Salant and Dale W. Henderson, "Market Anticipations of Government Policies and the Price of Gold."

Table 6-1. *Alternative Measures of Variability in the Nominal Exchange Value of the U.S. Dollar, Selected Periods, 1973–86*[a]

Percent appreciation (+) or depreciation (−)

Period and number of months[b]	Spot exchange rate with German deutsche mark	Spot exchange rate with Japanese yen	Weighted-average exchange rate, Federal Reserve series[c]	Weighted-average exchange rate, Morgan Guaranty series[d]
March 1973–July 1973 (4)	−17.0	+1.0	−7.3	−3.9
July 1973–January 1974 (6)	+20.5	+12.6	+15.5	+9.9
January 1974–March 1975 (14)	−17.6	−3.4	−12.3	−7.1
March 1975–September 1977 (30)	+0.2	−7.3	+10.5	+7.8
September 1977–October 1978 (13)	−20.9	−31.2	−17.1	−13.4
October 1978–May 1979 (7)	+3.8	+19.0	+5.0	+4.9
May 1979–July 1980 (14)	−8.4	+1.2	−6.3	−3.6
July 1980–August 1981 (13)	+43.2	+5.5	+32.6	+19.8
August 1981–November 1981 (3)	−10.9	−4.4	−6.9	−5.4
November 1981–November 1982 (12)	+14.6	+18.3	+18.9	+14.8
November 1982–January 1983 (2)	−6.5	−11.8	−5.3	−4.6
January 1983–January 1984 (12)	+17.7	+0.5	+14.7	+8.6
January 1984–March 1984 (2)	−7.6	−3.7	−3.8	−3.1
March 1984–February 1985 (11)	+27.1	+15.6	+21.9	+18.2
February 1985–July 1986 (17)	−34.8	−39.1	−30.3	−23.8

a. Underlying spot exchange rates and weighted indexes are monthly averages of daily rates.

b. Periods defined by peak and trough months in which dollar reached interim highs or lows.

c. Weighted average of the currencies of Group of Ten countries, with multilateral trade weights (each currency weighted by the share of that country in the *total* 1972–76 trade of the group of countries). Source: Board of Governors of the Federal Reserve System.

d. Weighted average of fifteen currencies (Group of Ten countries other than the United States plus Australia, Austria, Spain, Denmark, and Norway), with bilateral trade weights (each currency weighted by the share of that country in the 1980 trade of the United States). Source: Morgan Guaranty Trust Company of New York.

cross-currency financial transactions. In particular, exchange rates may become "misaligned" with, or fluctuate excessively in relation to, variables deemed to be their fundamental determinants over the long run. Foreign-exchange markets may experience speculative bubbles.

Consider table 6-1, which shows percentage changes in the nominal exchange value of the U.S. dollar for various subperiods since 1973. The changes are calculated for the spot exchange rates of the dollar against the German deutsche mark and the Japanese yen and for two of the many possible measures of a weighted-average exchange rate (the average value of the dollar against a basket of currencies). One of the weighted averages is an index constructed by the staff of the Federal Reserve Board; it averages the exchange rates of the dollar against the currencies of the other Group of Ten countries (including Switzerland), using as weights the shares of each country in the

Figure 6-1. *Nominal Exchange Value of the U.S. Dollar, Monthly-Average Data, 1973–86*

Index, March 1973 = 100

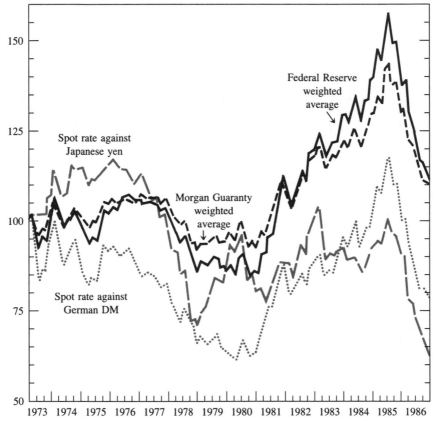

Sources: Board of Governors of the Federal Reserve System, "Federal Reserve Statistical Release" G.5 (405), various issues; and Morgan Guaranty Trust Company of New York, *World Financial Markets*, various issues. See table 6-1 and text footnotes for details.

total worldwide trade of the G-10 countries ("multilateral" trade weights).[18] The other weighted average, an index published by Morgan Guaranty Trust Company, combines spot exchange rates for the dollar against the currencies of fifteen major foreign countries. The Morgan index assigns weights to currencies according to the shares of each country in the trade of the United States

18. For a description of the series, see Peter Hooper and John Morton, "Summary Measures of the Dollar's Foreign Exchange Value." The data are published regularly in the *Federal Reserve Bulletin*.

Figure 6-2. *Nominal Exchange Value of the German Deutsche Mark, Monthly-Average Data, 1973–86*

Index, March 1973 = 100

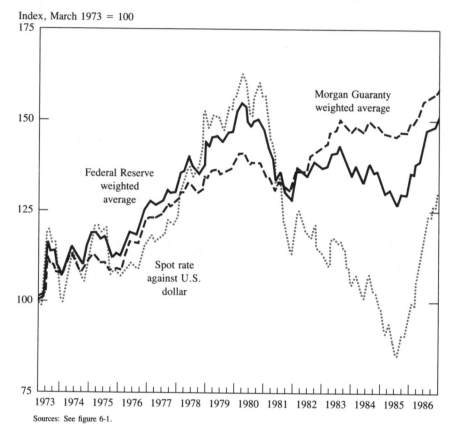

Sources: See figure 6-1.

("bilateral" trade weights).[19] The monthly observations used for calculating the percentage changes in table 6-1 are monthly averages of daily exchange rates. The subperiods shown in the table are not of equal duration. The peak and trough months that define the subperiods correspond to months in which the dollar reached interim highs or lows.

Figure 6-1 charts the four series for the dollar, providing a visual summary of the data used in preparing table 6-1. Analogous series for the exchange values of the deutsche mark and the yen are shown in figures 6-2 and 6-3. The

19. See Morgan Guaranty Trust Company of New York, "Effective Exchange Rates: Nominal and Real," "Effective Exchange Rates Compared," and "Dollar Index Confusion." The data are published regularly in *World Financial Markets*.

Figure 6-3. *Nominal Exchange Value of the Japanese Yen,*
Monthly-Average Data, 1973–86

Index, March 1973 = 100

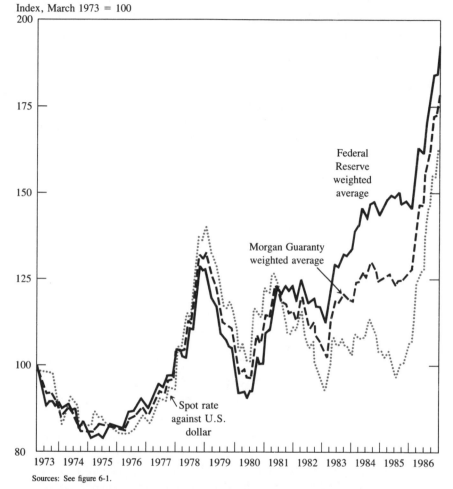

Sources: See figure 6-1.

series plotted in figures 6-2 and 6-3 are each currency's spot exchange rate
with the U.S. dollar plus Federal Reserve staff and Morgan Guaranty indexes
comparable in concept to the weighted averages used in figure 6-1.

Since the advent of generalized floating in 1973, as the table and figures
make clear, the magnitudes of medium-run swings in exchange rates, and even
month-to-month changes, have been remarkable. The exchange values of the
dollar, the deutsche mark, and the yen each exhibit large variability. Data for
most other currencies show commensurately large changes.

The variability is most striking for bilateral spot rates (first two columns of table 6-1, for example). The swings would be still more striking if measured from peaks to troughs for individual days instead of monthly averages. To give one illustration, the dollar strengthened against the DM by 35 percent between March 6, 1984, and February 26, 1985, whereas the change between the March 1984 and February 1985 monthly averages was only 27 percent. The size of changes for individual spot exchange rates within single days has often exceeded 2 percentage points.

A weighted-average measure is typically a much better gauge of "the" exchange rate for a nation's currency than its bilateral rate with any single foreign currency. Variability of the weighted averages is often somewhat less than for the underlying bilateral rates (third and fourth columns of table 6-1, for example). The apparent degree of variability is also sensitive to the choice of weighted average. For the United States, indexes calculated with bilateral-trade weights fluctuate less than indexes based on multilateral-trade weights, and indexes that include developing countries' currencies fluctuate less than indexes from which those currencies are excluded.[20]

Even if one appraises variability with weighted averages and even if one focuses on the averages exhibiting the least large fluctuations, however, the size of changes is still very substantial. For example, for the 1980–86 subperiods shown in table 6-1, the Morgan Guaranty series for the dollar's exchange value went up by 20 percent, down by 5½ percent, up by 15 percent, down by 4½ percent, up by 8½ percent, down by 3 percent, up by 18 percent, and down by 24 percent.

At the least, there are presumptive grounds for skepticism that the large short-run changes and very large medium-run swings in exchange rates can be completely accounted for by fundamental determinants.

What are the relevant fundamentals? The prices of goods at home and abroad are one set of candidate variables. A venerable theory in international economics, purchasing power parity (PPP), asserts that nominal exchange rates move to offset changes in the ratio of home and foreign price levels. Empirical tests of the different variants of this theory, however, have shown

20. Many alternative measures of weighted-average exchange rates may be calculated. Each has advantages and limitations, and no single average is preferable for all analytical purposes. An average using bilateral-trade weights emphasizes the particular geographical characteristics of a nation's trade but does not allow for the effects of trade competition in third markets. An average based on multilateral-trade weights allows for third-market competition but may overstate its importance. Neither trade-weighted measure takes any account of international financial transactions—an obviously serious omission, especially if one's purpose is to analyze shorter-run variability in exchange rates.

conclusively that PPP does not hold over short runs of one or a few years.[21] If a nominal exchange rate is adjusted for differential movements in home and foreign price levels—the adjusted series is typically labeled a "real" exchange rate—the failure of the adjustments to account for the bulk of exchange-rate fluctuations is glaringly apparent. The variability of real exchange rates, in other words, is still very large. This fact is illustrated in the two panels of figure 6-4, which repeat the nominal weighted-average indexes shown in figure 6-1 but also chart "real" (inflation-adjusted) counterparts.[22]

Other macroeconomic variables that are candidates for the fundamentals include relative (home versus foreign) interest rates, relative levels or rates of growth of output and employment, and imbalances in the current account of the balance of payments. All macroeconomic theories for open economies postulate interrelations of these variables with the exchange value of a nation's currency. When these variables are examined for their potential contributions to an empirical explanation of exchange-rate variability, however, a presumptive puzzle still remains. The variances of such variables, like the variances of price levels, tend to be an order of magnitude smaller than the variances of exchange rates.

The raw data for the variances of nominal exchange rates and their supposed fundamental determinants are, of course, no more than suggestive. Whether the variability of exchange rates is excessive relative to the variability

21. Evidence about the applicability of PPP over long time horizons is mixed and subject to alternative interpretations. Most economists accept the hypothesis that long-run trends in exchange rates are associated, weakly if not strongly, with divergent trends in national price levels. In hyperinflationary contexts, the tendency toward PPP may even hold in shorter runs. For reviews of the different variants of PPP and the empirical evidence, see Peter Isard, *Exchange-Rate Determination: A Survey of Popular Views and Recent Models*; Rudiger Dornbusch and Dwight Jaffee, eds., "Purchasing Power Parity: A Symposium" (see especially the papers by Kravis-Lipsey and Frenkel); Jacob A. Frenkel, "The Collapse of Purchasing Power Parities during the 1970s"; Robert E. Cumby and Maurice Obstfeld, "International Interest Rate and Price Level Linkages under Flexible Exchange Rates: A Review of Recent Evidence"; and Craig S. Hakkio, "A Re-examination of Purchasing Power Parity: A Multi-country and Multi-period Study."

22. The weighted-average real exchange-rate indexes are obtained by multiplying the nominal weighted average (foreign-currency price of home currency) by the ratio of a home price index to an index of foreign prices. The foreign price index is a weighted average of price indexes for individual foreign countries, with the same weights used in constructing the nominal exchange-rate index. For some analytical purposes—for example, appraisals of changes in the trade "competitiveness" of countries—real exchange-rate indexes are much more appropriate than nominal indexes. In particular, nominal indexes can give misleading impressions of changes in competitiveness where the countries whose currencies are included experience very different rates of inflation.

Figure 6-4. *Nominal and Real Exchange Values of the U.S. Dollar,*
1973–86

Index, March 1973 = 100

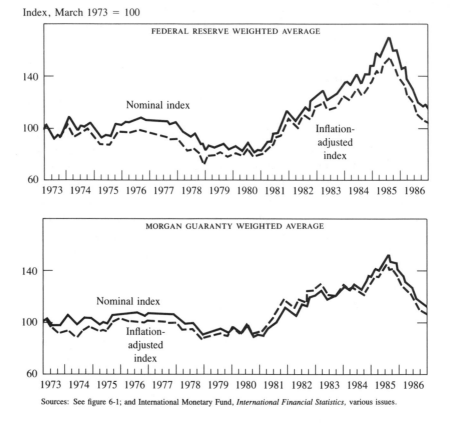

Sources: See figure 6-1; and International Monetary Fund, *International Financial Statistics,* various issues.

of other variables can be examined analytically only in the context of some
explicit model of the fundamentals. Unfortunately, researchers have not yet
been able to construct models of the fundamentals that satisfactorily explain
most of the variability in exchange rates.

Simplified models that try to explain exchange-rate fluctuations in terms of
changes in a few key macroeconomic variables have performed very poorly.
The explanatory variables most commonly included in small simplified models are relative price levels, relative interest rates, relative levels of output,
relative money supplies, and current-account imbalances. These postulated
fundamentals, as specified in the models, contribute something to an understanding of exchange-rate fluctuations. For example, changes in inflation-

adjusted interest differentials are somewhat helpful in explaining changes in inflation-adjusted exchange rates. But no simplified model based on these fundamentals has been able to account for most of the observed variance in exchange rates.[23]

In more complex structural models of open economies and their interactions, researchers treat price levels, interest rates, levels of output and employment, and current-account imbalances as "endogenous" variables. That is, together with exchange rates, such variables are jointly determined by still other economic forces (treated in the models as "exogenous"). With more complex models, therefore, it is possible not only to take account of the interactions between exchange rates and other endogenous variables, but also to look behind all the endogenous variables at deeper fundamentals—macroeconomic policies at home and abroad and various types of nonpolicy exogenous shocks (for example, changes in wage-bargaining behavior, OPEC-induced changes in energy prices, and changes in asset preferences induced by political events).

Analysis of deeper fundamentals in the context of structural models is, eventually, likely to provide a more satisfactory explanation of exchange-rate changes. The study of medium-run swings seems especially likely to yield to such approaches. Nonetheless, these approaches are as yet still primitive (especially in their treatment of expectations). So far they have not been notably successful, even in accounting for medium-run swings. No modeling of fundamental determinants, proximate or deeper, has come close to accounting for the bulk of short-run variability. And no approach has yet gained widespread acceptance among international economists. A recent thoughtful survey by Peter Isard concludes that "the empirical modelling of exchange rates over the past decade has been predominantly a failure."[24]

Despite the lack of consensus about models of the fundamentals determining exchange rates, researchers in recent years have begun to apply the ideas

---

23. In a series of well-known studies, Meese and Rogoff compared the most widely used of the small simplified models of exchange-rate determination with naive random-walk models. They showed that the small behavioral models could not outperform the naive models in forecasting, even when the forecasts were based on ex post realized values of the explanatory variables. See Richard A. Meese and Kenneth Rogoff, "Empirical Exchange Rate Models of the Seventies: Do They Fit Out of Sample?" "The Out-of-Sample Failure of Empirical Exchange Rate Models: Sampling Error or Misspecification?" and "Was It Real? The Exchange Rate-Interest Differential Relation, 1973–1984."

24. "The Empirical Modeling of Exchange Rates: An Assessment of Alternative Approaches."

of excessive volatility and speculative bubbles to exchange-rate data. Several of the early papers, using simplified models to represent the fundamentals, concluded that the empirical evidence was consistent with the existence of excess volatility or bubbles.[25]

Applying the excess-volatility and speculative-bubble hypotheses to exchange rates is, in principle, substantially more difficult than applying them to stock or bond prices. One additional difficulty is that exchange rates are prices of unique complexity. A purchase of foreign exchange is the purchase of an asset, and exchange rates do behave in many respects as though they were financial or asset prices. For example, exchange rates are set minute by minute through a continuous auction clearing of market supplies and demands; a variety of futures and options contracts exist alongside spot trading. Paradoxically, however, exchange rates have important functions that cannot be accurately described as merely financial. Although an exchange rate between countries A and B can be said to represent the relative price of A and B monies and the relative price of securities denominated in the A and B currencies, it can equally well be said to represent the relative price of *goods* produced in A and B. Expectations of future changes in exchange rates may depend as much, or more, on expectations of goods-market developments for entire economies as on expectations of financial activity or the returns on particular financial assets.

Another major problem in applying excess-volatility and speculative-bubble hypotheses to exchange rates is the difficulty of specifying an appropriate model to represent the fundamentals. As observed already, the choice of a model of exchange-rate fundamentals is substantially more uncertain and controversial than the choice of a model to represent the fundamental determinants of stock or bond prices.

25. For early applications of variance-bounds tests to the hypothesis of excessive variability in exchange rates, see, for example, Richard A. Meese and Kenneth J. Singleton, "Rational Expectations, Risk Premia, and the Market for Spot and Forward Exchange"; Roger D. Huang, "The Monetary Approach to Exchange Rate in an Efficient Foreign Exchange Market: Tests Based on Volatility"; Richard A. Meese and Kenneth J. Singleton, "Rational Expectations and the Volatility of Floating Exchange Rates"; Stephen S. Golub, "International Financial Markets, Oil Prices and Exchange Rates," chap. 4; and R. H. Vander Kraats and L. D. Booth, "Empirical Tests of the Monetary Approach to Exchange-Rate Determination." See also Robert P. Flood, "Explanations of Exchange-Rate Volatility and Other Empirical Regularities in Some Popular Models of the Foreign Exchange Market."

For the early application of speculative-bubble hypotheses to exchange rates, see, for example, Rudiger Dornbusch, "Equilibrium and Disequilibrium Exchange Rates"; and Wing T. Woo, "Speculative Bubbles in the Foreign Exchange Markets."

As in the analogous research on asset prices in domestic financial markets, the choice of a model is far and away the most crucial step in research on the possible malfunctioning of exchange markets. Tests of misalignments, excess volatility, or bubbles are necessarily tests of a joint hypothesis about the behavior of exchange rates and the analytical model. For example, when researchers test the null hypothesis that exchange rates are no more variable than predicted by the fundamentals, their test is inevitably contingent on the postulated model. If the test leads to rejection of the null hypothesis, which it usually does, the researchers and those evaluating their work inevitably face ambiguity in interpreting the results. One can infer that exchange rates fluctuate "excessively" *or* that the research has used an incorrect model of the fundamentals (or, possibly, both).

The research on excess volatility and speculative bubbles in financial activity continues to ferment. New studies are being produced each year, with most of the research still focused on stock prices. Not surprisingly, the empirical evidence and the interpretation of it are still very much in dispute.[26]

For example, the technical literature contains vigorous defenses of the view that stock prices are *not* excessively volatile. One line of attack taken by these defenders is to argue that dividends—and, by extension of the argument, other economic variables such as aggregate consumption and aggregate investment—are "smoothed either by the behavior of the economic agents that control them or by the statistical methods which are used to measure them." This smoothing, it is argued, masks the much larger fluctuations of intrinsic (fundamental) valuations. From this perspective, the puzzle to be explained is why dividends exhibit so little volatility, not why stock market prices exhibit so much.[27]

---

26. For overviews of the research on excess volatility, see Stephen F. LeRoy, "Efficiency and the Variability of Asset Prices"; Stanley Fischer and Robert C. Merton, "Macroeconomics and Finance: The Role of the Stock Market"; and Lawrence H. Summers, "Does the Stock Market Rationally Reflect Fundamental Values?" For extensions of the research, including studies critical of the early conclusions, see, for example, Marjorie A. Flavin, "Excess Volatility in the Financial Markets: A Reassessment of the Empirical Evidence"; N. Gregory Mankiw, David Romer, and Matthew D. Shapiro, "An Unbiased Reexamination of Stock Market Volatility"; Werner F.M. De Bondt and Richard Thaler, "Does the Stock Market Overreact?"; Allan W. Kleidon, "Variance Bounds Tests and Stock Price Valuation Models"; and Joe Mattey and Richard Meese, "Empirical Assessment of Present Value Relations." For recent research on bubbles, see Robert P. Flood, Robert J. Hodrick, and Paul Kaplan, "An Evaluation of Recent Evidence on Stock Market Bubbles."

27. See, for example, Terry A. Marsh and Robert C. Merton, "Dividend Variability and Variance Bounds Tests for the Rationality of Stock Market Prices." For a rejoinder, see Robert J. Shiller, "The Marsh-Merton Model of Managers' Smoothing of Dividends."

A similar attack can be mounted against the view that exchange rates are excessively volatile. Convinced believers in market efficiency can argue that exchange-rate fluctuations correctly reflect large changes in and uncertainties about underlying economic conditions among countries. In their view, the surprising feature of empirical data is the "modest" volatility in domestic variables like price levels and outputs, not the "large" volatility in exchange rates. With no risk of logical contradiction, proponents of this view can attribute apparent test findings of excess volatility entirely to inadequacy of the postulated models of the fundamentals.[28]

The unsettled status of the research about excess volatility, speculative bubbles, and misalignments in asset prices does not yet permit a consensus summary of the empirical evidence. Resolution of the differing views about the applicability of these ideas to exchange rates seems especially distant. Unfortunately, individual analysts can still respond to the evidence as they would to a Rorschach test. For every macroeconomic skeptic who sees the inkblots of stock exchanges and foreign-exchange markets as afflicted by serious blemishes, there seems to be at least one professor of finance to whom they appear surpassingly attractive and efficient.

Potential Fragility and Instability of Financial Activity

Episodes of financial instability, when participants in financial markets exhibit panicky behavior, have been observed for centuries.[29] During financial panics, real or rumored events can induce crowd behavior and a mob psychology. As Bernard Baruch was fond of observing: "Anyone taken as an individual is tolerably sensible and reasonable—as a member of a crowd, he at once becomes a blockhead."[30]

28. For recent research on the application of excess-volatility and speculative-bubble ideas to exchange markets, see, for example, Daniel Gros, "On the Volatility of Exchange Rates: A Test of Monetary and Portfolio Balance Models of Exchange Rate Determination"; Kunio Okina, "Empirical Tests of 'Bubbles' in the Foreign Exchange Market"; Jeffrey A. Frankel, "The Dazzling Dollar"; and Jeffrey A. Frankel and Kenneth A. Froot, "The Dollar as an Irrational Speculative Bubble: A Tale of Fundamentalists and Chartists."

29. For example, see Charles MacKay, *Extraordinary Popular Delusions and the Madness of Crowds;* Hyman P. Minsky, "Financial Instability Revisited: The Economics of Disaster"; Minsky, "The Financial Instability Hypothesis: A Restatement"; Charles P. Kindleberger, *Manias, Panics and Crashes: A History of Financial Crises*; and Charles P. Kindleberger and Jean-Pierre Laffargue, eds., *Financial Crises: Theory, History, and Policy.*

30. See Baruch's foreword to MacKay, *Extraordinary Popular Delusions and the Madness of Crowds.*

Even without perverse crowd behavior, a financial crisis, if allowed to run its course unchecked, may result in the bankruptcy of otherwise viable organizations. Because financial assets are bought and sold in auction markets, prices can change quickly and by large amounts. Confidence in financial institutions is a fragile thing. A decline in confidence in one financial intermediary can lead to a decline in confidence in its creditors, and contagion can occur so that even healthy institutions come under suspicion. In customer markets for goods and real tangible assets, where price changes are more viscous, contagion tends to spread much less quickly.

Contagion and herd behavior do not arise solely because of the actions of the customers of financial institutions. The financial institutions are quite capable of this behavior themselves, thereby exacerbating the adverse consequences of distressed financial conditions.

The instability that can occur in financial markets does not necessarily imply that individual economic agents act irrationally. Careful analysts of economic and social behavior have identified numerous instances in which noncooperative competition and unconstrained maximization by individual agents, while rational for each individual, can be irrational for all individuals together.[31] In this context, the contention is that a financial crisis unchecked by any actions taken by a lender of last resort is a situation in which each financial institution and customer can behave rationally and yet still produce a collective outcome that is highly undesirable for society as a whole.

In several ways the international aspects of financial intermediation can compound the consequences of distressed financial conditions. The causes of the distress may even originate abroad (for example, a failure of an intermediary with all its business in foreign nations or in the Eurocurrency markets). But whatever the origins, cross-border and cross-currency transactions can exacerbate the distress.

For example, foreign-exchange and Eurocurrency markets, because they are dominated by financial institutions that are highly sensitive to changes in confidence, can rapidly spread a deterioration in confidence. The risks of contagion are at least as great for international as for domestic transactions. In

---

31. See, for example, Francis M. Bator, "The Anatomy of Market Failure"; Kenneth J. Arrow, "Uncertainty and the Welfare Economics of Medical Care"; Mancur Olson, *The Logic of Collective Action: Public Goods and the Theory of Groups;* Alfred E. Kahn, "The Tyranny of Small Decisions: Market Failures, Imperfections, and the Limits of Economics"; Kenneth J. Arrow, "The Economics of Moral Hazard: Further Comment"; Kenneth J. Arrow, "Limited Knowledge and Economic Analysis"; Thomas Schelling, "On the Ecology of Micromotives"; and Fred Hirsch, *Social Limits to Growth.*

addition, the supervision and examination of the international aspects of financial intermediation are less stringent than for the domestic aspects. Large financial institutions with significant cross-border assets and liabilities are de facto multinational in their operations. National supervisors and national central banks may be unable to supervise adequately all aspects of their operations. (These supervisory issues are discussed in subsequent chapters.) Moreover, financial intermediaries may have less adequate information on foreign customers than is available for their domestic borrowers and therefore be less able to make good judgments about creditworthiness in their international activities. Lending by financial intermediaries to sovereign governments involves political risks that are not present in domestic lending. And individual financial institutions, in addition to all the other ways they have of getting into trouble in a closed economy, can get into trouble because of poorly managed foreign-exchange positions.[32]

At the very least, the capacity for financial shocks originating in one country to spread and cause problems in other countries has substantially increased. Thus the international dimensions of fragility, at a minimum, introduce additional layers of complexity into government oversight of financial activity.

Use of Scarce Resources

A final economic consideration on the cost side of the ledger is that markets and financial institutions use up resources that could be employed elsewhere. Innovations are costly to implement. New financial instruments, new patterns of financial behavior, and the setting up of new financial markets all take people and capital resources. They also tend to elicit new efforts by governments to oversee and police, which in turn use up additional resources. James Tobin has remarked that "the country cannot afford all the markets that enthusiasts may dream up." He would have the regulatory authorities approve new types of financial instruments or contracts only when they can be shown to fill genuine "gaps in the menu and enlarge the opportunities for Arrow-Debreu insurance," rather than merely adding to the opportunities for speculation and financial arbitrage.[33]

32. For an entertaining, but exaggerated, view of the incremental risks of financial instability due to international banking transactions—written at a time when fears of instability were prevalent—see John J. Fialka, "World Banking Bust: One Plot for a Tragedy in 8 Scenes and 12 Days."

33. "On the Efficiency of the Financial System," p. 10.

Analogous opportunity costs exist for the world as a whole. At the current stage of evolution of the world financial system, most of the innovations promoting internationalization may have yielded efficiency benefits greater than the resources devoted to them. But even if Tobin's cautionary observation can be shown to be less applicable to international innovations than to recent domestic ones, it could become more pertinent in the future. It is easy to imagine many future uses of the world's scarce resources that would generate larger social benefits than the likely returns from establishment of all the new international financial instruments and markets that enthusiasts are sure to propose.

Some Political Considerations

From the perspective of some observers, the enhanced integration of nations' financial markets can have favorable political consequences. For example, such observers argue that the freedom of residents to transfer their wealth outside a nation, acquiring financial or physical assets abroad, holds the government of the nation more politically accountable than it otherwise would be. The fear of capital flight is said to exert a strong discipline, forcing a government to behave better—especially when choosing its economic policies, but perhaps other policies as well—than it might otherwise be tempted to behave. Seen from the perspective of individual residents, the possibility of wealth transfer abroad is, to use Hirschman's distinction, an "exit" option. Rather than remaining fully engaged in the nation's economic and political life, exercising "voice" to influence their government, they can merely withdraw their wealth and disengage.[34] In extreme circumstances, the individuals themselves can leave the country and establish residence elsewhere. For such exit options to exist, a nation must have a relatively low, or at least poorly monitored, separation fence for financial transactions and it must freely permit emigration.

The normative values underlying this political perspective are, of course, highly controversial. For every individual holding such views there may exist another who supports essentially the opposite perspective. Transfer of residents' wealth abroad, these other observers argue, is a highly negative, not

---

34. The contrast between voice and exit options in political and economic life is analyzed in the seminal book by Albert O. Hirschman, *Exit, Voice, and Loyalty: Responses to Decline in Firms, Organizations, and States.*

positive, influence in the domestic political situation. Only the wealthier of the nation's residents have effective access to the option of capital flight. They alone have the requisite information and established connections with foreign financial institutions. Such observers are also likely to perceive the holding of wealth outside the nation as being highly correlated with domestic corruption and tax evasion. Instead of being a constructive discipline on national governments, the option of wealth transfer abroad is seen as reducing the incentives of residents to participate actively in helping to achieve political resolution of the nation's problems. Because exit is too easy, voice and loyalty are not nurtured.

Both of these political perspectives, or variants of them, are frequently encountered in a nation's political life. Recall, for example, the recent experiences of Latin American countries with large external debts. In the first half of the 1980s, some residents in many of those countries accumulated significant amounts of assets abroad. Was this "capital flight" a constructive pressure or an adverse contributing factor to their crises? The issue has been vociferously argued both ways. Those unconcerned or approving of the capital flows argue that the debtor governments, in the absence of the pressures from the capital exports, would have moved even more slowly to adopt the adjustment policies that were required. The opposite view emphasizes that the capital flight seriously exacerbated the countries' economic situations, thereby necessitating much harsher internal adjustments than would otherwise have been required.

Balancing Costs and Benefits

If the various blessings and blemishes associated with international financial intermediation are weighed against each other, do the scales tilt unambiguously to one side or the other?

Polar positions are simple to state and often command the greatest public attention. It thus may seem tempting to adopt one or the other extreme view— that the consequences on balance have been overwhelmingly beneficial, or that world welfare, and even more so the welfare of particular nations, has been seriously harmed. But that temptation should be resisted. Neither polar position can withstand careful scrutiny.

One polar view is preoccupied with the costs side of the report card. It perceives financial transactions among nations as unbridled and unstable.

It yearns for government actions to reverse this "out-of-control" situation. It deemphasizes benefits, or is altogether blind to them.

But that preoccupation is neither practical nor persuasive. The considerable advantages of the automobile are coupled with road congestion in urban areas, pollution of the environment, and increased loss of life in accidents. Yet no sensible person emphasizes the social costs of the automobile to the exclusion of its benefits. In an analogous way, modern financial activity comes associated with serious risks and problems. A practical man will have little interest in comparing financial activity as it actually exists with a nirvana in which financial activity is risk free and problem free. The relevant issue is whether some feasible alternative process exists that could channel funds from ultimate savers to ultimate investors, within countries and among countries, in a way that would be obviously superior.

To ensure that the negative aspects of financial activity are seen in perspective, two basic points need continuing emphasis. First, economic activity, quite apart from its financial aspects, is inherently uncertain and potentially unstable. Surprises occur at least as frequently in the political and social dimensions of life. This uncertainty and instability outside the financial sector cannot be eliminated. It is thus fruitless to wish for the elimination of uncertainty and potential instability in finance. In many of its aspects, financial activity mirrors the uncertainty and instability in the society at large. When the weather is stormy outside the financial sector, there is no conceivable way for the surface of the financial reservoir to stay tranquil. Nor would such tranquillity be socially desirable even if it could be attained. The fragility of financial intermediaries and financial markets could not be eliminated without simultaneously abandoning the essence of the useful functions that financial activity performs.

Second, the advantages of liquidity and negotiability supplied by financial intermediaries and financial markets likewise cannot be supplied without risks and problems. What the financial sector provides to individual savers and investors in sunny times cannot possibly be provided—in either sunny or stormy times—to society as a whole. Moreover, the advantages of liquidity and negotiability have to be bought, ineluctably, it appears, at the expensive price of facilitating speculative activity that can be shortsighted and socially inefficient.

As noted earlier, Keynes believed that securities markets could generate valuations out of touch with the long-run fundamentals. He therefore regarded the liquidity of such markets as a mixed blessing. Tobin has frequently articulated a similar view.[35] Analogously, in times of distressed financial conditions the liquidity of deposits in financial intermediaries can be a mixed blessing.

Nonetheless, illiquidity would probably be the worse evil. Keynes and Tobin, and other thoughtful critics of financial activity, have recognized this inherent dilemma. As Keynes observed the "spectacle of modern investment markets," for example, he wistfully longed for some device (he even floated the trial balloon of a "substantial government transfer tax on all transactions") that would "force the investor to direct his mind to the long-term prospects and to those only." But, he then cautioned,

> a little consideration of this expedient brings us up against a dilemma, and shows us how the liquidity of investment markets often facilitates, though it sometimes impedes, the course of new investment. For the fact that each individual investor flatters himself that his commitment is "liquid" (though this cannot be true for all investors collectively) calms his nerves and makes him much more willing to run a risk. If individual purchases of investments were rendered illiquid, this might seriously impede new investment, so long as *alternative ways* in which to hold his savings are available to the individual. This is the dilemma. So long as it is open to the individual to employ his wealth in hoarding or lending *money,* the alternative of purchasing actual capital assets cannot be rendered sufficiently attractive (especially to the man who does not manage the capital assets and knows very little about them), except by organising markets wherein these assets can be easily realised for money.[36]

The preceding points are at least as important for the international as for the domestic aspects of financial activity. For many nations, events in the outside world are more uncertain and potentially disruptive than those inside. Political and economic turbulence among nations, leading to numerous international financial transactions and financial-sector turbulence, is inevitable. Because the financial turbulence most often originates outside the financial sectors of national economies, however, it is pointless to assign primary blame to financial interdependence.

Consider two recent examples. The debt crises of developing countries in the early 1980s were caused more by inappropriate policies in the borrowing

35. For example, in "On the Efficiency of the Financial System." See also James Tobin, "A Mean-Variance Approach to Fundamental Valuations."
36. *General Theory of Employment, Interest and Money,* vol. 7, pp. 160, 161.

countries and by a severe, unforeseen recession in the OECD countries (partly traceable in turn to their inappropriate macroeconomic policies) than by inappropriate behavior of the commercial banks who had loaned large amounts of money to the developing countries during preceding years. The banks were far from blameless, of course. With the wisdom of hindsight, it is apparent that the lending policies of many banks were incautious and in some degree marred by herdlike decisions. After a period of excessive eagerness to lend to developing countries and insufficient monitoring of potential risks, the banks did a U-turn and individually wanted to withdraw when it was collectively impossible for all of them to do so. Nevertheless, the most important underlying causes of the debt crises cannot plausibly be laid on the doorstep of the lending banks. Nor is it plausible to look primarily to them for a resolution of the crises.

Similarly, the enormous appreciation of the U.S. dollar in 1980–85 was probably exacerbated by speculative froth. By the second half of 1984— almost certainly by early 1985—the dollar had been carried well beyond a range consistent with long-run external and internal balance for the economies of the United States and its major trading partners. But can one convincingly attribute the major part of the *sustained* appreciation to events originating within exchange markets and U.S. or foreign financial sectors—for example, to "nonfundamentals" such as speculative bubbles, excess volatility, or other not-easily-explained shifts in preferences for assets denominated in U.S. dollars? In my judgment, clearly not. The place to start when trying to understand the large swings in exchange rates during 1980–85 is with the burgeoning structural deficit in the U.S. government budget, the relatively tight monetary policies of the Federal Reserve, and the contracting deficits characteristic of budgetary policies in Germany, Japan, and several other large industrial countries.

A vigorously growing world economy requires flexibility for substantial intercountry transfers of savings. If that transfer process is to function smoothly, creditors in the nations exporting savings must have confidence that their claims on the recipient countries are sound. Individual creditors will also need the illusion that their cross-border and cross-currency claims are liquid and negotiable. Without that illusion, the intercountry transfer of savings would be greatly constrained. "Illusion" is an appropriate term because, for the international as for the domestic aspects, the individual creditor can have liquidity but the world as a whole (and, often, even particular nations) cannot. Here as elsewhere, liquidity is a mixed blessing. For countries wanting to pursue divergent macroeconomic policies, the closer linking of national financial sectors makes that goal less attainable. As within countries, however, illiquidity—impeding the efficient intercountry transfer of savings—could be the worse evil.

What about the opposite polar view, preoccupied with the benefits side of the report card? Is international financial intermediation efficient enough to justify ignoring the associated risks and problems? The perspective that answers "yes" may be labeled, only a little unfairly (and with apologies to Voltaire), semi-Panglossian. If only financial intermediaries and financial markets could be allowed to function without impediments, asserts this view, all would be for the best in this nearly best of all possible worlds.

An extreme efficient-markets view, I believe, is no more practical or persuasive than the opposite preoccupation with negative points—just as it would not be prudent to ignore the evidence that automobiles, while enormously enhancing welfare, nonetheless cause congestion, pollution, and accidental loss of life.

Although turbulence in financial activity often merely reflects events originating outside the financial sector, the resulting financial turbulence can nonetheless exacerbate the adverse consequences of nonfinancial disturbances. And, in a minority of cases, the uncertainty and instability can even originate within the financial sector. If financial prices drift away from fundamental valuations, the allocation of new investment can be deflected from a socially efficient outcome. Such problems cannot convincingly be dismissed as negligible. And only when there is no reasonable prospect for mitigating the problems should nations passively accept financial-sector outcomes that are unfavorable. The virtually universal decision of societies with advanced financial sectors to establish a government-sponsored lender of last resort (see chapters 7 and 8), for example, is a decisive rejection of the semi-Panglossian position that financial activity should run its course untrammeled by any government intervention.

Could economists and lawyers draft a blueprint for financial revolution—radical changes that would represent, if implemented, a wholesale improvement in financial structure and financial activity? I am doubtful that such a brave new world can be devised, even in principle. Nor is a wholesale transformation likely to be politically feasible. There is limited potential for reform even within a single nation (where at least the political institutions exist through which reformers can try to shape a consensus on needed changes). The likelihood of obtaining international agreement on sweeping changes in financial structure is, for the foreseeable future, extremely small.

Even so, there is no justification for being sanguine, much less complacent. Individual nations, and the world community of nations, can realistically aspire to incremental improvements in the performance of financial intermediaries and financial markets. The most promising possibilities involve adjustments in government regulations, tax policies, and supervision procedures. As the world economy continues to evolve, there will be growing opportunities— and a greater need—for international cooperation in the supervision, regulation, and taxation of financial activity. I turn to these subjects in the chapters that follow.

Readers forming their own judgments about the issues discussed in this book can draw comfort from the knowledge that they are, in essence, on familiar ground, participating in a debate that is several centuries old. Thoughtful economists have always recognized a tension between market efficiency and market failure. The decentralized decisionmaking embodied in market supplies and demands can accomplish allocative feats of marvelous complexity. But markets can also malfunction. Decentralized, noncooperative decisionmaking in some circumstances produces outcomes decidedly inferior to those attainable through collective action. Governmental institutions can supply, or induce others to supply, collective goods (including the amelioration of collective "bads") that would not be provided at all, or would be provided inadequately, in the absence of the governmental catalyst.

An eclectic and agnostic position about international financial intermediation is essentially the same mainstream stance that makes sense in resolving the tension between market efficiency and market failure.[37] The view that international finance is out of control is second cousin to the traditional extreme criticism of capitalist society that sees Adam Smith's allocative virtues as a small island in a sea of market imperfections. The semi-Panglossian view is a nephew of the conviction that potential sources of market failure are a few fleas on the thick hide of an ox, requiring only a flick of the tail to be brushed away.

In international finance, as in the broader debate, eclecticism is the judicious response to extreme views. After all, economic analysis both supports a presumptive belief in the efficiency of market allocations and provides the tools for an incisive critique. Suppose one is being lectured by a *dirigiste*

---

37. In these concluding sentences, I have shamelessly adapted several passages from the introductory paragraphs of Robert M. Solow's 1979 presidential address to the American Economic Association ("On Theories of Unemployment," p. 2). If Solow were less successful in crafting the right phrase, we other economists would succumb less often to plagiarism.

official of a European ministry of finance, asserting that Eurocurrencies are legions without commanders roaming the financial markets of the world. One's mind should promptly flood with thoughts of the mischief caused by anachronistic government regulations, the beneficial discipline of interbank and intercountry competition, the wide range of substitutes for existing financial instruments, the merits of lending decisions decentralized to where information about credit risk is most reliable, and the potential for improved resource allocation and faster growth resulting from savings being channeled to investment projects yielding the highest returns. Conversely, suppose one should be cornered by a vice-president of Citicorp or the Hong Kong and Shanghai Banking Corporation, arguing that across-the-board financial deregulation will work supply-side miracles in the world economy. The mind should then overflow with thoughts of bank executives who behave like sheep in choosing a Latin American loan portfolio, drug-smuggling proceeds laundered through banks in offshore financial centers, exchange rates fluctuating in response to false rumors started by market participants in order to make exploitive trades, and competition in laxity between governments trying to attract financial institutions to their jurisdictions by reducing taxation and the stringency of supervision—not to mention the failures of the Herstatt and Franklin National banks in 1974, the Credit-Anstalt in Vienna in 1931, and the South Sea Company in London in 1720.

The eclectic's position is unsatisfyingly bland. Yet there continues to be great wisdom in the advice given by Phoebus to the impetuous Phaethon: *medio tutissimus ibis* (you will go most safely by the middle way). The advice is not an infallible guide to sound policy. But, as it would have in Phaethon's case, it can often prevent those holding the reins from committing egregious errors.

CHAPTER SEVEN

The Regulation and Supervision
of Financial Intermediation

EARLIER CHAPTERS sought to adapt the analysis of financial intermediation to its increasingly important international dimensions. A similar adaptation is required with respect to its regulation, supervision, and taxation.

In virtually all nations, financial intermediaries are subjected to tighter
regulation and supervision than other types of business organizations. Commercial banks often attract greater scrutiny than other intermediaries. Financial markets tend to be closely monitored. Yet the reasons for this special
attention are seldom identified clearly. Before discussing the international
dimensions of regulation and supervision, therefore, I first review the rationales that have been used to justify government intervention in a domestic
context.

Basic Motives for Supervision and Regulation

The possible motives for supervision and regulation of financial intermediation include: prudential oversight of the stability of the financial system as a
whole (a "macroprudential" rationale), prudential oversight of the payments
mechanism (a corollary rationale that is also macroprudential), prudential protection of depositors and investors (the "microprudential" rationale), policy
control of the financial system and the economy, prevention of undue concentration of economic power and promotion of competition among financial
institutions, achievement of sectoral allocation objectives for credit flows, and
preservation of indigenous and small financial institutions.

Prudential Oversight of the Financial System

The macroprudential rationale is integrally associated with the role of a
central bank as lender of last resort. Policymakers and economists at least

119

since the time of Walter Bagehot have argued that, because society is prone to panicky crowd behavior in times of distressed financial conditions, some central financial institution is necessary that can provide banks and other intermediaries with temporary liquidity assistance during crises.[1]

This rationale for a lender of last resort need not presume that individual economic agents act irrationally. The maximization calculus that is rational for each individual acting alone can turn out to be irrational for all individuals together. In particular, if a financial crisis worsens progressively without any intervention by a lender of last resort, each financial institution and each customer may act rationally, and yet society as a whole may experience a collective outcome that is adverse for everyone.

If accepted, this argument for action in crises by a lender of last resort creates a fundamental dilemma. If financial institutions can confidently count on assistance from a lender of last resort on a rainy day, on sunny days they will have insufficient incentives to behave prudently. Financial intermediation necessarily entails the assumption of risks. Ultimate investors may not be able to service their borrowing, or may even go bankrupt. Ultimate depositors may unexpectedly withdraw their funds, requiring sudden and costly adjustment of intermediaries' asset portfolios. Some level of risk taking by financial institutions is of course socially desirable. But the institutions will be tempted to take risks that are excessive from society's point of view if they believe that emergency funding will always be readily available, at little cost to themselves, to bail them out of trouble. This temptation to excessive risk taking is a salient illustration of the general problem economists call "moral hazard."

This moral hazard dilemma thus leads many analysts to the prudential-oversight rationale for supervision and regulation of financial intermediation. These analysts argue that the government cannot acknowledge its residual responsibility for stability of the financial system unless it also engages in oversight of financial institutions to ensure sound practices and prevent excessive risk taking.[2]

1. See Walter Bagehot, *Lombard Street: A Description of the Money Market*; Charles P. Kindleberger, *Manias, Panics, and Crashes: A History of Financial Crises*; Charles P. Kindleberger and Jean-Pierre Laffargue, *Financial Crises: Theory, History, and Policy*; and Fred Hirsch, "The Bagehot Problem."

2. Essentially similar considerations are at stake when governments provide deposit insurance. The classic case against a guarantee of the deposits of financial intermediaries is that such a guarantee will mitigate the threat of withdrawal of deposits, thereby removing a check on imprudent risk taking and irresponsibility by the management of the intermediaries. If made, however, a decision to provide deposit insurance leads logically to concomitant regulation of the intermediaries to avert the moral hazard problem that would otherwise exist. (The moral hazard issue arises in its most acute form with "level-premium" insurance. Proposals for the reform of deposit insurance that recommend relating the premium paid by a financial intermediary to the riskiness of

Prudential Oversight of the Payments Mechanism

A modern exchange economy is unimaginable without at least one financial asset that serves as a widely accepted means of payment and generalized store of value. As checkable demand deposits in financial intermediaries became the predominant means of payment in modern economies, procedures for facilitating transactions through and among the intermediaries correspondingly assumed an increasingly vital role in the financial system. In future years, electronic arrangements for making transactions are likely to account for a progressively larger fraction of all payments and receipts. As that happens, the role of financial intermediaries in operating the society's payments mechanism is likely to become still more important.

Some analysts, laying great stress on the importance of a smoothly operating payments mechanism, would therefore supplement the preceding macroprudential rationale with a corollary. In their view, the government—as part of its role as lender of last resort and supervisor of the soundness of the financial system—should regulate, and thereby protect the integrity of, the society's payments mechanism. If pressed to state their position more formally, such analysts would describe the payments mechanism as a collective good that would not be supplied in an optimal way for society as a whole in the absence of governmental supervision.

For most of the twentieth century, commercial banks have been the main, if not exclusive, type of financial intermediary supplying payments services. In recent history, however, the payments mechanism in many countries has changed significantly. Merchant banks, nonbank financial institutions, and even nonfinancial businesses have encroached on the traditional domain of commercial banks. These developments have demonstrated in practice a point that monetary economists have long appreciated in theory: there is no logically inevitable correlation between commercial banking and the provision of the payments mechanism.[3]

Prudential Protection of Depositors and Investors

In contrast to macroprudential justifications for regulation and supervision, which emphasize systemic stability, a different set of arguments can be given for microprudential protection of depositors and investors in financial inter-

---

its asset portfolio are intended to mitigate the moral hazard problem.) For a survey of the deposit insurance system in the United States and proposals for its change, see U.S. General Accounting Office, *Deposit Insurance: Analysis of Reform Proposals*.

3. See, for example, James Tobin, "Commercial Banks as Creators of 'Money'."

mediaries. This rationale emphasizes individual institutions—for example, the risks of failure of particular financial intermediaries and the regulations or supervisory oversight that might avert such failures.[4]

A substantial part of the legal regulation of ordinary nonfinancial corporations is designed to ensure disclosure of relevant information to investors and to inhibit insider misconduct. In many respects, therefore, a prudential-protection rationale for the regulation of financial institutions does not raise issues or problems peculiar to the financial industry. Some defenders of such a rationale, however, do believe it to be peculiarly applicable to banks and other financial intermediaries.[5]

Policy Control of the Financial System

Another set of arguments appeals to the role of central banks in influencing financial and economic activity in normal times as well as in situations of financial crisis. Even in the absence of financial crises, financial activity can exert powerful influences on the pace of real activity and on the general level of prices. It is also widely acknowledged that a nation's central bank—more generally, its monetary authorities—can strongly influence the volume of overall financial activity. The monetary authorities have this power because, in effect, the financial system is like an inverted pyramid balanced on a small tip, the balance sheet of the monetary authorities.

The relationships between the tip of the pyramid and all the upper layers of the structure (the balance sheets of the various private-sector financial institutions) are complex and elastic. The inverted pyramid is a flexible, rather than rigid, structure. Especially over a long period, it is capable of dramatic changes in size and shape that are independent of changes in the small tip controlled by the monetary authorities.

The flexibility of the pyramid does not mean, of course, that a nation's monetary authorities are unable to influence the rate at which the national financial system expands. Other things being equal, an incremental expansion of the central bank's balance sheet will stimulate an expansion of the pyramid as a whole, and vice versa for an incremental contraction. Nonetheless, the

<hr/>

4. Examples of the regulations intended to achieve this microprudential protection include the various legal guidelines forcing intermediaries to disclose adequate information about their activities. Still other examples are the guidelines for capital-to-assets ratios imposed by government examiners and the restrictions pertaining to self-dealing, conflicts of interest, and other types of insider misconduct by the managements of intermediaries.

5. See, for example, Robert Charles Clark, "The Soundness of Financial Intermediaries."

authorities can control the financial pyramid only within some range of tolerance. When international economic interdependence is strong, the control may be very imprecise.

These observations lead to a possible further rationale for the regulation and supervision of financial activity. The general argument asserts that the monetary authorities should regulate the activities of intermediaries and transactions in financial markets to facilitate control of the financial system. The more specific argument is that the monetary authorities should be empowered to use supplementary devices—for example, reserve requirements against the deposit liabilities of the intermediaries—that would render their main control instrument, the expansion or contraction of their own balance sheet, more powerful or less uncertain than it would otherwise be.

An extension of this line of reasoning, discussed in chapter 6, asserts that financial activity, when unregulated and unsupervised, can generate asset prices that fluctuate excessively or get out of line with fundamental valuations. If someone believes that government institutions have the requisite information and capacity for carrying out market transactions to offset excessive variability or misalignment in asset prices, then he may also believe that a strong public policy case exists for such intervention. Similarly, a belief that governments can establish socially beneficial deterrents to shortsighted and inefficient speculative transactions can lead to a policy-control argument for particular types of regulations or supervisory procedures for financial institutions.

Concentration and Competition

A further family of arguments used to justify the regulation of financial institutions may be labeled the concentration-competition rationale. Those accepting this rationale tend to believe that regulation is required to obviate an undue concentration of economic power. Such a situation could develop, it is feared, unless governmental restraints prevent a few financial institutions from becoming very large and thereby acquiring an excessively dominant position in the financial system. A related line of reasoning asserts that regulation can promote or manage competition among financial institutions, thus improving the allocation of the economy's financial and real resources. Still another strand of thought, related but not identical, suggests that regulation can be helpful in assuring competitive equity among financial institutions. Bankers have competitive equity in mind when they say that the various categories of financial institutions should operate on a "level playing field" where like institutions are treated alike.

Unlike the previously discussed rationales for regulation, this one is not peculiarly applicable to financial institutions. No doubt financial institutions pose some special regulatory problems because the nature of their business differs from that of nonfinancial organizations. But the same general issues of concentration and competition arise in connection with virtually all types of economic activity in the private sectors of mixed capitalist economies.

Sectoral Allocation Objectives

The desire to achieve sectoral allocation objectives is yet another conceivable rationale for regulating financial institutions. For example, policymakers may seek to bolster economic activity in certain industries or regions of a country and discourage activity in others. As one device for achieving this objective, they may design regulations intended to channel credit toward the favored destinations or away from those that are disfavored.

Indigenous and Small Institutions

Two final rationales—for preserving indigenous institutions and small institutions—are less often encountered in the United States. But in some countries at some times they have been a significant factor in debates about regulation and supervision.

The indigenous-institution rationale asserts that it may be important for communities or regions to have financial institutions that are organized, owned, and controlled locally. Those making this assertion presume that institutions rooted locally will provide better financial services for the community or region than nonlocal institutions. This presumption depends on, among other things, the view that local residents have better information about the community or region and are more likely to respond to its needs and problems.

The small-institution rationale asserts that small financial institutions may perform valuable functions that would not be served, or would be served less well, by a financial system composed entirely of large institutions. The underlying thought behind this assertion may be a presumption that small institutions help to foster innovation and entrepreneurship. Those holding this view may wish to preserve small institutions to affect the distribution of income and wealth (in favor of the owners and customers of the small institutions). Some may hold this view because they like to help the underdog.

The wish to maintain indigenous institutions can be logically differentiated from the wish to maintain small institutions. The two are often encountered together, however. Note that the meanings of "indigenous" and "small" critically depend on the contexts in which they are used. A large, nonlocal institution from the perspective of a community may well be a small, indigenous institution from the perspective of a region or the nation as a whole.

Whether used singly or together, these two arguments can become justifications for preferential regulatory treatment. Most often, the arguments appear when the activities of indigenous or small institutions seem threatened in some way.

Costs of Regulation and Supervision

The preceding summary of rationales refers to regulation and supervision in general, rather than specific types of regulatory devices and supervisory procedures.[6] Yet regulation of financial institutions can take a wide variety of forms—for example, mandatory reserve requirements, interest-rate ceilings, limitations on capital-asset ratios, requirements for disclosure of information, restrictions on entry and merger, differential tax or subsidy treatment of types of activities or intermediaries, geographical limitations on activities, and quantitative limitations on the amounts of particular categories of assets and liabilities. Supervision can be exercised in alternative ways—for example, through monitoring of accounting reports, on-site examinations, and consultations with high-level management. Self-evidently, some types of regulation, supervision, and taxation are more appropriate than others for any one of the rationales summarized above. Not much can be usefully said about financial regulation at a high level of generalization. Particular regulations, taxes, and supervisory procedures need to be evaluated in specific contexts.

Because of its focus on the potential benefits of regulation and supervision, the preceding review is limited in a second way. Every aspect of a government's relationships with financial institutions can be rationalized, initially, if not also currently, as a response to externalities or market imperfections. One fundamental rationale for government, after all, is to supply, or induce others to supply, collective goods that would not be provided, or would be provided

6. The analysis here pays only limited attention to the taxation of financial institutions, partly because my knowledge is insufficient to discuss tax aspects in any detail. Taxation, however, is probably as important as regulation and supervision.

inadequately, in the absence of the governmental catalyst. Alternatively, government can ameliorate collective "bads" (for example, through assistance as the lender of last resort in distressed financial conditions). The identification of externalities, however, is invariably controversial. Where one observer perceives a presumptive need for collective action catalyzed by government, another may not. In the case of each motive for regulation and supervision summarized above, some group can be found that questions the motive's validity.

Even if agreement could be reached on the worthiness of a particular motive, it would be insufficient to focus only on the potential benefits of regulation and supervision. The fact that markets often fail in adequately supplying collective goods does not justify the presumption that government action can remedy the market failures. Regulation and supervision may not succeed in achieving their intended goals. The costs of government regulations can exceed the benefits. Unanticipated side effects can be adverse. Conceivably, regulation and supervision can induce sclerosis in the financial system, thereby inadvertently inhibiting needed adjustments to changed circumstances. For example, a regulation may initially facilitate a specific goal (say, improved policy control of the financial system or the maintenance of indigenous institutions), yet may also, indirectly if not directly, undermine the adaptability of the financial system to new technology. More generally, even if a regulatory measure is an appropriate response when first implemented, a solution to today's problem is an admission ticket to new problems when circumstances change. A balanced analysis of any regulation must therefore evaluate its costs and side effects, not merely its intended benefits, and must subject it to periodic reevaluation.

For virtually all the specific regulations and supervisory procedures that can be devised, some groups or some individuals assess the intended benefits as less consequential than the costs and side effects. Some authors who have studied government regulation of financial institutions in a variety of nations perceive a general pattern of overregulation that has inhibited economic development.[7] This enthusiasm for deregulation of banks and other financial institutions, however, is not shared by all observers.[8]

---

7. See, for example, Edward S. Shaw, *Financial Deepening in Economic Development*; and Ronald I. McKinnon, *Money and Capital in Economic Development*.

8. For examples pertinent to the recent debate in the United States, see John H. Kareken, "Bank Regulation and the Effectiveness of Open Market Operations," and "Deregulating Commercial Banks: The Watchword Should Be Caution"; Albert M. Wojnilower, "The Central Role

Public opinion about the regulation and supervision of financial institutions tends to be strongly influenced by recent experience. Lengthy periods unsullied by distressed conditions cause regulation issues to recede into the background. The failure or near failure of intermediaries—in particular, highly publicized problems of large institutions such as those of the Franklin National Bank and the Herstatt Bank in 1974, the Continental Illinois Bank in 1984, and the state-insured savings and loan associations in Ohio in 1985—brings the issues back into prominence.[9]

Innovation in Response to Regulation

The operating procedures and services provided by financial institutions change over time. Significant innovations have occurred especially rapidly in recent decades.[10]

The importance of changing technology in inducing new types of financial intermediation, not least across national borders, has already been highlighted in chapter 4. Domestically and internationally, improvements in communications methods and in electronic data processing have made many former banking practices obsolete or inefficient.

The higher and more variable rates of inflation experienced in the 1970s and early 1980s were also a significant catalyst for change. Inflation caused a secular upward drift and a greater volatility in nominal interest rates, which in turn forced financial institutions and the nonfinancial sectors of the economy to adapt their behavior.

---

of Credit Crunches in Recent Financial History''; and Robert E. Litan, ''Evaluating and Controlling the Risks of Financial Product Regulation,'' and ''Taking the Dangers Out of Bank Deregulation.''

9. The tendency of the public and financial intermediaries themselves to forget incidents of distressed conditions in the more distant past—dubbed ''disaster myopia''—is analyzed in Jack M. Guttentag and Richard J. Herring, ''Credit Rationing and Financial Disorder,'' and *Disaster Myopia in International Banking*.

10. For recent surveys of the numerous innovations in financial intermediation and some of their implications, see, for example, Thomas D. Simpson and Patrick M. Parkinson, ''Some Implications of Financial Innovations in the United States''; Bank of England, ''The Nature and Implications of Financial Innovation'' and ''Competition, Innovation and Regulation in British Banking''; M. A. Akhtar, *Financial Innovations and Their Implications for Monetary Policy: An International Perspective;* J. David Germany and John E. Morton, ''Financial Innovation and Deregulation in Foreign Industrial Countries''; Yoshio Suzuki and Hiroshi Yomo, eds., *Financial Innovation and Monetary Policy: Asia and the West*; and Bank for International Settlements, *Recent Innovations in International Banking*.

Scarcely less important, however, have been private-sector innovations responding to the existing pattern of governmental regulation, supervision, and taxation. If regulations are successful in inhibiting changes in financial activity, financial institutions and their customers have incentives to circumvent the regulatory constraints. The more stringent the constraints, the stronger the incentives for circumvention.

When financial institutions develop a new type of contract or a new practice that undermines a regulatory constraint, the governmental authorities responsible for the regulations may try to change the regulations to cover the new circumstances. If so, the private-sector institutions may in turn try to adapt their behavior in still other ways. In retrospect the process of interaction may seem like a disorderly scramble, with the private institutions and the authorities each vainly trying to get one step ahead of the other.[11]

International Aspects of Regulation and Supervision

The possible rationales for regulation and supervision of financial activity, the costs of implementing such measures, and the tendency for private-sector innovations to erode existing regulations warrant analysis and debate in a purely domestic context. And, for the most part, those domestic aspects have received the lion's share of attention. When the international aspects have been considered, they have usually been discussed independently in specialized and less publicized forums. This separate treatment of the domestic and international aspects, however, has become increasingly anachronistic.

The supervisory, regulatory, and tax environments governing the operations of financial institutions differ in important ways from one nation to another. These disparities generate competitive inequities among national financial systems. Disadvantaged financial institutions thus have strong incentives to locate their borrowing and lending activities in countries with lower taxes and less stringent regulations and supervision. In a world where cross-border financial transactions are growing rapidly, the disparities in national regulatory and tax environments become still more difficult to maintain.

All nations are affected in minor ways by the erosion of the disparities in national regulatory environments. A few large industrial countries are beginning to encounter serious problems because of their more stringent and pervasive regulations. Some financial business that is primarily domestic in

11. See, for example, Donald D. Hester, "Innovations and Monetary Control."

nature is being conducted through international transactions, thereby enabling intermediaries and their customers to avoid domestic regulatory restrictions. For practical purposes, the traditional distinction between domestic and international banking is becoming elusive. Scarcely a single regulatory issue that formerly was viewed solely as a domestic matter can now be intelligently discussed without reference to international flows of funds and the regulatory environments in foreign countries.

The erosion of national regulatory environments associated with the internationalization of financial intermediation is a salient example of the general phenomenon of innovations in response to regulations. In a closed domestic context, financial institutions trying to avoid regulations must devise a new financial instrument or discover some other innovation that will allow them to escape the existing regulatory constraint. In an open economy, another and potentially more powerful alternative exists: a financial institution experiencing stringent regulation can decide to move the regulated activities outside the jurisdiction of the national regulators. Unless the home authorities can induce their counterparts in other countries to adopt a posture as stringent as theirs, the financial institution may succeed in escaping the home regulations. Alternatively, the national regulators may see that they cannot prevent the relocation of the institution's activities, and may therefore decide to relax their regulations sufficiently to keep the activities at home.

When the international aspects are acknowledged, the conventional arguments for and against regulation of financial intermediation acquire additional nuances and encounter new difficulties.

In a significantly open economy, the prudential-oversight and prudential-protection rationales must take into account the many complexities associated with cross-border and foreign-currency transactions. Individual financial institutions are exposed to new types of risks when they have extensive asset-liability relationships with foreign residents. Similarly, denomination of assets and liabilities in foreign currencies as well as in the home nation's currency introduces additional elements of risk. To be sure, cross-border and foreign-currency transactions also permit a greater diversification of risk. The net consequences of international intermediation for the safety and soundness of a nation's financial institutions are thus complex. No simple generalization about the consequences may be possible. At the least, however, it is clear that the regulatory authorities of a single open economy concerned with the microprudential protection of that nation's depositors and investors have a much more difficult job than would their counterparts in a hypothetical closed economy.

Similarly, macroprudential oversight of the financial system in a single national economy becomes increasingly problematic as the economy becomes more open. The moral hazard dilemma—the temptation of financial intermediaries with ready access to assistance from a lender of last resort to take risks that are excessive from a social point of view—may be heightened in an economic environment characterized by extensive cross-border and foreign-currency transactions. In any case, a single nation's decisions about the intensity of regulation and supervision and its formulation of criteria for providing lender-of-last-resort assistance become more complex.

For some circumstances, a qualitatively new set of difficulties arises. When a banking office located in nation A with its head office located in nation B gets into financial trouble, which central bank should have responsibility for providing lender-of-last-resort support, assuming such assistance is merited? Should the allocation of the central-bank responsibility differ according to the nature of the banking office in nation A—for example, whether the office is a branch or a subsidiary of the parent bank in nation B? How should consortium banks—joint ventures located in A but owned by banks or investors in B and several other nations—be treated? Is there a risk that national central banks will individually behave too timidly, thereby exposing the world financial system as a whole to inadequate provision of lender-of-last-resort assistance? If international agreement on such assistance is thought necessary to assure world financial stability, does the moral hazard dilemma require a commensurate degree of international cooperation in the supervision and regulation of financial institutions?[12]

Analogous points can be made about macroprudential protection of (speaking loosely) the world's payments mechanism. A small number of the world's largest banks are the operators of the existing clearing arrangements for foreign-exchange transactions and other cross-border payments—for example, the Clearing House Interbank Payments System (CHIPS), an electronic funds transfer arrangement based in New York that processes the bulk of large-value international payments denominated in U.S. dollars, and the Society for Worldwide Interbank Financial Telecommunication (SWIFT), a cooperative company created under Belgian law that processes international transactions among banks. If unexpected disruptions in these arrangements should occur, the responsibility for managing the restoration of normal activity would necessarily have to be shared among the large private banks and central banks of

---

12. For a study analyzing some of these issues, see Jack M. Guttentag and Richard J. Herring, *The Lender-of-Last-Resort Function in an International Context.*

several nations, not merely one nation. Consider, for example, the large volume of interbank U.S. dollar clearings arranged daily in Tokyo under the auspices of the Chase Manhattan Bank. If the viability of those dollar-clearing arrangements should ever be threatened, how would the responsibility for remedial action be shared between the Bank of Japan and the Federal Reserve?[13]

The possibility of disruptions in international payments arrangements is more than theoretical. In June 1974 the failure of the Bankhaus I.D. Herstatt temporarily shattered confidence in CHIPS and demonstrated its potential vulnerability.[14] Other instances are said to have occurred in association with the Iranian hostage crisis in 1980 and the Brazilian debt-servicing crisis of 1982–83.[15]

The policy-control motive for regulation and supervision likewise acquires greater force and encounters new difficulties when international aspects are taken into account because the increasing openness of a nation's economy undermines the autonomy of national monetary policy and the controllability of the national economy (chapter 6). As a central bank perceives a weakening of its control of the nation's financial system, and more broadly its control of the ultimate target variables for the nation's economy, it may conceivably decide—rightly or wrongly—that the benefits from economic interdependence are outweighed by the costs of the erosion of controllability of the

13. National payments systems are described and compared in Bank for International Settlements, *Payment Systems in Eleven Developed Countries*. The international aspects of payments system issues are analyzed in Allen B. Frankel and Jeffrey C. Marquardt, "International Payments and EFT Links." For more details on CHIPS and SWIFT, see Herbert F. Lingl, "Risk Allocation in International Interbank Electronic Fund Transfers: CHIPS & SWIFT."

14. Herstatt was declared officially closed by the German authorities at 4:00 P.M. Frankfurt time, while financial markets in New York were open. Dollar settlements of Herstatt's preclosure spot exchange contracts through CHIPS were not completed that afternoon in New York even though the corresponding deutsche mark settlements in Germany had already resulted earlier in the day in transfers of funds to Herstatt in Cologne. Given the sudden uncertainties about CHIPS and international payments, spot and forward foreign-exchange trading all around the world fell to low volumes. Several days after Herstatt's failure, the twelve largest New York commercial banks, which control the New York Clearing House, felt obliged to establish a special emergency rule allowing banks to recall payments up to a day after they had been put into the system. The emergency procedure encouraged a recovery of more normal trading in exchange markets. But the disruption of CHIPS, combined with the troubles and impending failure of the Franklin National Bank, kept exchange markets and Eurocurrency banking in a nervous, low-volume state for months thereafter. Court cases connected with the incident were not settled until some five years later. For a description of the events, see Joan Edelman Spero, *The Failure of the Franklin National Bank: Challenge to the International Banking System*, pp. 101–18.

15. See, for example, John E. Hoffman, Jr., and Ian H. Giddy, "Lessons from the Iranian Experience: National Currencies as International Money."

economy. If so, it may attempt in one way or another to inhibit cross-border financial transactions. If the separation fence around the national financial system had earlier been lowered, it might now be raised. Such an effort to enhance the autonomy of national monetary policy is, analytically speaking, a particular case of the policy-control rationale for regulation. The various conceivable controls on international capital movements could include restraints on the nonfinancial sectors of the economy as well as on financial institutions. However, because financial intermediaries play such a key role in financial markets—and not least in foreign exchange markets—the central bank is likely to assert that an especially strong case exists for regulating financial institutions, or in any event for regulating them to a greater extent than nonfinancial corporations and households.

Many economists and policymakers believe that exchange rates are good illustrations of financial variables that can fluctuate excessively or become misaligned with fundamental valuations. The available evidence about these issues (chapter 6), and about the efficacy of exchange-market intervention in dealing with them (chapter 5), is inconclusive. I mention these controversial subjects again to remind the reader that they are the obverse side of the coin of "disequilibrating" capital flows. Changes in separation fences to deter disequilibrating capital flows are, par excellence, international issues of regulating and supervising financial institutions.

The justification for regulation and supervision to preserve indigenous institutions has a straightforward international extension. And it invites a correspondingly straightforward rebuttal. In a world of numerous nations, "indigenous" is likely to be a synonym for "national." The maintenance of national institutions, including the prevention of significant inroads in domestic activity by foreigners, is an objective that may have significant political appeal to home citizens. Local control can be defended as desirable to keep financial institutions sensitive to national needs and problems. Some may even allege that indigenous financial institutions are essential for national security. The standard rebuttal to these arguments is based on the traditional objection to economic autarky: protective regulations encourage an inefficient allocation of resources and deny the nation as a whole the full benefits of commerce with the rest of the world.

In fact, many nations maintain some form of discrimination in favor of financial institutions owned by local residents. Most others apply some variant of the principle of "reciprocity" in their treatment of financial institutions owned by foreign nationals. If the government of country A applies reciprocity to conditions of entry, financial institutions owned by nationals of country B will be permitted to establish offices in *A* only if the government of *B* permits financial institutions owned by *A* nationals to establish offices in *B*. The principle of reciprocity is often extended to the powers granted to foreign-owned financial institutions; in such cases, *B*-owned institutions will be permitted to conduct within *A* only those types of financial activities that *A*-owned institutions are permitted to conduct in *B*. "National treatment" prevails if foreign-owned financial institutions are allowed to compete in a host country on essentially equal terms with domestic-owned institutions. Among the major nations, only the United States adheres closely to the principle of national treatment.[16]

The rationale for regulation to prevent undue concentration is usually advocated in a form implicitly presuming that concentration and competition should be measured and evaluated in a domestic context. For a significantly open economy, that presumption needs to be severely questioned. Why should a national economy be the relevant geographical market for judging concentration, rather than a regional economy or the world economy as a whole? Can national governments have separate and different antitrust policies for their economies when firms and financial institutions engage in integrated activities across national borders?

16. For detailed discussions of the regulatory treatment of foreign-owned banks in all the major and many smaller countries, see the extensive compendium in U.S. Department of the Treasury, *Report to Congress on Foreign Government Treatment of U.S. Commercial Banking Organizations,* and *Report to Congress on Foreign Government Treatment of U.S. Commercial Banking Organizations: 1984 Update.*

CHAPTER EIGHT

International Collective-Goods Problems in Regulation and Supervision

THE ISSUES raised in chapter 7 are obviously germane for the industrial nations that have well-developed financial systems. Everything that has been said applies in some degree to banking and other types of intermediation in such financial centers as New York, Tokyo, London, Zurich, Frankfurt, and Paris. But still other geographical loci for international intermediation have become important. Issues about the internationalization of financial activity arise in an especially interesting way in the so-called offshore financial centers.

Offshore Financial Centers

The locations commonly referred to as offshore centers include Anguilla, the Bahamas, Barbados, Bermuda, the Cayman Islands, the Netherlands Antilles, Panama, and the British West Indies in the Caribbean area; Bahrain, Lebanon, and the United Arab Emirates in the Middle East; Guam, Hong Kong, the Philippines, Singapore, and Vanuatu (New Hebrides) in Asia and Oceania; and Luxembourg, the Channel Islands (Jersey and Guernsey), and the Isle of Man in Europe.

Banking transactions conducted from, or booked in, these offshore centers have grown especially rapidly. Table 8-1 provides some selective data for the centers that had the greatest volume of activity as of the mid-1980s. When available, two indicators are shown in the table. The first is a measure of the total size of the balance sheets of some or all of the banking offices located in the country, as published by the national monetary authority. The second is a measure, published by the International Monetary Fund, of the claims of local banking offices on foreigners (nonresidents). For comparison, the final line gives figures for a broad aggregate in international banking that excludes data from offshore centers.

Neither set of indicators, especially those of the second type, is fully satisfactory as a yardstick for the growth of banking activities in the countries shown. The coverage of reporting banks differs significantly from one center to another. All the figures are expressed in U.S. dollars even though some of the assets of the banks are denominated in other currencies. As with many of the tables in chapter 3, therefore, interpretation of the data is complicated by fluctuations in the exchange value of the U.S. dollar against other currencies. Nonetheless, the figures in the last four columns of the table do give a correct overall impression of the relatively faster expansion of banking in offshore centers.

Consider first Singapore and Hong Kong. As the proxy measures in table 8-1 show, international banking activity in Singapore grew at a compounded rate of some 44–49 percent per year over 1970–85. The international dimensions of the balance sheets of banks in Hong Kong grew at an annual rate of around 30 percent during that period. Even during 1982–85, a troubled time for the world economy, the growth rates of banking in the two centers were on the order of 15 percent. This expansion in Singapore and Hong Kong, as can be seen by contrasting it with the bottom line in the table, was markedly faster than in Europe, North America, and Japan. By 1986 financial institutions in Singapore and Hong Kong combined had total assets of more than US$350 billion.

In Bahrain, neither the Bahrain Monetary Agency nor Offshore Banking Units—entities specially created to conduct international banking—even existed in 1970. The Bahrain Monetary Agency was established in late 1973; in late 1975 it invited international banks to establish Offshore Banking Units (OBUs). By 1982–83 the OBUs in Bahrain had some US$60 billion of total assets on their books.

In the Bahamas, banks' claims on foreign residents grew at nearly a 50 percent annual rate during 1970–76. Bahamian growth in the late 1970s and early 1980s was much slower, partly because many banks shifted their Caribbean emphasis to the Cayman Islands. Even so, by the early 1980s the foreign assets of banking offices in the Bahamas had risen to some US$150 billion. Statistics for the Cayman Islands that became available in the early 1980s indicate that the total assets of banks there (not only the branches of U.S. banks but also banking offices owned by parent banking organizations in other foreign countries) were US$126 billion at the end of 1982 and rose to US$174 billion by December 1985. Panama and the Netherlands Antilles also experienced extremely rapid growth during 1970–82.

Table 8-1. Indicators of Banking Growth in Selected Offshore Centers, 1970–85

Country of location of banking offices	Billions of U.S. dollars at current exchange rates				Compound annual rate of growth[a]			
	1970	1976	1982	1985	1970–76	1976–82	1982–85	1970–85
Singapore								
Total assets of Asian Currency Units[b]	0.4	17.4	103.3	155.4	88.3	34.6	14.6	49.1
Banks' claims on foreigners[c,d]	0.5	14.6	81.3	120.4	73.8	33.1	14.0	43.6
Hong Kong								
Total assets of banks[e]	3.5	18.5	91.9	141.0	31.7	30.7	15.3	27.8
Total assets of deposit-taking companies[e]	n.a.	n.a.	41.0	58.2	n.a.	n.a.	12.4	n.a.
Total assets of all deposit-taking institutions[e]	n.a.	n.a.	132.9	199.2	n.a.	n.a.	14.4	n.a.
Claims of deposit-taking institutions on foreigners[c,f]	1.2	12.4	58.2	101.2	46.8	29.4	20.2	34.1
Bahrain								
Total assets of Offshore Banking Units[g]	...	6.2	59.0	56.8	n.a.	45.5	-1.3	n.a.
Banks' claims on foreigners[c]	0.1	6.1	49.8	50.7	115.7	42.1	0.6	56.7
Bahamas								
Banks' claims on foreigners, old series[c,h]	7.2	77.7	129.5	122.8	48.9	8.7	-1.8	20.8
Banks' claims on foreigners, new series[c,h]	n.a.	n.a.	154.4	143.1	n.a.	n.a.	-2.5	n.a.
Cayman Islands								
Banks' claims on foreigners,[c,i]	n.a.	22.0	126.0	173.9	n.a.	33.8	11.3	n.a.
Panama								
Banks' claims on foreigners[c]	0.3	10.4	43.5	33.1	78.6	27.0	-8.7	36.2

Netherlands Antilles								
Banks' claims on foreigners[c]	0.1	1.6	11.9	6.6	53.2	40.4	−17.6	30.7
Luxembourg								
Total assets of banks[j]	4.8	47.5	127.6	151.5	46.8	17.9	5.9	26.0
Banks' claims on foreigners[c]	3.7	37.9	109.7	131.5	47.3	19.4	6.2	26.9
Memorandum								
Aggregate claims on foreigners of banks in all industrial countries excluding Luxembourg[c]	141.7	488.0	1625.5	2081.4	22.9	22.2	8.6	19.6

n.a. Not available.

a. Calculated from unrounded data.

b. Balance-sheet data for Asian Currency Units (total assets, including claims on Singapore financial institutions and nonbank Singapore residents) as published in Monetary Authority of Singapore, *Monthly Statistical Bulletin*, various issues.

c. These series appear in International Monetary Fund, *International Financial Statistics*. In principle, they refer to "deposit banks'" claims on foreign residents; the foreign assets of monetary authorities are excluded. Figures for 1970 and 1976 are from International Monetary Fund, *International Financial Statistics Yearbook 1985*, p. 61. Figures for 1982 and 1985 are from *International Financial Statistics Yearbook 1986*, p. 69, and *International Financial Statistics* (August 1986), p. 51.

d. Includes the foreign assets of Asian Currency Units (ACUs) and domestic banking units. This IFS series incorrectly treats the entire amount of the claims of ACUs on nonbanks as claims on foreigners; in fact, a modest fraction of the ACUs' claims on nonbanks involves lending to Singapore residents.

e. Balance-sheet data for banks and deposit-taking companies as published in Hong Kong, Census and Statistics Department, *Hong Kong Monthly Digest of Statistics*. Historical data for 1970 and 1976 for the banks have been adjusted by the author to the same conceptual definition as the 1982 and 1985 data (making use of unpublished data kindly supplied by the Hong Kong Commissioner of Banking). Data for the deposit-taking companies are available only for 1978 and subsequent years.

f. This IFS series for years after 1978 includes figures for the identified foreign assets of the deposit-taking companies as well as the identified foreign assets of the banks.

g. Balance-sheet data for Offshore Banking Units (total assets, including claims on domestic residents) as published in Bahrain Monetary Agency, *Quarterly Statistical Bulletin*, various issues.

h. In the spring of 1986 the IMF Bureau of Statistics began publishing a somewhat more comprehensive figure in *International Financial Statistics* for the claims on foreigners of banking offices in the Bahamas. The new series is based on data reported twice a year, for dates beginning in December 1983, by certain banking operations with international licenses. The first row for the Bahamas in this table is the old series, updated with a figure for 1985 that is the author's estimate. The second row is the new series, with the figure for 1982 an estimate by the author.

i. Based on the revised series published for the first time in the January 1985 issue of *International Financial Statistics*, which in turn is derived from Cayman Islands Department of Finance and Development, Government Statistics Unit, *Statistical Abstract*.

j. Balance-sheet data for all "*établissements bancaires et d'épargne*" in Luxembourg as published in Institut Monétaire Luxembourgeois, *Bulletin Trimestriel*, various issues.

From some perspectives, Luxembourg should not be labeled an offshore center. In several respects, however, banks with head offices in Germany and other industrial countries did regard Luxembourg in the 1970s as offering benefits similar to those in other offshore centers. Between 1970 and 1976, bank balance sheets and the (dominant) international parts of the balance sheets both increased at annual rates of some 47 percent. Quite rapid growth persisted through 1981; after 1981, the U.S. dollar value of bank assets declined somewhat, and then sharply increased again during 1985.[1]

A time series that begins from an initial base near zero can appear in its early years to grow at an explosive rate merely because of its small initial base. The rapid growth of some of the series in table 8-1 is partly attributable to this statistical phenomenon. For the most part, however, the growth rates in the table reflect basic economic forces that encouraged banking activity in the offshore centers to grow very much faster than domestic financial intermediation in the industrial countries, and even considerably faster than international banking conducted from the industrial countries.

As pointed out in the final section of chapter 3, the securitization of lending in the 1980s and the associated growth of off-balance-sheet business caused a marked slowdown in the measured rate of growth of international banking. These new trends affected measured activity in offshore centers at least as much as in the main industrial countries. Another factor leading to slower growth of the international banking numbers after 1982–83 was the debt crises of numerous developing countries and the resulting financial uncertainties. These events, too, influenced offshore centers especially strongly. Depositors in international banks worried generally about possible financial instability of banks that had large claims on the troubled debtor countries. More specifically, some of them also worried that deposit claims on banking offices in offshore centers were unusually vulnerable to financial instability. An October 1983 episode in the Philippines, an aspiring offshore financial center, fueled such worries.[2] As can be seen from the next to the last column of table 8-1, growth in all the offshore financial centers was much slower during 1982–85.

---

1. The growth rates for Luxembourg in the 1980s were very strongly affected by the large 1980–85 appreciation and the subsequent 1985–86 depreciation of the U.S. dollar against European currencies. Over half of the Luxembourg banks' assets and liabilities are denominated in deutsche marks and other European currencies. Hence growth rates for 1981–84, for example, are much smaller calculated in U.S. dollars than calculated in a European currency.

2. The Philippines government temporarily froze banks' assets as part of an emergency package of policies to deal with its debt crisis. The branches of foreign-owned banks in the Philippines were prevented from paying off depositors, including other banks, who had placed funds with the Philippines branches. In a subsequent court case, Wells Fargo Asia Limited sued Citibank for

The balance sheets of banks in Bahrain and the Bahamas declined modestly over those three years. Panama and the Netherlands Antilles experienced large contractions.

Throughout recent economic history, financial intermediation in general and banking in particular have grown relatively faster than output of goods and services (chapters 2, 3, and 4). This faster growth of financial intermediation, emphasized by Goldsmith and Gurley-Shaw, might be expected to be still more pronounced for developing nations than for industrial nations at an advanced stage of development. Nevertheless, for most if not all of the individual political units shown in table 8-1, the rapid growth in banking cannot plausibly be ascribed to the secular trends identified by Goldsmith and Gurley-Shaw—at least not to such trends *within* their national economies.

Instead, one must look elsewhere for a major part of the explanation. Financial intermediation is more "footloose" than most other economic activities. It can shift locations with less difficulty and without incurring prohibitively large costs. The many innovations in electronic communications and data processing have probably enhanced this differential mobility. Even more than for industry in general, therefore, the scope exists for an individual locality or nation to try to lure financial activity within its borders by imposing less stringent regulation, taxation, and supervision than that prevailing elsewhere. When framing their policies, the governments of the offshore financial centers have been very much aware of this relocation possibility. And almost surely, a major part of the rapid expansion of banking in most offshore centers is attributable to the differential location incentives created by governmental policies.

Viewed from a cosmopolitan world perspective, the regulatory, tax, and supervisory incentives designed to attract financial activity to offshore centers can be described—provocatively—as a "competition in laxity." Similarly, one may ask whether the largest nations in the world could be indefinitely satisfied with an ever higher proportion of their citizens' financial transactions being conducted from offices located in the offshore centers. Even if one resists the temptation to be provocative, the growing importance of offshore centers raises several questions that merit analysis in a systemic, global context.

---

nonpayment of deposits placed with the Manila branch of Citibank. The incident was widely commented on in international banking circles and was said to have induced nervousness about other offshore financial centers—for example, Panama.

The offshore financial centers are diverse in nature. And "offshore" is one of several terms in international finance that is used widely but has ambiguous connotations. A careful analysis of the offshore centers should differentiate among them according to their economic and financial structures and the types of regulatory, tax, and supervisory environments they have established.[3]

Global Public Policy Problems

The international aspects of government policies identified in the preceding chapter pose issues and problems for each nation individually. But the disparities among nations' regulatory, tax, and supervisory environments are also a collective, global problem.

For example, it is a striking fact that virtually all nations discriminate in favor of banking activities conducted in foreign currencies, especially when the banks' customers are nonresidents. Until the 1980s the United States was an exception to this generalization. With the authorization of International Banking Facilities (IBFs) as of December 1981, however, the United States reversed its position and went along with the global trend.[4] During 1982–84 Japan and Australia considered regulatory changes designed to enhance such favorable discrimination; in 1986 Japan authorized the establishment of offshore banking facilities (similar in many respects to the IBFs in the United States).[5] Differential regulatory, tax, and supervisory incentives that favor international banking are strongest of all in the offshore financial centers.

For these regulatory issues, each nation or political unit in effect regards itself as individually small in relation to the rest of the world. It regulates intensively only those domestic aspects of financial intermediation that are perceived as most directly affecting its own economy. It then adopts a hands-off policy, or in any event a less stringent regulatory posture, with respect to the remaining international activities of financial institutions located within its

---

3. Some of the issues are discussed in my draft manuscript, "International Banking in Singapore and Hong Kong." Early versions of some of this material were circulated as Brookings Discussion Papers in International Economics: "The Progressive Internationalization of Banking," and "Financial Structure and International Banking in Singapore." Also see Bryant, "The Evolution of Singapore as a Financial Center."

4. Sydney J. Key, "International Banking Facilities"; and Henry S. Terrell and Rodney H. Mills, "International Banking Facilities and the Eurodollar Market."

5. See Institute for Financial Affairs, *World Financial Centres;* Eisuke Sakakibara and Akira Kondoh, *Study on the Internationalization of Tokyo's Money Markets*; Jeffrey A. Frankel, *The Yen/Dollar Agreement: Liberalizing Japanese Capital Markets*; and John R. Hewson, "Offshore Banking in Australia."

borders. This greater leniency for international activities is subtly associated with the tendency of most national governments to discriminate in favor of financial institutions owned by local residents. Nations regulate domestic business more stringently and simultaneously accord it limited protection from competition by foreign-owned financial institutions. For international business conducted from offices within the nation, on the other hand, foreign-owned and locally owned institutions often compete under the same, somewhat looser, regulations. In effect, many nations implement the principle of national treatment for *international,* but not for domestic, financial intermediation.

Implicitly if not explicitly, the typical attitude is to let every other nation cope with its own problems as best it can. No nation has developed a systemic, global view about the regulation, taxation, and supervision of financial intermediation.

In such a world environment, no nation can effectively act on its own to deal with any adverse consequences attributable to this situation. Unilateral tightening of supervision and regulation by a single nation, for intermediary offices within its borders or for intermediary offices located abroad controlled by national residents, might merely induce a transfer away from its intermediary offices to those of other nations.

If action of some sort is called for, only collective action is likely to be successful. International cooperation in these circumstances, however, is yet another example of a collective good. The supply of international regulatory cooperation is likely to fall short of what would be mutually beneficial because each nation, acting rationally on an individual basis, ignores the potential benefits of the greater cooperation for others. Each nation tends to assume that it is small enough to ignore the consequences of its actions for the rest of the world; this tendency is an integral part of the collective problem. As is characteristic of such situations, the actual outcome for all nations can be inferior to outcomes potentially attainable through mutual consultation and cooperative bargaining. The larger the group of nations involved, furthermore, the higher the probability that some nations will act as "free riders" and hence the less likely that the group of nations will further their mutual interests.[6] Only

6. To the extent that a collective good is supplied, all who value it tend to benefit whether or not they contribute to the cost of supplying it. Hence a disproportionately large share of the costs tends to be borne by a few "less small" participants in the collective action. For discussion of the analytical issues, see Mancur Olson, *The Logic of Collective Action: Public Goods and the Theory of Groups*; and Brian Barry and Russell Hardin, eds., *Rational Man and Irrational Society?: An Introduction and Sourcebook.*

the exercise of political leadership by some national governments and the gradual evolution of international political institutions can correct this inherent bias against cooperative responses to systemic, global problems.

Some Examples

To see the general issue in clearer perspective, consider three examples. The first is indicative of the problems that supervisory authorities can encounter in their prudential oversight of individual intermediaries. When examining the branch or subsidiary in country A of a multinational bank, suppose the country-A supervisors discover some loans that, in their judgment, are of questionable quality. Perhaps the supervisors even have reliable information demonstrating that the borrowers in question are poor credit risks. Alternatively, suppose the supervisors learn that the branch or subsidiary in A has made loans to a single customer that amount to a disproportionately large proportion of the office's total balance sheet. The A-country supervisors might be especially concerned if the borrowing customers are residents of country A, but they would have grounds for concern even if the customers were residents of other countries.

To redress these perceived problems, the supervisors in A may be able to require the bank to make adjustments in the balance sheet of its country-A office. But the supervisors in A may not be able to prevent the A office of the bank from transferring the bad loans or the imprudently large loans with a single customer to the balance sheets of offices of the bank in country B or country C. The A supervisors will have, at best, incomplete information about the banking organization's operations in B and C. The supervisors in B and C will be at an analogous disadvantage with respect to the bank's operations in A. Given their information, for example, the B and C supervisors may have no basis for questioning the soundness of the loans transferred into their jurisdiction from A even though the loans may in fact be unsound and had been judged so correctly by the supervisors in A. (The likelihood of the A supervisors having superior information is higher, other things being equal, if the ultimate borrowers are residents of A.) If country C happens to attach a higher priority to attracting banking business within its borders than to supervision of that business, moreover, the C supervisors may in any case be reluctant to ask uncomfortable questions. A multinational bank with offices in many national jurisdictions thus could conceivably play one nation's supervisory authorities off against others, effectively escaping in its worldwide operations from the constraints imposed by any one authority.

This class of problems would arise most urgently for financial intermediaries that were irresponsibly or fraudulently managed. Yet even when fraud or outright irresponsibility are absent, differences in judgments are inevitable among banks and supervisors about what constitutes a "bad" loan or "imprudently large lending," not least because conditions can unexpectedly change after loan agreements are made. In the absence of considerable communication of information among national supervisory authorities, such differences tend—in the case of multinational banks—to be effectively resolved in the banks' favor. What is more, cooperation in supervision tends to be no more effective than the least strong link in the chain. In the preceding example, if the supervisors in country C have the least adequate information or ask the fewest questions, the bad loans will be transferred from the bank's offices in A to its offices in C. Extensive communication and cooperation between the supervisors in A and B will not be sufficient to generate a satisfactory outcome.

Taxation policies are a second area in which important examples of international externalities arise. Suppose one country abolishes withholding taxes on interest payments to foreign residents and accords preferential tax treatment to profits earned by banking offices within its borders when those profits are generated by lending to foreigners.[7] Suppose the tax incentives then induce multinational banks to shift some banking activity to that country away from other countries where the activity would otherwise have been booked. Then suppose that numerous other countries, observing this experience, decide to abolish withholding taxes on interest payments to foreigners and to accord preferential tax treatment to profits on lending to foreigners.[8] Finally, suppose this trend were to lead eventually to a worldwide adoption of the preferential tax policies. The inadvertent outcome of the sequence of independent national actions could be an effective loss, for all governments, of tax revenues on their own residents' profits and interest incomes.

I have stated this example in an extreme form. In practice, only some nations have taken such tax actions. I cannot confidently generalize about actual national experiences; nor can I identify a hypothetical "optimal" stan-

7. For example, Singapore took these actions in the late 1960s and early 1970s and extended the preferential tax treatment to various other types of offshore income and profits during the late 1970s and 1980s.

8. Many of the offshore financial centers accord preferential tax treatment to bank profits and do not withhold tax on interest payments to foreigners. In 1984 the United States abolished withholding taxes on interest paid to foreigners on U.S. Treasury securities. In 1984–85 Japan considered analogous steps in conjunction with proposals for "offshore" banking facilities in Japan.

dard for withholding taxes and the tax treatment of financial institutions' profits (more precisely, a hypothetical set of guidelines for the world as a whole that could be adopted by national tax authorities if all of them were prepared to cooperate in designing the guidelines—see chapter 9). Yet it is not implausible to conjecture that the net result of sequential and independent changes in national tax policies can be—indeed, at times has been—inadvertently harmful to the interests of many nations.[9]

The third example pertains to the policy-control rationale for regulation and supervision. Suppose nation A, as part of its separation fence, maintains policies intended to inhibit the "internationalization" of its currency. Singapore is a salient example. (Japan was an example before its policy changes in the mid-1980s.) The various regulations having this objective make it more difficult for foreign residents to hold assets or incur liabilities denominated in the A currency, especially if the assets and liabilities are not directly associated with transactions with residents of A.

Now suppose that banks begin to facilitate, within nation B, the activities in currency A that the government of A is trying to discourage, for example, accepting deposits in the A currency and beginning to make a secondary market in A-currency deposit instruments.[10] What obligations, if any, do the policy and supervisory authorities in B have to inform the authorities in A about these activities? Should the B authorities assist the A authorities in their effort to discourage the internationalization of the A currency? What would it mean for the B government to stay neutral with respect to abetting or undercutting the objectives of the A government? At the least, a cooperative dilemma is inherent in this type of situation. Action, or the lack of action, by the B government can importantly affect the ability of the A government to achieve its goals.

Nascent Cooperative Efforts

In the last decade international collective-goods problems of the type just identified have received increasing attention from national governments.

9. There is an analogy here with the experience of state governments within the United States. After a few state governments extended fiscal incentives to induce firms to relocate plants within their states, other state governments emulated the policies. Arguably, the eventual result after several decades was only a small change in the geographical location of industry but significant revenue losses for all of the state governments.

10. For example, some "international" uses of the yen and the Singapore dollar occurred in Hong Kong on a limited scale during the first half of the 1980s.

The most important forum for catalyzing consultations and cooperation among banking supervisory authorities is the so-called Basel Supervisors' Committee, or Cooke committee, meeting under the auspices of the Bank for International Settlements. The committee grew out of the concerns generated by the Herstatt and Franklin National Bank crises in 1974. Before the formation of this committee in 1975, consultations among the national authorities were infrequent and primarily bilateral. The committee now meets regularly, usually three or four times a year, and has made significant progress on several fronts.[11]

One of the committee's early achievements was the drafting of a "Concordat" on the "Supervision of Banks' Foreign Establishments." The first version of the Concordat was agreed upon in December 1975. A somewhat modified version was prepared during 1983.[12] The Concordat sets out agreed principles and guidelines covering the division of responsibilities among national authorities for the supervision of banks that operate in more than one national jurisdiction. The most important principles in the document are that the supervision of foreign-owned banking establishments should be the joint responsibility of host and parent authorities, that no foreign-owned banking establishment should escape supervision, and that the supervision should be adequate as judged by both host and parent authorities. Recommendations are made to deal with possible gaps in supervision (for example, if host authority supervision is deemed inadequate by the parent authority, if parent authority supervision is judged inadequate by the host authority, if banking groups contain both banks and nonbank organizations, or if the existence of holding companies cither at the head or in the middle of a banking group constitutes an impediment to adequate supervision). Detailed guidelines deal with solvency, liquidity, and foreign-exchange operations and positions. For example, the Concordat states that the supervision of solvency for the foreign branches of a

---

11. W. P. Cooke, of the Banking Supervision Division at the Bank of England, is the current chairman of the committee; it was chaired in the initial years by George Blunden, another official of the Bank of England. The formal title of the group is the Committee on Banking Regulations and Supervisory Practices. For published accounts of the committee's activities, see Bank of England, "Developments in Co-operation among Banking Supervisory Authorities"; W. P. Cooke, "The International Banking Scene: A Supervisory Perspective"; and G. G. Johnson with Richard K. Abrams, *Aspects of the International Banking Safety Net*, app. I.

12. The text of the revised version was published in Richard C. Williams and others, *International Capital Markets: Developments and Prospects, 1983*. The initial version was reprinted in Williams and others, *International Capital Markets: Recent Developments and Short-Term Prospects, 1981*.

bank is primarily a matter for the parent authority. The supervision of solvency for foreign subsidiaries, on the other hand, is identified as a joint responsibility of host and parent authorities; subsidiaries are separate legal entities incorporated in the country of host authorities, yet supervision of the parent authorities is also required because the solvency of parent banks cannot be adequately judged without taking account of all their foreign establishments and because parent banks cannot be indifferent to the situation of their foreign subsidiaries.

Another achievement of the committee was an agreement on the principle that banks' international business should be monitored on a consolidated basis. After some delays, most countries represented on the committee took steps to implement the principle. The 1983 version of the Concordat reformulated some of the 1975 provisions to take account of this agreement that the soundness of individual banks can be adequately appraised only by examining the totality of each bank's worldwide business through the technique of consolidation. In conjunction with another BIS standing committee, the Cooke committee has also encouraged the collection of more complete and improved data for international banking. Examples of the improved data include statistics on the maturity composition of banks' international assets and liabilities and on the country distribution of banks' lending.

Through the efforts of the Basel committee, supervisory authorities from countries not represented at BIS meetings were invited to a broader international conference held in London in 1979. Similar conferences were held in Washington in 1981 and in Italy in 1984. An associated development was the formation of an Offshore Group of Banking Supervisors (a first meeting was held in October 1980) and a Commission of Latin American and Caribbean Banking Supervisory and Inspection Organizations (a first meeting was held in July 1981). The members of the Offshore Group have accepted the principles of the Basel committee's Concordat. As best one can tell, these latter two groups have been much less active than the Basel committee itself.

After several of the new trends in international financial intermediation in the 1980s had become increasingly apparent, in early 1985 the central-bank governors of the Group of Ten countries established a study group under BIS auspices to examine the trends and their policy implications. The report of the study group was made available to the public in April 1986.[13] Among other things, the report described in detail the growing importance to banks of off-balance-sheet business—note issuance facilities, currency and interest-rate

13. Bank for International Settlements, *Recent Innovations in International Banking*.

swaps, foreign-currency and interest-rate options, forward rate agreements, and various guarantee backup facilities.

Concurrently with the work of the study group, the Basel Supervisors' Committee examined the problem of off-balance-sheet exposures. In March 1986 the committee circulated an agreed "preliminary assessment" of how banks and supervisory authorities should manage such exposures.[14] This assessment concluded that "the individual types of risk associated with most off-balance-sheet business are in principle no different from those associated with on-balance-sheet business." All members of the committee endorsed the general approach summarized in the document. It was also observed, however, that "the precise way in which supervisory policies are developed to take account of the growth in off-balance-sheet activity is a matter for national consideration in the light of the legal and other institutional circumstances which may bear on the determination of policy." Supervisory authorities were thus able to develop some common guidelines but left detailed implementation to national discretion. Shortly after the committee's paper was made public, several national authorities moved promptly to modify their regulations and supervisory procedures.[15]

In another noteworthy respect, the BIS study group report drew attention to the need for enhanced international cooperation. The report identified ways in which the securitization of lending, its unbundling of different types of risks, and its growth of off-balance-sheet business has eroded the quality of the existing statistics on international financial intermediation. It then went on to argue that governments should consider steps to broaden the coverage and quality of the statistics. In particular, the report recommended that governments collect fuller and more detailed information on banks' involvement in the securities markets; information on the arrangements and use of NIFs and other backup facilities; information from outside the banking sector on outstanding bond indebtedness and short-term securities, using where possible data from trade associations and other sources; and information on banks' off-balance-sheet business, "arranging when possible for data to be collected by supervisory authorities in a manner useful for macro-analysis."[16]

The 1986 report of the BIS study group and the 1986 paper on off-balance-sheet exposures of the Supervisors' Committee constitute strong evidence that

14. Bank for International Settlements, "The Management of Banks' Off-Balance-Sheet Exposures: A Supervisory Perspective."

15. See, for example, Bank of England, "Innovation in International Banking" and "Supervision and Competitive Conditions."

16. BIS, *Recent Innovations in International Banking,* pp. 6–7.

the international dimensions of supervisory and regulatory issues were, by the mid-1980s, commanding greater attention within national governments.[17]

Statements by government officials about the work of the Basel Supervisors' Committee assert that it has responsibility only for supervisory and some regulatory issues. In particular, the officials insist that the committee has no mandate to discuss the international aspects of lender-of-last-resort assistance. The international aspects of "monetary control" issues are likewise said to be beyond the committee's jurisdiction.[18]

In principle, there is no logically defensible way to separate the narrower supervision issues from the broader questions of lender-of-last-resort assistance and regulations that have a bearing on monetary control. This point is implicitly, but not explicitly, acknowledged in the April 1986 report of the BIS study group. That report contains chapters on "the impact of financial innovations on financial stability," "issues for macro-prudential policy," and "consequences for the conduct and effectiveness of monetary policy." Eventually, the mandate of the Supervisors' Committee will need to be formally broadened. Alternatively, other channels—outside the BIS, or under different auspices within the BIS—will need to be used for intergovernmental discussion and cooperation on these issues.

The current mandate of the Supervisors' Committee covers only banking regulations and supervisory practices. Because securities firms and other nonbank financial institutions have likewise become increasingly active in cross-border and cross-currency transactions, international cooperation in financial

17. In January 1987 international cooperation on issues of bank regulation and supervision took another significant step forward. The Bank of England and the U.S. bank regulatory agencies jointly issued for public comment a proposal for the assessment of capital adequacy and the establishment of minimum capital standards on an international basis. The principal objective of the proposal is "to promote the convergence of supervisory policies on capital adequacy assessments among countries with major banking centers." In a pointed remark in their announcement, the supervisory authorities expressed the "hope that the approach adopted by the United States and the United Kingdom will provide a basis which other countries can follow." For details, see "Agreed Proposal of the United States Federal Banking Supervisory Authorities and the Bank of England on Primary Capital and Capital Adequacy Assessment," issued in a joint release dated January 8, 1987, by the Comptroller of the Currency, the Federal Deposit Insurance Corporation, and the Federal Reserve Board.

18. The following quotation summarizes the official position on the nonresponsibilities of the Basel Supervisors' Committee for lender-of-last-resort issues: the Concordat "sets out guidelines covering the responsibilities of the different supervisory authorities for the ongoing supervision of banks where those banks operate in more than one national jurisdiction. It is not, and was never intended to be, an agreement about responsibilities for the provision of lender of last resort facilities to the international banking system, and there should not necessarily be considered to be any automatic link between acceptance of responsibility for ongoing supervision and the assumption of a lender of last resort role." Bank of England, "Developments in Co-operation among Banking Supervisory Authorities," p. 240.

regulation and supervision must eventually extend to securities transactions. In effect, the Securities and Exchange Commission in the United States, the Securities and Investment Board in the United Kingdom, and their supervisory counterparts in other nations will have to organize consultations and cooperative actions analogous to those initiated through the Basel Supervisors' Committee.

The difficulties of international collaboration are compounded by the somewhat arbitrary division of supervisory responsibilities within some national governments. In countries such as Germany and the United Kingdom, no sharp legal distinction exists between banking (direct intermediation) and securities transactions (indirect intermediation). Regulatory overlaps between different agencies of government are common (for example, in the United Kingdom between the Bank of England and the Securities and Investment Board). In other countries, for example the United States and Japan, laws and regulations enforce a separation between commercial banking and securities underwriting. It seemed natural in those countries to establish a parallel separation of supervisory responsibilities within the government. Even in those countries, however, the de facto distinction between banking and securities transactions has been gradually eroding. The rationale for separating supervisory responsibilities has correspondingly eroded. In the not too distant future, as borrowers and lenders shift with increasing ease between banking and securities markets, banking and securities supervisors will experience growing pressures to regulate jointly within national jurisdictions and to consult jointly in international forums.

The European Economic Community (EEC) has created several institutions for discussing regulatory and supervisory problems. The "Groupe de Contact," whose members are the banking supervisors of the EEC countries, has met periodically since 1969. The Banking Advisory Committee is a steering group set up under the First Banking Coordination Directive of 1977 with responsibilities for the planning and coordination of bank regulation. An example of the work of these groups was the European Community Directive on "Supervision of Credit Institutions on a Consolidated Basis."[19]

The Organization for Economic Cooperation and Development has also sponsored studies of these issues in recent years, conducted by an Expert Group on Banking responsible to the Committee on Financial Markets. Several publications resulting from this effort are now available.[20]

19. This document is reprinted in Williams and others, *International Capital Markets, Developments and Prospects, 1983*.

20. See, for example, Rinaldo Pecchioli, *The Internationalisation of Banking: The Policy Issues*; and T. R. G. Bingham, *Banking and Monetary Policy*.

The International Monetary Fund has participated only indirectly in these nascent efforts to provide some prudential oversight of international financial intermediation. National governments, and the Fund staff itself, have presumed that collective action on these subjects would, if needed, be undertaken outside the Fund.

Two developments in the early 1980s suggest that the traditional lack of IMF participation in this area might undergo a reevaluation. The first development was a growing commitment of Fund staff resources to the analysis of international financial markets. As one manifestation of this analysis, in 1980 the Exchange and Trade Relations Department began publishing an annual survey of developments and prospects in international banking and bond markets. The Fund's Bureau of Statistics, in cooperation with the BIS, likewise augmented its efforts to collect and interpret data for these markets. The enhanced concern in 1982–84 about the debt situation of developing countries gave a further stimulus to this increased commitment of staff resources.[21]

The second development, potentially of great significance, occurred in conjunction with the IMF's 1982–86 lending to developing nations caught up in debt-servicing crises. In a major departure from previous experience, the Fund became actively involved in negotiations between debtor countries and their commercial-bank creditors. For example, the IMF played a decisive role in resolving the debt-management crises in 1982 and 1983 of Mexico, Brazil, and several other Latin American nations. Its involvement in debt renegotiations continued through 1986, apparently no less extensively. In effect, the IMF became a "financial orchestrator," helping a country to negotiate a combined financing and adjustment program satisfactory to the country and all its creditors. In cases where commercial banks were reluctant to maintain or increase their lending, the IMF made its own lending contingent on the continued participation of the banks. This so-called concerted lending, described as "bailing in" rather than "bailing out" the commercial banks, brought the IMF into much closer proximity with private financial institutions than at any earlier time in its history. It also raised some important questions about future relationships between the Fund and private financial institutions.

21. For a recent annual survey, see Maxwell Watson and others, *International Capital Markets: Developments and Prospects*. The Bureau of Statistics' new data for international banking are described in the *IMF Survey* for March 18, 1985, pp. 81, 89–92; and in Joslin Landell-Mills, *The Fund's International Banking Statistics*.

CHAPTER NINE

Broad Choices for the Evolution
of Government Policies

THERE is little reason to believe that the shrinking of effective economic distances between nations has reached its limits. Nonpolicy technological innovations in communications and transportation will continue to be made, which will generate further changes in the economic preferences of firms and consumers. Probably, therefore, assets denominated in different currencies and issued in different locations will continue to become better substitutes.

Governments will be under continuing pressure to adjust their domestic regulation and supervision of financial activity. The impetus for headlong deregulation has probably lost steam in the United States and in several other industrial countries. Nonetheless, financial innovations—many of them designed explicitly for cross-border and cross-currency applications—have continued at a rapid pace. These innovations will require governments to review and in some cases amend their current regulations. Such amendments will induce further innovations and changes in behavior, leading to still more alterations in the financial structures of national economies. All the changes may generate significant side effects for cross-border and cross-currency financial activity.

Governments seem likely to face conflicting pressures about the remaining separation fences around national financial markets. Some governments may face strong demands to raise their fences (see below). At the same time, however, the trend toward discrimination in favor of conducting financial transactions in foreign currencies and with foreign residents seems likely to continue. Some governments, in other words, will probably continue to try to lure financial intermediaries to relocate business in their jurisdictions by extending additional regulatory and tax incentives.

If these broad speculations about nonpolicy innovations and policy adjustments are correct, the net effect over the next decade will be a further strengthening of the interconnectedness of financial markets. This evolution will in turn pose still greater challenges for government policies, especially for those nations whose regulatory, tax, and supervisory environments are more stringent than the world average.

Drift in the Short Run

Is this further drift toward a unified world capital market sustainable? Will public opinion and national governments understand and accept its consequences? *Should* they accept them?

For the time being, general public interest in these issues is very low. Most citizens, in all countries, are relatively uninformed. Financial activity and its regulation are widely perceived as arcane subjects, especially the international dimensions. Average opinion is thus inattentive, even somnolent. The autonomy of any one country's policy actions declines over time, but not in a dramatic way that calls attention to the persistent trend. The nations with the most stringent regulations and supervision experience an erosion of their environments, but the erosion is gradual and not highly visible to the general public.

In the private sector, the exceptions to this lack of awareness are individuals in the financial community itself and a few academics. Unsurprisingly, the people who make their living in the financial community have a favorable view of what has happened in the last several decades. Among them, many hold the efficient-markets, semi-Panglossian position, or views tending toward it. A few nervous observers, who see things as out of control, want to find a way to put on the brakes.

As with the general public, the average civil servant or parliamentary representative tends to be poorly informed and inattentive. A minority of officials in finance ministries, central banks, supervisory agencies, and international organizations have been following the evolution closely, and often with some concern. During the 1980s, especially after the debt crises of 1982, a somewhat wider group within national governments became aware of the trends and issues. In this period there were also signs of growing regulatory and supervisory attention, including more intensive international consultations (chapter 8). Only a few government policies changed, however, and then only in relatively minor ways and in lagged response to developments. Policies were not designed to deliberately manage the evolution of international financial intermediation.

Because the mass of public opinion is inattentive and only a minority within governments is engaged, government policies in the short and medium run can continue to drift. Public opinion is not likely to force the underlying issues onto the agendas of government policymakers. The further integration of national financial sectors can proceed relatively unchallenged. By default, the typical government policy is little different from benign neglect—a situation regarded as appropriate by semi-Panglossians. This short- and medium-run drift could last through the rest of the 1980s.

Over a longer run, however, I conjecture that this drift will prove unsustainable—for political reasons. It may take a major economic or financial crisis to catalyze a widespread awareness of the underlying trends. Once the trends have been widely recognized, however, public reactions are likely to force governments to confront the difficult choices more explicitly. At some point, the large mass of public opinion that is now relatively oblivious to the issues will divide, with individual views gravitating toward one of three broad positions.

One of the three would be the semi-Panglossian perspective. Those moving in that direction would become aware of what has been happening and, more or less enthusiastically, embrace it. They would want to push the financial deregulation movement further within their own countries. Simultaneously, they would resist efforts to replace parts of national regulation and supervision with international or supranational substitutes.

I doubt that the semi-Panglossian view will become widely popular. My conjecture is that the bulk of public opinion will eventually shift toward one of the other two possibilities: "dis-integration," or "enhanced multilateral decisionmaking."

Dis-Integration

In the areas of regulation, taxation, and supervision of financial activity, dis-integration would entail the rebuilding of separation fences. By deliberate choice, governments would try to inhibit the free flow of funds between national reservoirs.

More broadly, one can imagine governments retreating from the implications of interdependence across the whole range of economic policies. For monetary policies, for example, central banks would seek ways to regain some of the differential impact on home ultimate targets that had been dissipated through financial interdependence. The nonpolicy factors bringing nations closer together, such as continuing advances in communications technology, cannot be effectively controlled by governments. Thus the only feasible way to recapture lost autonomy—to reverse market integration and to reduce the substitutability among assets denominated in different currencies and issued in different nations—is to establish stronger barriers or frictions at national borders.

Dis-integration could occur in a disorderly way. Within each nation influential private groups, the communications media, and the national government itself could espouse a narrow definition of national (and private) interests. Through a sequence of decentralized and noncooperative decisions, national governments could revert to protectionist policies designed to promote their own residents' interests at the expense of foreigners. New forms of protectionist policies could apply to trade in goods and services as well as financial transactions. If carried out in this way, dis-integration could easily represent yet another illustration of the classic dilemma of collective action in which members of a group inadvertently damage their common interests.

But the course of dis-integration could also, in principle, be cooperatively managed. Conceived in that way, dis-integration can plausibly be portrayed in a positive rather than negative light—as a constructive effort to permit nations to experience divergent macroeconomic and financial conditions suited to their own needs and circumstances. Intergovernmental cooperation that self-consciously managed a mutually agreed sequence of national actions could prevent the dis-integration from going too far or collapsing into self-defeating anarchy. Separation fences inhibiting financial transactions would be partially rebuilt in accord with internationally agreed guidelines. Conceivably, international cooperation could also specify amended guidelines for restraints on current-account transactions, for example, modifications of existing arrangements under the General Agreement on Tariffs and Trade (GATT).

One approach to cooperative guidelines would specify a differential favoring of current-account transactions. Trade in goods and services would remain relatively unhampered, with perhaps no more restrictions than at present, while an attempt would be made to reverse the integration of national financial reservoirs by imposing restrictions on various categories of financial transactions. Cooperative guidelines to prohibit restrictions on certain classes of cross-border goods-and-services transactions require, at a minimum, a corresponding absence of restrictions on the financial settlements (payments and receipts) for that goods-and-services trade. As under the original GATT and International Monetary Fund articles, therefore, new international guidelines that differentially favored goods-and-services trade would have to distinguish

among financial transactions according to whether they were or were not settlements for current-account transactions.

A differential favoring of current-account transactions would represent a
return to the attitudes about international capital flows prevailing at the end of
World War II. The architects of the postwar international agreements believed
that many types of international capital movements should be discouraged, if
not prevented. Yet at the same time they aspired to liberalize international
trade in goods and services (chapter 4). As with the postwar agreements, any
new guidelines along these lines would presumably be rationalized by assertions that "disequilibrating" capital flows caused by speculative excesses
could influence national economies adversely rather than beneficially. The old
assertion would no doubt be intellectually refurbished by appealing to the
more recent research on speculative bubbles and excess variability in
exchange rates (chapter 6).

James Tobin has put forward a second type of approach to foster cooperatively managed dis-integration. His suggestion is that governments impose an
internationally uniform transfer tax on transactions across currencies, thereby
diminishing the substitutability of assets denominated in different currencies.[1]
Tobin's tax would differ from the selective restrictions on capital flows used
extensively after World War II. It would apply to all spot foreign-exchange
transactions, including those that were payments or receipts for goods and
services. Tobin's intent is to increase the transactions costs of short-run sales
and purchases of assets made for speculative purposes. He does not wish to
make current-account transactions more expensive. By applying the tax to all
types of spot transactions, however, Tobin avoids perhaps insuperable difficulties that would otherwise arise in the administration of the tax (distinguish-
ing between speculative financial transactions that would be taxed and beneficial transactions that would not).[2]

Suggestions for cooperatively managed dis-integration are attractive in
principle. They deserve serious analysis and debate. In particular, Tobin's

1. Tobin first made the proposal in *The New Economics, One Decade Older*, pp. 88–92, and
subsequently elaborated it in "A Proposal for International Monetary Reform." The proposal is
reprinted in the third volume of his collected papers, *Essays in Economics: Theory and Policy*,
chap. 20. Tobin's proposal draws inspiration from Keynes's idea of a government transfer tax on
financial transactions; see John Maynard Keynes, *The General Theory of Employment, Interest
and Money*, p. 160.

2. Tobin argues that, while the incremental impediment to goods trade is unfortunate, it
would be only a small additional cost. The disincentive for in-and-out, speculative financial
transactions would be proportionately much greater. And Tobin would be prepared to accept the
costs of marginally discouraging trade in goods and services as the price for achieving restraint on
nonproductive financial transactions.

proposal for an internationally uniform transfer tax deserves more careful examination than it has so far received.

In practice, however, I surmise that cooperative dis-integration would prove infeasible or excessively costly. It would be an extraordinarily difficult task to rebuild separation fences between national financial reservoirs in a way that yields a large gain in autonomy while sacrificing only a small part of the benefits of interdependence. Whatever the agreed guidelines might be, the sacrifice of benefits might still be considerable. And the politically easy way to reerect separation fences—catering to localized and individually differentiated demands for protection without abiding by international guidelines—would probably be very costly indeed.

During the years of the Bretton-Woods adjustable-peg regime for exchange rates, many academic economists argued that flexibility in exchange rates would substantially insulate nations' economic policies from the effects of interdependence. Though the argument appeared to be justified by economic theory, the analytical basis for it was in fact faulty. Economists and policymakers have now abandoned that earlier hope, recognizing that exchange-rate variability cannot itself bring about dis-integration of national economies.[3]

For many countries, there may be no administratively feasible way to maintain an effective separation fence for financial transactions. So many pipes and pumping stations now connect national reservoirs—and so many new channels could be established in response to controls on existing channels—that governments simply may not have the capacity to prevent international movements of funds. To change the analogy, recapturing lost autonomy might well be like trying to squeeze toothpaste back into its tube.

It would be difficult—perhaps impossible—to restore exchange and capital controls of the type prevalent after World War II. Such controls would have to try to distinguish helpful financial transactions from undesirable, disequilibrating transactions. Each country would have difficulties working out independent guidelines for its own situation. To design and implement internationally agreed guidelines would be still more difficult since what would be judged undesirable by some nations would be deemed helpful by others.

Tobin's proposal for an internationally uniform transfer tax would avoid some of the difficulties of old-fashioned exchange and capital controls. But it would encounter severe administrative difficulties nonetheless. To prevent effective evasion, the tax would have to be applied to forward as well as spot

---

3. See Ralph C. Bryant, *Financial Interdependence and Variability in Exchange Rates,* especially pp. 18–21 ("Can Exchange-Rate Variability Insulate National Economies?").

transactions in foreign exchange. Similarly, it might have to be applied to options and futures contracts on currencies and to currency swaps and various combinations of currency swaps with interest-rate swaps. At the least, implementation would require extensive monitoring of transactions and sizable expenditures for administrative staff. More serious still, the tax would not be effective unless major countries and the offshore financial centers all agreed to implement it. If only a few nations (for example, one or two offshore financial centers) refused to cooperate, financial transactions could be shifted into those jurisdictions to escape the tax, thereby largely negating the effects of the tax even for those countries implementing the proposal.

All things considered, the prospects for cooperatively managed dis-integration seem poor. High levels of overt conflict among nations could, it is true, create a political climate in which the rebuilding of separation fences would be popular. Stringent restrictions might then be implemented quickly. A little war here or there, for example, would be a marvelous shot in the arm for exchange controls. But dis-integration achieved in that way would certainly not be cooperatively managed. It would represent disintegration in the more common sense of that word, namely a destruction rather than a pulling back that is controlled and mutually agreed.

Enhanced Multilateral Decisionmaking

Difficult though it will prove to be, therefore, a course that involves strengthening the ability of national governments to cooperate through enhanced procedures of multilateral decisionmaking seems the most likely prospect for the last years of this century and the first decades of the next. Rather than pulling back from financial interdependence, this posture would actively try to adapt to it and manage it better.

Nations would not try to rebuild separation fences for financial transactions—not even cooperatively. Rather, they would accept, perhaps even in some ways encourage, the integration of national financial sectors. One rationale for this approach would be to gain the substantial benefits from international financial intermediation. Another reason would be the judgment that a cooperative dis-integration approach is infeasible.

What would this broad choice imply for regulation, supervision, and taxation? National governments would have to grope toward a world environment for financial intermediation in which there would be less divergence and more cooperation among countries. The first steps in this process would be some further internationally agreed improvements in the collection and compilation of statistics and the development of some agreed principles that would foster less heterogeneity in national regulations, tax treatments, and supervisory procedures. Such "world standard" principles need not imply uniformity in national policies. But they would constrain national behavior more than the "anything goes" presumption that is now the formal state of affairs. The Concordat on the supervision of banks' foreign establishments and the principles for handling banks' off-balance-sheet business worked out by the Basel Supervisors' Committee (chapter 8) are first hesitant steps along these lines.

Agreement on some world principles would have the corollary effect of halting the drift toward discrimination in favor of financial intermediaries' transactions with foreign residents in foreign currencies. And it would imply that nations should gradually implement the world principles. Countries with high taxes and stringent regulations would thus remain under some pressure to reduce their taxes and regulations. But there would also be resistance to competition in laxity that, if unresisted, could drive regulation, supervision, and taxation toward a least common denominator for the world as a whole. Countries whose tax and regulatory environments were much less stringent than average would have to tighten their policies toward the emerging set of world standards.

How could a set of world standards be formulated? Merely taking an unweighted average of existing national standards has no compelling logic to recommend it, economically or politically. Insisting that smaller countries conform to the existing standards of the most powerful nations has a political logic, but not one with appeal to those who must conform. Ideally, one would like to see world standards based on objective criteria, or criteria as objectively formulated as possible. Wherever it proved infeasible to maintain heterogeneity in regulations across countries, criteria would need to be developed to judge whether high taxes and stringent regulations were inappropriately restrictive or whether low taxes and loose regulations were inappropriately permissive. Much groundwork would have to be laid at the analytical level before it would be reasonable to schedule intergovernmental discussions about the possibility of such world standards.

What would enhanced multilateral decisionmaking mean more generally—for example, for nations' macroeconomic policies?

At a minimum, governments would need to pay greater attention to the consequences of their macroeconomic policies for other nations. The growing importance of such spillovers raises the likelihood of the world economy inadvertently experiencing mutually inferior outcomes (chapters 6 and 8). More intensive intergovernmental consultation, and eventually "coordination" of national policies, could reduce the frequency and adverse consequences of such outcomes. The broad objective of enhanced cooperation about macro-economic policies, therefore, would be to develop analytical and institutional procedures that fostered mutually beneficial consultation and coordination. Presumptively, a crucial part of such enhancement would be a strengthening of international organizations, such as the IMF and the Organization for Economic Cooperation and Development, to serve as a monitor of and catalyst for multilateral decisionmaking.

National governments for several years have stated that they intend to strengthen the process of "multilateral surveillance" (a code term for enhanced cooperation about macroeconomic policies). At successive economic summit meetings among the largest seven industrial countries, beginning at Versailles in June 1982, the communiqués have asserted that goal. For example, at the end of the May 1986 summit meeting in Tokyo the heads of state boldly proclaimed, "It is important that there should be close and continuous coordination of economic policy among the seven summit countries. . . . Additional measures should be taken to insure that procedures for effective coordination of international economic policy are strengthened further."[4] Summit communiqués since 1982 have also envisaged an increased role for the IMF in catalyzing multilateral surveillance.

What happened during 1982–86 to strengthen multilateral surveillance? Very little, a frank evaluation has to acknowledge. The rhetoric in favor of enhanced cooperation ran far ahead of actual measures to facilitate it.

Several obstacles continue to stand in the way of significant progress. One of them is the inherent asymmetry of pressures experienced by nations with balance-of-payments deficits or weakening currencies relative to the pressures on nations with balance-of-payments surpluses or strengthening currencies. Countries with deficits or weakening currencies, because they will in any event be forced to take some sort of policy actions, tend to have a stronger interest in consultation and policy coordination than do countries with surpluses or strengthening currencies. Yet the ultimate causes of systemic inconsistencies in nations' policies do not emanate exclusively from nations with deficits. A careful appraisal of systemic inconsistencies (for example, by the IMF in its role as catalyst for multilateral decisionmaking) would suggest an

4. "Text of Economic Declaration Issued at End of Tokyo Summit Conference," *New York Times*, May 7, 1986, p. A10.

evenhanded pressuring of not only deficit but also surplus countries. But no effective leverage, in the IMF or elsewhere, exists to encourage such an evenhanded approach.

Another obstacle to progress is a lack of political will. Though national governments have aspirations to cooperate, the aspirations are seldom rooted in genuine political commitment. In effect, an individual government favors multilateral consultations and surveillance when they would induce helpful behavior by other nations, but not when the process would uncomfortably constrain options for the home nation. Just as superstition tends to be defined as some other person's religion and protectionism as some other nation's commercial policy, stubborn attachment to outmoded ideas of national sovereignty is perceived as the attribute of other nations' attitudes toward international surveillance.

The lack of a commonly accepted analytical framework for assessing the cross-border interactions among nations' economies is still another obstacle to joint discussions of macroeconomic policies. Enormous uncertainty exists about how policy actions and nonpolicy shocks originating in one country influence economic developments in other countries. Thus governments do not have an analytically sound basis to coordinate their decisions, even if they were politically disposed to do so.

There is not even an adequate analytical framework for evaluating the effects of external forces on the domestic economy for any individual nation. Worse still, neither governments, international institutions, nor academic economists have an analytical framework capable of modeling the interactions among individual national economies in an internally consistent, systemic fashion.[5] Yet some degree of consensus among objective analysts about the direction and quantitative size of such interactions is a necessary—albeit far from sufficient—condition for significant progress in facilitating coordination of national macroeconomic policies.

Flexibility in exchange rates, as noted earlier, cannot insulate nations' economic policies from the effects of interdependence and cannot by itself engender dis-integration. Could a return to a Bretton-Woods system of fixed (that is, infrequently adjusted) exchange rates be a substitute for cooperation about

5. These problems were extensively discussed at a conference on "Empirical Macroeconomics for Interdependent Economies: Where Do We Stand?" held at the Brookings Institution in March 1986. Participants included virtually all groups in the world, official and private, who had developed empirical models of macroeconomic interactions among the main industrial countries. The papers and associated materials derived from this conference will be published in Ralph C. Bryant, Dale W. Henderson, Gerald Holtham, Peter Hooper, and Steven A. Symansky, eds., *Empirical Macroeconomics for Interdependent Economies*.

macroeconomic policies? More generally, is there any one-time reform of international monetary arrangements that could eliminate the need for enhanced multilateral decisionmaking?

Alas, salvation is not simple. The yearning for an ideal set of exchange-rate arrangements is misguided. The two traditional policy views about fluctuations in exchange rates, the minimum-variance position and the untrammeled-market position, are each analytically deficient. In itself, variability in exchange rates is neither good nor bad. Neither its presence nor its absence makes sense as an *objective* for most nations' macroeconomic policies. For most individual nations, and hence for the world generally, some type of intermediate exchange regime that permits period-to-period discretionary adjustments—call it "managed fixing" or "managed flexibility"—is likely to prove more viable than either untrammeled flexibility or minimized variability around infrequently changed pegs.[6]

If analytical consensus were eventually to be reached either about "excessive" variability in exchange rates or about techniques for calculating "misaligned" exchange rates, such consensus would doubtless have significant implications for the design of exchange-rate arrangements and for guidelines governing official intervention in exchange markets. But consensus is not yet in sight. Even if it were, moreover, the yearnings for an ideal or "optimum" exchange regime would still be somewhat misguided.

The manner and degree of exchange-rate variability are not, in themselves, issues of overriding importance. There is no set of exchange-rate arrangements under which the oil shocks and policy mistakes of the 1970s and 1980s would not have had traumatic consequences. It is impossible to imagine any arrangements that would not have transmitted major inflationary and contractionary impetuses back and forth among national economies. I doubt that the competence and appropriateness of domestic macroeconomic policies in the 1970s and 1980s was much influenced, positively or negatively, by the exchange-rate arrangements that actually existed. I even doubt that those policies would have been greatly improved under alternative exchange arrangements—for example, "crawling pegs" or "target zones."[7]

Lamentable though the fact is, the next several decades in the world economy are likely to be difficult no matter what alternative rules and procedures

6. For further discussion, see again Bryant, *Financial Interdependence and Variability in Exchange Rates*.

7. Crawling peg arrangements are analyzed in John Williamson, ed., *Exchange Rate Rules: The Theory, Performance and Prospects of the Crawling Peg*. For one version of the target-zone proposal, see John Williamson, *The Exchange Rate System*.

for exchange rates are incorporated in the Articles of Agreement of the International Monetary Fund. Policymakers in the major countries would be ill advised, even quixotic, if they hoped to rely on some optimum design for exchange arrangements as a substitute for—instead of merely a complement to—enhanced cooperation about the entire range of their macroeconomic policies.

The European Monetary System (EMS) is an instructive illustration. It is an arrangement under which exchange rates among the European currencies normally vary within margins of moderate width around central parities but infrequently change by discrete larger amounts at the time of mutually agreed adjustments in the central parities. No thoughtful observer of the EMS believes it has been a substitute for enhanced multilateral decisionmaking within Europe. Quite the contrary: the EMS has strengthened the pressure on European governments to consult and cooperate about their domestic economic policies.

What Is Cooperation?

Cooperation among national governments, as I envisage it here, has a limited and precise meaning. Cooperation occurs when several governments take into account the interactions between their economies and polities and as a result mutually adjust their national policies or jointly undertake an international policy. The essential ingredient in cooperation is an agreement among the governments to behave differently in certain circumstances than they would have behaved without the agreement. To be durable, agreements need to be binding and enforceable. In contrast, noncooperative decisions are characterized by an unwillingness to enter into binding commitments. Each government adapts its decisions to what it observes or expects others to do, but without constraints on its own independence of action and without assurances of constraints on the actions of others.

This concept of cooperation is not a synonym for amity, harmony, or altruism. Cooperation is merely a self-interested mutual adjustment of behavior. Cooperation does not imply that national governments have identical or compatible goals. It implies nothing about goals. The goals of national governments are plainly different and often incompatible. Yet the potential for cooperation may be greatest when goals are inconsistent and discord is high.

Heightened cooperation in the sense of self-interested mutual agreements will of course be difficult to achieve, even with better awareness of the need for it. It will have to be conducted the way porcupines make love—very cautiously. Without it, however, there may be no satisfactory evolution of the world economy and financial system. Managed dis-integration would require a large dose of it. It will be the very essence of enhanced multilateral decisionmaking.

Bibliography

Akhtar, M. A. *Financial Innovations and Their Implications for Monetary Policy: An International Perspective.* BIS Economic Papers no. 9. Basel: Bank for International Settlements, Monetary and Economic Department, 1983.

Argy, Victor. *Exchange-Rate Management in Theory and Practice.* Princeton Studies in International Finance no. 50. Princeton University, Department of Economics, International Finance Section, 1982.

Arrow, Kenneth J. "The Economics of Moral Hazard: Further Comment." *American Economic Review,* vol. 58 (June 1968), pp. 537–39.

———. "Limited Knowledge and Economic Analysis." *American Economic Review,* vol. 64 (March 1974), pp. 1–10.

———. "Uncertainty and the Welfare Economics of Medical Care." *American Economic Review,* vol. 53 (December 1963), pp. 941–73.

Bagehot, Walter. *Lombard Street: A Description of the Money Market.* London: Kegan, Paul and Co., 1873. Reprint. London: John Murray, 1924.

Bank of England. "Competition, Innovation and Regulation in British Banking." *Bank of England Quarterly Bulletin,* vol. 23 (September 1983), pp. 363–76.

———. "Developments in Co-operation among Banking Supervisory Authorities." *Bank of England Quarterly Bulletin,* vol. 21 (June 1981), pp. 238–44.

———. "Developments in International Banking and Capital Markets in 1985." *Bank of England Quarterly Bulletin,* vol. 26 (March 1986), pp. 58–70.

———. "Innovation in International Banking." *Bank of England Quarterly Bulletin,* vol. 26 (June 1986), pp. 225–29.

———. "The Nature and Implications of Financial Innovation." *Bank of England Quarterly Bulletin,* vol. 23 (September 1983), pp. 358–62.

———. "Recent Innovations in International Banking." *Bank of England Quarterly Bulletin,* vol. 26 (June 1986), pp. 209–10.

———. "Supervision and Competitive Conditions." *Bank of England Quarterly Bulletin,* vol. 26 (June 1986), pp. 242–44.

Bank for International Settlements. "The Management of Banks' Off-Balance-Sheet Exposures: A Supervisory Perspective." Basel: BIS Committee on Banking Regulations and Supervisory Practices, March 1986. Circulated in the United States with a covering press release by the Comptroller of Currency, Federal Deposit Insurance Corporation, and the Federal Reserve Board, March 17, 1986.

———. *The Nationality Structure of the International Banking Market and the Role of Interbank Operations.* Basel: Monetary and Economic Department, May 1985.

———. *Payment Systems in Eleven Developed Countries.* Rev. ed. Basel: Bank Administration Institute, 1985.

———. *Recent Innovations in International Banking.* Basel: Report of a study group established by the central banks of the Group of Ten countries. Basel: BIS, 1986.

Barry, Brian, and Russell Hardin, eds. *Rational Man and Irrational Society?: An Introduction and Sourcebook.* Beverly Hills, Calif.: Sage Publications, 1982.

Bator, Francis M. "The Anatomy of Market Failure." *Quarterly Journal of Economics,* vol. 72 (August 1958), pp. 351–79.

Bingham, T. R. G. *Banking and Monetary Policy.* Paris: Organization for Economic Cooperation and Development, 1985.

Blanchard, Olivier J., and Mark W. Watson. "Bubbles, Rational Expectations, and Financial Markets," in Paul Wachtel, ed., *Crises in the Economic and Financial Structure.* Lexington, Mass.: Lexington Books, 1982.

Boothe, Paul, Kevin Clinton, Agathe Côté, and David Longworth. "International Asset Substitutability: Theory and Evidence for Canada," *Bank of Canada Review* (February 1985), pp. 9–10.

Boothe, Paul, and David Longworth. "Foreign Exchange Market Efficiency Tests: Implications of Recent Empirical Findings." *Journal of International Money and Finance,* vol. 5 (June 1986), pp. 135–52.

Brainard, William C., John B. Shoven, and Laurence Weiss. "The Financial Valuation of the Return to Capital." *Brookings Papers on Economic Activity* (2:1980), pp. 453–502.

Braudel, Fernand. *Civilization and Capitalism: 15th–18th Century.* Vol. 3: *The Perspective of the World.* New York: Harper and Row, 1984.

Brown, Seyom, Nina W. Cornell, Larry L. Fabian, and Edith Brown Weiss. *Regimes for the Ocean, Outer Space, and Weather.* Washington, D.C.: Brookings Institution, 1977.

Bryant, Ralph C. "Eurocurrency Banking: Alarmist Concerns and Genuine Issues." *OECD Economic Studies,* no. 1 (Autumn 1983), pp. 7–41.

———. "The Evolution of Singapore as a Financial Center," in K. S. Sandhu and P. Wheatley, eds., *Singapore: The Management of Success.* New York: Oxford University Press, forthcoming.

———. *Financial Interdependence and Variability in Exchange Rates.* Washington, D.C.: Brookings Institution, 1980.

———. "Financial Structure and International Banking in Singapore." Brookings Discussion Papers in International Economics no. 29. May 1985.

———. *Money and Monetary Policy in Interdependent Nations.* Washington, D.C.: Brookings Institution, 1980.

———. "The Progressive Internationalization of Banking." Brookings Discussion Papers in International Economics no. 14. April 1984.

Bryant, Ralph C., and Patric H. Hendershott. "Empirical Analysis of Capital Flows: Some Consequences of Alternative Specifications," in Fritz Machlup, Walter S. Salant, and Lorie Tarshis, eds., *International Mobility and Movement of Capital.* New York: Columbia University Press for National Bureau of Economic Research, 1972.

———. *Financial Capital Flows in the Balance of Payments of the United States: An Exploratory Empirical Study.* Princeton Studies in International Finance no. 25. Princeton University, Department of Economics, International Finance Section, 1970.

Bryant, Ralph C., Dale W. Henderson, Gerald Holtham, Peter Hooper, and Steven A. Symansky, eds. *Empirical Macroeconomics for Interdependent Economies.* Washington, D.C.: Brookings Institution, forthcoming.

Cameron, Rondo, ed. *Banking and Economic Development: Some Lessons of History.* New York: Oxford University Press, 1972.

Cameron, Rondo, with Olga Crisp, Hugh T. Patrick, and Richard Tilly. *Banking in the Early Stages of Industrialization: A Study in Comparative Economic History.* New York: Oxford University Press, 1967.

Caprio, Gerard, Jr., and David H. Howard. "Domestic Saving, Current Accounts, and International Capital Mobility." International Finance Discussion Papers no. 244. Washington, D.C.: Board of Governors of the Federal Reserve System, June 1984.

Caves, Richard E., and Ronald W. Jones. *World Trade and Payments: An Introduction.* 4th ed. Boston: Little, Brown and Co., 1985.

Claassen, Emil-Maria, and Charles Wyplosz. "Capital Controls: Some Principles and the French Experience." *Annales de l'INSEE,* no. 47–48 (1982), pp. 237–67.

Clark, Robert Charles. "The Soundness of Financial Intermediaries." *Yale Law Journal,* vol. 86 (November 1976), pp. 3–102.

Cooke, W. P. "The International Banking Scene: A Supervisory Perspective." *Bank of England Quarterly Bulletin,* vol. 23 (March 1983), pp. 61–65.

Cooper, Richard N. "International Cooperation in Public Health as a Prologue to Macroeconomic Cooperation." Brookings Discussion Papers in International Economics no. 44. March 1986.

Cumby, Robert E., and Frederic S. Mishkin. "The International Linkage of Real Interest Rates: The European-U.S. Connection." NBER Working Paper no. 1423. Cambridge, Mass.: National Bureau of Economic Research, August 1984.

Cumby, Robert E., and Maurice Obstfeld. "International Interest Rate and Price Level Linkages under Flexible Exchange Rates: A Review of Recent Evidence," in John F. O. Bilson and Richard C. Marston, eds., *Exchange Rate Theory and Practice.* Chicago: University of Chicago Press for National Bureau of Economic Research, 1984.

De Bondt, Werner F. M., and Richard Thaler. "Does the Stock Market Overreact?" *Journal of Finance,* vol. 40 (July 1985), pp. 793–805.

Despres, Emile, Charles P. Kindleberger, and Walter S. Salant. "The Dollar and World Liquidity: A Minority View." *Economist,* vol. 218 (February 5, 1966), pp. 526–29. Reprinted in Lawrence H. Officer and Thomas D. Willett, eds., *The International Monetary System: Problems and Proposals.* Englewood Cliffs, N.J.: Prentice-Hall, 1969.

Diaz-Alejandro, Carlos F. "Latin American Debt: I Don't Think We Are in Kansas Anymore." *Brookings Papers on Economic Activity* (2:1984), pp. 335–89.

Dooley, Michael P., and Peter Isard. "Capital Controls, Political Risk, and Deviations from Interest-Rate Parity." *Journal of Political Economy,* vol. 88 (April 1980), pp. 370–84.

Dornbusch, Rudiger. "Equilibrium and Disequilibrium Exchange Rates." NBER Working Paper no. 983. Cambridge, Mass.: National Bureau of Economic Research, September 1982.

Dornbusch, Rudiger, and Dwight Jaffee, eds. "Purchasing Power Parity: A Symposium." *Journal of International Economics,* vol. 8 (May 1978).

Downing, Thomas E., and Robert W. Kates. "The International Response to the Threat of Chlorofluorocarbons to Atmospheric Ozone." *American Economic Review,* vol. 72 (May 1982, *Papers and Proceedings, 1981*), pp. 267–72.

Fama, Eugene F. "Efficient Capital Markets: A Review of Theory and Empirical Work." *Journal of Finance,* vol. 25 (May 1970), pp. 383–417.

———. *Foundations of Finance: Portfolio Decisions and Securities Prices.* New York: Basic Books, 1976.

Feldstein, Martin. "Domestic Saving and International Capital Movements in the Long Run and the Short Run." *European Economic Review,* vol. 21 (March–April 1983), pp. 129–51.

Feldstein, Martin, and Charles Horioka. "Domestic Savings and International Capital Flows." *Economic Journal,* vol. 90 (June 1980), pp. 314–29.

Fialka, John J. "World Banking Bust: One Plot for a Tragedy in 8 Scenes and 12 Days." *Wall Street Journal,* November 10, 1982.

Fischer, Stanley, and Robert C. Merton. "Macroeconomics and Finance: The Role of the Stock Market," in Karl Brunner and Allan H. Meltzer, eds., *Essays on Macroeconomic Implications of Financial and Labor Markets and Political Processes.* Carnegie-Rochester Conference Series on Public Policy, vol. 21 (Autumn 1984), pp. 57–115.

Flavin, Marjorie A. "Excess Volatility in the Financial Markets: A Reassessment of the Empirical Evidence." *Journal of Political Economy,* vol. 91 (December 1983), pp. 929–56.

Flood, Robert P. "Explanations of Exchange-Rate Volatility and Other Empirical Regularities in Some Popular Models of the Foreign Exchange Market," in Karl Brunner and Allan H. Meltzer, eds., *The Costs and Consequences of Inflation.* Carnegie-Rochester Conference Series on Public Policy, vol. 15 (Autumn 1981), pp. 219–49.

Flood, Robert P., and Peter M. Garber. "Bubbles, Runs, and Gold Monetization," in Paul Wachtel, ed., *Crises in the Economic and Financial Structure.* Lexington, Mass.: Lexington Books, 1982.

Flood, Robert P., Robert J. Hodrick, and Paul Kaplan. "An Evaluation of Recent Evidence on Stock Market Bubbles." Northwestern University, March 1986.

Forbes, John F. "International Cooperation in Public Health and the World Health Organization," in Todd Sandler, ed., *The Theory and Structures of International Political Economy.* Boulder, Colo.: Westview Press, 1980.

Frankel, Allen B., and Jeffrey C. Marquardt. "International Payments and EFT Links," in Elinor Harris Solomon, ed., *Electronic Funds Transfers and Payments: The Public Policy Issues.* Boston: Kluwer-Nijhoff, 1987.

Frankel, Jeffrey A. "The Dazzling Dollar." *Brookings Papers on Economic Activity* (1:1985), pp. 199–217.

———. "International Capital Mobility and Crowding Out in the U.S. Economy: Imperfect Integration of Financial Markets or of Goods Markets?" Paper presented at a conference at the Federal Reserve Bank of St. Louis, October 1985.

———. *The Yen/Dollar Agreement: Liberalizing Japanese Capital Markets.* Policy Analyses in International Economics no. 9. Washington, D.C.: Institute for International Economics, 1984.

Frankel, Jeffrey A., and Kenneth A. Froot. "The Dollar as an Irrational Speculative Bubble: A Tale of Fundamentalists and Chartists." *Marcus Wallenberg Papers on International Finance* (International Law Institute), vol. 1 (1986), pp. 27–55.

Frenkel, Jacob A. "The Collapse of Purchasing Power Parities during the 1970's." *European Economic Review,* vol. 16 (May 1981), pp. 145–65.

Germany, J. David, and John E. Morton. "Financial Innovation and Deregulation in Foreign Industrial Countries." *Federal Reserve Bulletin,* vol. 71 (October 1985), pp. 743–53.

Gerschenkron, Alexander. *Continuity in History and Other Essays.* Cambridge, Mass.: Harvard University Press, 1968.

———. *Economic Backwardness in Historical Perspective: A Book of Essays.* Cambridge, Mass.: Harvard University Press, 1962.

Goldsmith, Raymond W. *Comparative National Balance Sheets: A Study of Twenty Countries, 1688–1978.* Chicago: University of Chicago Press, 1985.

————. *The Determinants of Financial Structure*. Paris: Development Center of the OECD, 1966.

————. *Financial Intermediaries in the American Economy Since 1900*. Princeton: Princeton University Press, 1958.

————. *Financial Structure and Development*. New Haven: Yale University Press, 1969.

————. *The National Balance Sheet of the United States, 1953–1980*. Chicago: University of Chicago Press, 1982.

————. *A Study of Saving in the United States*. Princeton: Princeton University Press, 1955.

Golub, Stephen S. "International Financial Markets, Oil Prices and Exchange Rates." Ph.D. dissertation, Yale University, 1983.

Gros, Daniel. "On the Volatility of Exchange Rates: A Test of Monetary and Portfolio Balance Models of Exchange Rate Determination." IMF Working Paper WP/86/6. Washington, D.C.: International Monetary Fund, October 1986.

Gurley, John G., and Edward S. Shaw. "Financial Intermediaries and the Saving-Investment Process." *Journal of Finance*, vol. 11 (May 1956), pp. 257–76.

————. "The Growth of Debt and Money in the United States, 1800–1950: A Suggested Interpretation." *Review of Economics and Statistics*, vol. 39 (August 1957), pp. 250–62.

————. *Money in a Theory of Finance*. Washington, D.C.: Brookings Institution, 1960.

Guttentag, Jack M., and Richard J. Herring. "Credit Rationing and Financial Disorder." *Journal of Finance*, vol. 39 (December 1984), pp. 1359–82.

————. *Disaster Myopia in International Banking*. Princeton Essays in International Finance no. 164. Princeton University, Department of Economics, International Finance Section, 1986.

————. *The Lender-of-Last-Resort Function in an International Context*. Princeton Essays in International Finance no. 151. Princeton University, Department of Economics, International Finance Section, 1983.

Hakkio, Craig S. "A Re-examination of Purchasing Power Parity: A Multi-country and Multi-period Study." *Journal of International Economics*, vol. 17 (November 1984), pp. 265–77.

Harberger, Arnold C. "Vignettes on the World Capital Market." *American Economic Review*, vol. 70 (May 1980, *Papers and Proceedings*, 1979), pp. 331–37.

Hartman, David G. "The International Financial Market and U.S. Interest Rates." *Journal of International Money and Finance*, vol. 3 (April 1984), pp. 91–103.

Henderson, Dale W. "Exchange Market Intervention Operations: Their Role in Financial Policy and Their Effects," in John F. O. Bilson and Richard C. Marston, eds., *Exchange Rate Theory and Practice*. Chicago: University of Chicago Press for the National Bureau of Economic Research, 1984.

Henderson, Dale W., and Stephanie Sampson. "Intervention in Foreign Exchange Markets: A Summary of Ten Staff Studies." *Federal Reserve Bulletin*, vol. 69 (November 1983), pp. 830–36.

Hester, Donald D. "Innovations and Monetary Control." *Brookings Papers on Economic Activity* (1:1981), pp. 141–89.

Hewson, John R. "Offshore Banking in Australia." *Australian Financial System Inquiry: Commissioned Studies and Selected Papers*. Pt. 2: *Macroeconomic Policy: External Policy*. Canberra: Australian Government Publishing Service, 1982.

Hirsch, Fred. "The Bagehot Problem." *Manchester School of Economic and Social Studies*, vol. 45 (September 1977), pp. 241–57.

————. *Social Limits to Growth*. Cambridge, Mass.: Harvard University Press, 1976.

Hirschman, Albert O. *Exit, Voice, and Loyalty: Responses to Decline in Firms, Organizations, and States*. Cambridge, Mass.: Harvard University Press, 1970.

Hoffman, John E., Jr., and Ian H. Giddy. "Lessons from the Iranian Experience: National Currencies as International Money." *Journal of Comparative Corporate Law and Securities Regulation,* vol. 3 (1981), pp. 271–86.

Hooper, Peter, and John Morton. "Summary Measures of the Dollar's Foreign Exchange Value." *Federal Reserve Bulletin,* vol. 64 (October 1978), pp. 783–89.

Huang, Roger D. "The Monetary Approach to Exchange Rate in an Efficient Foreign Exchange Market: Tests Based on Volatility." *Journal of Finance,* vol. 36 (March 1981), pp. 31–41.

Institute for Financial Affairs. *World Financial Centres*. Report of the Offshore Banking Survey Mission 1982. Tokyo: Institute for Financial Affairs, 1983.

Isard, Peter. "The Empirical Modeling of Exchange Rates: An Assessment of Alternative Approaches," in Ralph C. Bryant, Dale W. Henderson, Gerald Holtham, Peter Hooper, and Steven Symansky, eds., *Empirical Macroeconomics for Interdependent Economies*. Washington, D.C.: Brookings Institution, forthcoming.

————. *Exchange Rate Determination: A Survey of Popular Views and Recent Models*. Princeton Studies in International Finance no. 42. Princeton University, Department of Economics, International Finance Section, 1978.

Johnson, G. G., with Richard K. Abrams. *Aspects of the International Banking Safety Net*. Occasional Paper no. 17. Washington, D.C.: International Monetary Fund, 1983.

Kahn, Alfred E. "The Tyranny of Small Decisions: Market Failures, Imperfections, and the Limits of Economics." *Kyklos,* vol. 19 (1966), pp. 23–45.

Kaizuka, Keimei, and Tadao Hata. "Internationalization in Financial Activities in Japan." Paper presented at the Symposium on Internationalization of Banking and Finance, Seoul, Korea, December 1985.

Kareken, John H. "Bank Regulation and the Effectiveness of Open Market Operations." *Brookings Papers on Economic Activity* (2:1984), pp. 405–44.

————. "Deregulating Commercial Banks: The Watchword Should Be Caution." *Federal Reserve Bank of Minneapolis Quarterly Review,* vol. 5 (Spring–Summer 1981), pp. 1–5.

Key, Sydney J. "International Banking Facilities." *Federal Reserve Bulletin,* vol. 68 (October 1982), pp. 565–77.

Keynes, John Maynard. *The Collected Writings of John Maynard Keynes*. Vol. 7: *The General Theory of Employment, Interest and Money*. London: Macmillan and St. Martin's Press for the Royal Economic Society, 1973. Vol. 25: *Activities 1940–1944: Shaping the Post-War World: The Clearing Union*. Edited by Donald Moggridge. New York and Cambridge: Macmillan and Cambridge University Press for the Royal Economic Society, 1980. Vol. 26: *Activities 1941–1946: Shaping the Post-War World: Bretton Woods and Reparations*. Edited by Donald Moggridge. New York and Cambridge: Macmillan and Cambridge University Press for the Royal Economic Society, 1980.

Kindleberger, Charles P. *Balance-of-Payments Deficits and the International Market for Liquidity*. Princeton Essays in International Finance no. 46. Princeton University, Department of Economics, International Finance Section, 1965.

————. "Financial Institutions and Economic Development: A Comparison of Great

Britain and France in the Eighteenth and Nineteenth Centuries.'' *Explorations in Economic History,* vol. 21 (April 1984), pp. 103–24.

——. *The Formation of Financial Centers: A Study in Comparative Economic History.* Princeton Studies in International Finance no. 36. Princeton University, Department of Economics, International Finance Section, 1974.

——. *Manias, Panics, and Crashes: A History of Financial Crises.* New York: Basic Books, 1978.

Kindleberger, Charles P., and Jean-Pierre Laffargue, eds. *Financial Crises: Theory, History, and Policy.* Cambridge: Cambridge University Press, 1982.

Kleidon, Allan W. ''Bias in Small Sample Tests of Stock Price Rationality.'' *Journal of Business,* vol. 59 (April 1986), pp. 237–61.

——. ''Variance Bounds Tests and Stock Price Valuation Models.'' *Journal of Political Economy,* vol. 94 (October 1986), pp. 953–1001.

Kuznets, Simon. *Economic Growth of Nations: Total Output and Production Structure.* Cambridge, Mass.: Harvard University Press, 1971.

Landell-Mills, Joslin. *The Fund's International Banking Statistics.* Washington, D.C.: International Monetary Fund, 1986.

Lave, Lester B. ''Mitigating Strategies for Carbon Dioxide Problems.'' *American Economic Review,* vol. 72 (May 1982, *Papers and Proceedings, 1981*), pp. 257–61.

LeRoy, Stephen F. ''Efficiency and the Variability of Asset Prices,'' *American Economic Review,* vol. 74 (May 1984, *Papers and Proceedings, 1983*), pp. 183–87.

LeRoy, Stephen F., and Richard D. Porter. ''The Present Value Relation: Tests Based on Variance Bounds.'' *Econometrica,* vol. 49 (May 1981), pp. 555–74.

Levich, Richard M. ''Empirical Studies of Exchange Rates: Price Behavior, Rate Determination and Market Efficiency,'' in Ronald W. Jones and Peter B. Kenen, eds., *Handbook of International Economics.* Vol. 2. New York: North Holland, Elsevier Science Publishers, 1985.

Lingl, Herbert F. ''Risk Allocation in International Interbank Electronic Fund Transfers: CHIPS & SWIFT.'' *Harvard International Law Journal,* vol. 22 (Fall 1981), pp. 621–60.

Litan, Robert E. ''Evaluating and Controlling the Risks of Financial Product Regulation.'' *Yale Journal on Regulation,* vol. 3 (Fall 1985), pp. 1–52.

——. ''Taking the Dangers Out of Bank Deregulation.'' *Brookings Review,* vol. 4 (Fall 1986), pp. 3–12.

Longworth, David, Paul Boothe, and Kevin Clinton. ''A Study of the Efficiency of Foreign Exchange Markets.'' *Bank of Canada Review* (October 1983), pp. 9–10.

MacKay, Charles. *Extraordinary Popular Delusions and the Madness of Crowds.* 1841. Reprint. Boston: L. C. Page and Co., 1932.

Mankiw, N. Gregory, David Romer, and Matthew D. Shapiro. ''An Unbiased Reexamination of Stock Market Volatility.'' *Journal of Finance,* vol. 40 (July 1985), pp. 677–87.

Marsh, Terry A., and Robert C. Merton. ''Dividend Variability and Variance Bounds Tests for the Rationality of Stock Market Prices.'' *American Economic Review,* vol. 76 (June 1986), pp. 483–98.

Marshall, Alfred. *Principles of Economics.* 9th (variorum) ed. New York: Macmillan, 1961.

Mattey, Joe, and Richard Meese. ''Empirical Assessment of Present Value Relations.'' University of California–Berkeley, August 1986.

Mayer, Helmut W. ''The BIS Concept of the Eurocurrency Market.'' *Euromoney* (May 1976), pp. 60–66.

McKenzie, Colin R. "Issues in Foreign Exchange Policy in Japan: Sterilized Intervention, Currency Substitution and Financial Liberalization." Ph.D. thesis, Australian National University, 1986.

McKinnon, Ronald I. *Money and Capital in Economic Development*. Washington, D.C.: Brookings Institution, 1973.

Meese, Richard A., and Kenneth Rogoff. "Empirical Exchange Rate Models of the Seventies: Do They Fit Out of Sample?" *Journal of International Economics*, vol. 14 (February 1983), pp. 3–24.

———. "The Out-of-Sample Failure of Empirical Exchange Rate Models: Sampling Error or Misspecification?" in Jacob A. Frenkel, ed., *Exchange Rates and International Macroeconomics*. Chicago: University of Chicago Press for National Bureau of Economic Research, 1983.

———. "Was It Real? The Exchange Rate-Interest Differential Relation, 1973–1984." International Finance Discussion Papers no. 268. Washington, D.C.: Board of Governors of the Federal Reserve System, August 1985.

Meese, Richard A., and Kenneth J. Singleton. "Rational Expectations, Risk Premia, and the Market for Spot and Forward Exchange." International Finance Discussion Papers no. 165. Washington, D.C.: Board of Governors of the Federal Reserve System, July 1980.

———. "Rational Expectations and the Volatility of Floating Exchange Rates." *International Economic Review*, vol. 24 (October 1983), pp. 721–33.

Merton, Robert C. "On the Current State of the Stock Market Rationality Hypothesis," in Stanley Fischer and Rudiger Dornbusch, eds., *Macroeconomics and Finance: Essays in Honor of Franco Modigliani*. Cambridge, Mass.: MIT Press, 1987.

Miles, Edward, ed. *Restructuring Ocean Regimes: Implications of the Third United Nations Conference on the Law of the Sea*. Special issue of *International Organization*, vol. 31 (Spring 1977).

Mills, Rodney H. "Foreign Lending by Banks: A Guide to International and U.S. Statistics." *Federal Reserve Bulletin*, vol. 72 (October 1986), pp. 683–94.

———. "The Regulation of Short-term Capital Movements: Western European Techniques in the 1960's." Staff Economic Studies no. 46. Washington, D.C.: Board of Governors of the Federal Reserve System, May 1968.

Minsky, Hyman P. "The Financial Instability Hypothesis: A Restatement." Thames Papers in Political Economy. London: School of Social Sciences, Thames Polytechnic, Autumn 1978.

———. "Financial Instability Revisited: The Economics of Disaster," in Board of Governors of the Federal Reserve System, *Reappraisal of the Federal Reserve Discount Mechanism*. Vol. 3. Washington, D.C.: Board of Governors of the Federal Reserve System, June 1972.

Mishkin, Frederic S. "Are Real Interest Rates Equal Across Countries? An Empirical Investigation of International Parity Conditions." *Journal of Finance*, vol. 39 (December 1984), pp. 1345–58.

Modigliani, Franco, and Richard A. Cohn. "Inflation, Rational Valuation, and the Market." *Financial Analysts Journal*, vol. 35 (March–April 1979), pp. 24–44.

Morgan Guaranty Trust Company of New York. "Dollar Index Confusion." *World Financial Markets* (October–November 1986), pp. 14–19.

———. "Effective Exchange Rates Compared." *World Financial Markets* (April 1979), pp. 6–13.

———. "Effective Exchange Rates: Nominal and Real." *World Financial Markets* (May 1978), pp. 3–15.

————. "Growth and Financial Market Reform in Latin America." *World Financial Markets* (April–May 1986), pp. 1–11.

————. "International Bank Lending Trends." *World Financial Markets* (July 1985), pp. 1–11.

————. "LDC Capital Flight." *World Financial Markets* (March 1986), pp. 13–15.

Morse, Edward L. "Managing International Commons." *Journal of International Affairs,* vol. 31 (Spring–Summer 1977), pp. 1–21.

Murphy, Robert G. "Capital Mobility and the Relationship between Saving and Investment Rates in OECD Countries." *Journal of International Money and Finance,* vol. 3 (December 1984), pp. 327–42.

Nurkse, Ragnar. *International Currency Experience: Lessons of the Inter-War Period.* League of Nations, Economic, Financial and Transit Department, 1944. Reprinted in U.S. by Princeton University Press.

Obstfeld, Maurice. "Can We Sterilize? Theory and Evidence." *American Economic Review,* vol. 72 (May 1982, *Papers and Proceedings, 1981*), pp. 45–50.

————. "Capital Mobility in the World Economy: Theory and Measurement," in Karl Brunner and Allan H. Meltzer, eds., *The National Bureau Method, International Capital Mobility and Other Essays.* Carnegie-Rochester Conference Series on Public Policy, vol. 24 (Spring 1986), pp. 55–103.

Okina, Kunio. "Empirical Tests of 'Bubbles' in the Foreign Exchange Market." *Bank of Japan Monetary and Economic Studies,* vol. 3 (May 1985), pp. 1–45.

Okun, Arthur M. *Prices and Quantities: A Macroeconomic Analysis.* Washington, D.C.: Brookings Institution, 1981.

Olson, Mancur. "Environmental Indivisibilities and Information Costs: Fanaticism, Agnosticism, and Intellectual Progress." *American Economic Review,* vol. 72 (May 1982, *Papers and Proceedings, 1981*), pp. 262–66.

————. *The Logic of Collective Action: Public Goods and the Theory of Groups.* 2d ed. Cambridge, Mass.: Harvard University Press, 1971.

Pecchioli, Rinaldo. *The Internationalisation of Banking: The Policy Issues.* Paris: Organization for Economic Cooperation and Development, 1983.

Penati, Alessandro, and Michael P. Dooley. "Current Account Imbalances and Capital Formation in Industrial Countries, 1949–81." *IMF Staff Papers,* vol. 31 (March 1984), pp. 1–24.

Ricardo, David. *The Works and Correspondence of David Ricardo.* Vol. 1, *On the Principles of Political Economy and Taxation.* Edited by Piero Sraffa. Cambridge: Cambridge University Press, 1962.

Rogoff, Kenneth. "On the Effects of Sterilized Intervention: An Analysis of Weekly Data." *Journal of Monetary Economics,* vol. 14 (September 1984), pp. 133–50.

Sachs, Jeffrey R. "Aspects of the Current Account Behavior of OECD Economies," in E. Claassen and P. Salin, eds., *Recent Issues in the Theory of Flexible Exchange Rates.* Amsterdam: North Holland, 1983.

————. "The Current Account and Macroeconomic Adjustment in the 1970s." *Brookings Papers on Economic Activity* (1:1981), pp. 201–68.

Sakakibara, Eisuke, and Akira Kondoh. *Study on the Internationalization of Tokyo's Money Markets.* JCIF Policy Study Series no. 1. Tokyo: Japan Center for International Finance, 1984.

Salant, Stephen W., and Dale W. Henderson, "Market Anticipations of Government Policies and the Price of Gold." *Journal of Political Economy,* vol. 86 (August 1978), pp. 627–48.

Salant, Walter S. "Capital Markets and the Balance of Payments of a Financial Center," in William Fellner and others, eds., *Maintaining and Restoring Balance in International Payments*. Princeton: Princeton University Press, 1966.

———. "Financial Intermediation as an Explanation of Enduring 'Deficits' in the Balance of Payments," in Fritz Machlup, Walter S. Salant, and Lorie Tarshis, eds., *International Mobility and Movement of Capital*. New York: Columbia University Press for National Bureau of Economic Research, 1972.

Schelling, Thomas. "On the Ecology of Micromotives," in Robin Marris, ed., *The Corporate Society*. New York: Macmillan, 1974.

Shaw, Edward S. *Financial Deepening in Economic Development*. New York: Oxford University Press, 1973.

Shiller, Robert J. "Do Stock Prices Move Too Much to Be Justified by Subsequent Changes in Dividends?" *American Economic Review*, vol. 71 (June 1981), pp. 421–36.

———. "The Marsh-Merton Model of Managers' Smoothing of Dividends." *American Economic Review*, vol. 76 (June 1986), pp. 499–503.

———. "Stock Prices and Social Dynamics." *Brookings Papers on Economic Activity* (2:1984), pp. 457–98.

———. "The Volatility of Long-Term Interest Rates and Expectations Models of the Term Structure." *Journal of Political Economy*, vol. 87 (December 1979), pp. 1190–1219.

Simpson, Thomas D., and Patrick M. Parkinson. "Some Implications of Financial Innovations in the United States." Staff Studies no. 139. Washington, D.C.: Board of Governors of the Federal Reserve System, September 1984.

Singleton, Kenneth J. "Expectations Models of the Term Structure and Implied Variance Bounds." *Journal of Political Economy*, vol. 88 (December 1980), pp. 1159–76.

Smith, Adam. *An Inquiry into the Nature and Causes of the Wealth of Nations*. Edited by Edwin Cannan. London: Methuen, 1961.

Solomon, Robert. "The United States as a Debtor in the Nineteenth Century." Brookings Discussion Papers in International Economics no. 28. May 1985.

Solow, Robert M. "On Theories of Unemployment." *American Economic Review*, vol. 70 (March 1980), pp. 2–11.

Soroos, Marvin S. "The Commons in the Sky: The Radio Spectrum and Geosynchronous Orbit as Issues in Global Policy." *International Organization*, vol. 36 (Summer 1982), pp. 665–77.

Spero, Joan Edelman. *The Failure of the Franklin National Bank: Challenge to the International Banking System*. New York: Columbia University Press for the Council on Foreign Relations, 1980.

Stiglitz, Joseph E. "Information and Economic Analysis: A Perspective." *Economic Journal*, vol. 95 (Conference Papers Supplement, 1985), pp. 21–41.

Stiglitz, Joseph E., and Andrew Weiss. "Credit Rationing in Markets with Imperfect Information." *American Economic Review*, vol. 71 (June 1981), pp. 393–410.

Summers, Lawrence H. "Does the Stock Market Rationally Reflect Fundamental Values?" *Journal of Finance*, vol. 41 (July 1986), pp. 591–601.

———. "Tax Policy and International Competitiveness." NBER Working Paper no. 2007. Cambridge, Mass.: National Bureau of Economic Research, August 1986.

Suzuki, Yoshio, and Hiroshi Yomo, eds. *Financial Innovation and Monetary Policy: Asia and the West*. Tokyo: University of Tokyo Press, 1986.

Terrell, Henry S., and Rodney H. Mills. "International Banking Facilities and the

Eurodollar Market.'' Staff Studies no. 124. Washington, D.C.: Board of Governors of the Federal Reserve System, August 1983.

Tobin, James. ''Commercial Banks as Creators of 'Money,' '' in Deane Carson, ed., *Banking and Monetary Studies*. Homewood, Ill.: Richard D. Irwin, 1963.

———. ''A Mean-Variance Approach to Fundamental Valuations.'' Cowles Foundation Discussion Paper no. 711R. Yale University, Cowles Foundation for Research in Economics, October 1984.

———. *The New Economics, One Decade Older*. Princeton: Princeton University Press, 1974.

———. ''On the Efficiency of the Financial System.'' Fred Hirsch Memorial Lecture. *Lloyds Bank Review* (July 1984), pp. 1–15.

———. ''A Proposal for International Monetary Reform.'' *Eastern Economic Journal*, vol. 4 (1978). Reprinted in *Essays in Economics: Theory and Policy*. Cambridge, Mass.: MIT Press, 1982.

Tobin, James, and William C. Brainard. ''Financial Intermediaries and the Effectiveness of Monetary Controls.'' *American Economic Review*, vol. 53 (May 1963, *Papers and Proceedings, 1962*), pp. 383–400.

Tobin, James. ''Comments on 'Domestic Savings and International Capital Flows.' '' *European Economic Review*, vol. 21 (March–April 1983), pp. 153–56.

Townsend, Robert M. ''Financial Structure and Economic Activity.'' *American Economic Review*, vol. 73 (December 1983), pp. 895–911.

U.S. General Accounting Office. Staff Study. *Deposit Insurance: Analysis of Reform Proposals*. 3 vols. GAO-GGD-86-32, 32A, 32B. Washington, D.C.: GAO, 1986.

U.S. Department of the Treasury. *Report to Congress on Foreign Government Treatment of U.S. Commercial Banking Organizations*. Washington, D.C.: Department of the Treasury, 1979.

———. *Report to Congress on Foreign Government Treatment of U.S. Commercial Banking Organizations: 1984 Update*. Washington, D.C.: Department of the Treasury, 1984.

Vander Kraats, R. H., and L. D. Booth. ''Empirical Tests of the Monetary Approach to Exchange Rate Determination.'' *Journal of International Money and Finance*, vol. 2 (December 1983), pp. 255–78.

Watson, Maxwell, and others. *International Capital Markets: Developments and Prospects*. Occasional Paper no. 43. Washington, D.C.: International Monetary Fund, 1986.

Westphal, Uwe. ''Comments on 'Domestic Savings and International Capital Flows.' '' *European Economic Review*, vol. 21 (March–April 1983), pp. 157–59.

Williams, Richard C., and others. *International Capital Markets: Developments and Prospects, 1983*. Occasional Paper no. 23. Washington, D.C.: International Monetary Fund, 1983.

———. *International Capital Markets: Recent Developments and Short-Term Prospects, 1981*. Occasional Paper no. 7. Washington, D.C.: International Monetary Fund, 1981.

Williamson, John, ed. *Exchange Rate Rules: The Theory, Performance and Prospects of the Crawling Peg*. New York: St. Martin's Press, 1981.

Williamson, John. *The Exchange Rate System*. Policy Analyses in International Economics no. 5. Rev. ed. Washington, D.C.: Institute for International Economics, 1985.

Wojnilower, Albert M. "The Central Role of Credit Crunches in Recent Financial History." *Brookings Papers on Economic Activity* (2:1980), pp. 277–326.

Woo, Wing T. "Speculative Bubbles in the Foreign Exchange Markets." Brookings Discussion Papers in International Economics no. 13. March 1984.

Working Group on Exchange Market Intervention. "Report of the Working Group on Exchange Market Intervention." Phillippe Jurgensen, chairman. March 1983.

Young, Oran R. *Compliance and Public Authority: A Theory with International Applications*. Baltimore: Johns Hopkins University Press for Resources for the Future, 1979.

Index